ECCLESIASTES

ABINGDON OLD TESTAMENT COMMENTARIES

ABINGDON OLD TESTAMENT COMMENTARIES

ECCLESIASTES

JULIE ANN DUNCAN

Abingdon Press
Nashville

CONTENTS

CONTENTS

FOREWORD

The Abingdon Old Testament Commentaries are offered to the reader in hopes that they will aid in the study of Scripture and provoke a deeper understanding of the Bible in all its many facets. The texts of the Old Testament come out of a time, a language, and socio-historical and religious circumstances far different from the present. Yet Jewish and Christian communities have held to them as a sacred canon, significant for faith and life in each new time. Only as one engages these books in depth and with all the critical and intellectual faculties available to us can the contemporary communities of faith and other interested readers continue to find them meaningful and instructive.

These volumes are designed and written to provide compact, critical commentaries on the books of the Old Testament for the use of theological students and pastors. It is hoped that they may be of service also to upper-level college or university students and to those responsible for teaching in congregational settings. In addition to providing basic information and insights into the Old Testament writings, these commentaries exemplify the tasks and procedures of careful interpretation.

The writers of the commentaries in this series come from a broad range of ecclesiastical affiliations, confessional stances, and educational backgrounds. They have experience as teachers and, in some instances, as pastors and preachers. In most cases, the authors are persons who have done significant research on the book that is their assignment. They take full account of the most important current scholarship and secondary literature, while not attempting to summarize that literature or to engage in technical academic debate. The fundamental concern of each volume is analysis and discussion of the literary, socio-historical, theological, and ethical dimensions of the biblical texts themselves.

The New Revised Standard Version of the Bible is the principal translation of reference for the series, though authors may draw upon other interpretations in their discussion. Each writer is attentive to the original Hebrew text in preparing the commentary. But the authors do not presuppose any knowledge of the biblical languages on the part of the reader. When some awareness of a grammatical, syntactical, or philological issue is necessary for an adequate understanding of a particular text, the issue is explained simply and concisely.

Each volume consists of four parts. An *introduction* looks at the book as a whole to identify *key issues* in the book, its *literary genre* and *structure*, the *occasion and situational context* of the book (including both social and historical contexts), and the *theological and ethical significance* of the book.

The *commentary* proper organizes the text by literary units and, insofar as is possible, divides the comment into three parts. The *literary analysis* serves to introduce the passage with particular attention to identification of the genre of speech or literature and the structure or outline of the literary unit under discussion. Here also the author takes up significant stylistic features to help the reader understand the mode of communication and its impact on comprehension and reception of the text. The largest part of the comment is usually found in the *exegetical analysis*, which considers the leading concepts of the unit, the language of expression, and problematical words, phrases, and ideas in order to get at the aim or intent of the literary unit, as far as that can be uncovered. Attention is given here to particular historical and social situations of the writer(s) and reader(s) where that is discernible and relevant as well as to wider cultural (including religious) contexts. The analysis does not proceed phrase by phrase or verse by verse but deals with the various particulars in a way that keeps in view the overall structure and central focus of the passage and its relationship to the general line of thought or rhetorical argument of the book as a whole. The final section, *theological and ethical analysis*, seeks to identify and clarify the theological and ethical matters with which the unit deals or to which it points. Though not aimed primarily at contemporary issues of faith and life, this section should provide readers a basis for reflection on them.

Each volume also contains a select bibliography of works cited in the commentary as well as major commentaries and other important works available in English.

The fundamental aim of this series will have been attained if readers are assisted not only in understanding more about the origins, character, and meaning of the Old Testament writings but also in entering into their own informed and critical engagement with the texts themselves.

Patrick D. Miller
General Editor

ACKNOWLEDGMENTS

It is hard to know where to begin in thanking everyone who has been a part of this journey.

My cohort at Garrett-Evangelical Theological Seminary heartened and supported me throughout the process, offering both haven and inspiration. In particular I want to give warm thanks to Lallene J. Rector and Jack L. Seymour, under whose deanships I was granted study leaves that made the completion of the book possible. My deepest thanks to my colleague Hendrik Pieterse, fellow explorer of the depths of Ecclesiastes, for engaging me in stimulating conversations about Qohelet, theology, and philosophy; his unwavering belief in the book greatly encouraged me. I was fortunate to have the help of skilled and enthusiastic research assistants Charlotte Heeg and Justin Lane. I'm grateful to Lisa M. Wolfe, my doctoral student at Garrett from 1997 to 1999, for her substantive contributions to the Ecclesiastes seminar of 1998, for her probing and thought-provoking dissertation on the book's theodicy, and for being such a spirited conversation partner in the years since. I am also grateful for my longtime friend and colleague Brooke Lester, who afforded me the sort of inspiration that comes from deep and wide-ranging conversation, and the resilience that comes from sharing hearty laughter.

Thanks go to my support network, of whom I can only mention a few. To my three dearest sisters, Lisa, Lori, and Amy, cheerleaders throughout the process, who knew when to bring comic relief and when to pray. This or any other moment would be unimaginable without them. To Barbara Bright, beloved friend, who brightened my days with pastries, cards, and her lovely works of art; she has blessed my life with her generosity of spirit. To Armando Rodriguez for his unbounded friendship. His heartfelt enthusiasm for the project buoyed me up many a time and helped take me to the end.

S. Dean McBride, mentor and cherished friend, opened up for me the depths of the Hebrew Bible, introduced me to the Epic of Gilgamesh in a way only he could have done, and heard my voice so many decades ago, thereby helping me begin to find it. I am content to be forever in his debt.

Three people in particular made the completion of this book possible: Brent A. Strawn, miracle-working problem-solver and most treasured friend of many years, enriched me with his breadth of knowledge on things Qohelet and beyond, offering incisive feedback and sustaining me with his sage counsel and warm encouragement throughout the process. My gratitude also goes to Karen A. Howe, dearest friend and my muse for the end of the journey; she piloted me in the final phases of writing, inspiring me with her love of Ecclesiastes, and nourishing me with her thoughts. Her true zeal for the project helped me bring it to fruition.

Finally, I am deeply indebted to Choon-Leong Seow. At a point when my studies in the book of Ecclesiastes were yet untested, he had faith in me and made my dream of writing a commentary on the book a reality. His vast knowledge, wisdom, formidable intelligence, and skilled guidance have made this a better book (any remaining flaws and deficiencies are my own responsibility). One could not hope for a more patient editor, or a truer friend for the journey.

This book is dedicated to my parents, Robert Lee Duncan and Betty Haygood Duncan, who have each, in their own way, reinforced the lessons and wisdom of Qohelet. My father, a professor of comparative literature, instilled in me a love of the classics. His affinities for such writers as Leo Tolstoy, Fyodor Dostoyevsky, and Albert Camus found their way into my heart early on, as did his abiding love for the Bible. Despite the ravages of Alzheimer's, his spirit of grace, of kindness, of gentle address remained intact, reminding me what it means to be human, finite, and beautiful for our very dependency on one another. My mother, my ever-stalwart supporter, has fed me lentil soup and muffins galore, but more than anything has fortified me with her unfailing love and belief in me. She continues to inspire me daily with her good spirits, resilience, and verve for life amid challenging circumstances. She has been and remains my mainstay.

ABBREVIATIONS

ABR *Australian Biblical Review*

AEL *Ancient Egyptian Literature: A Book of Readings.* Edited by Miriam Lichtheim. 3 vols. Berkeley: University of California, 1971–1980.

ANET *Ancient Near Eastern Texts Relating to the Old Testament.* Edited by J. B. Pritchard. 3rd ed. Princeton: Princeton University, 1969.

AT Author's translation

CEB Common English Bible

COS *Context of Scripture: Canonical Compositions, Monumental Inscriptions, and Archival Documents from the Biblical World.* Edited by William W. Hallo and K. Lawson Younger Jr. 3 vols. Leiden: Brill, 1997–2002.

GNT Good News Translation

JB Jerusalem Bible

JBL *Journal of Biblical Literature*

NAB New American Bible

NASB New American Standard Bible

NEB New American Bible

REB Revised English Bible

NIV New International Version

NJPS New Jewish Publication Society Version

NRSV New Revised Standard Version

TAD *Textbook of Aramaic Documents from Ancient Egypt.* Edited by B. Porten and A. Yardeni. 3 vols. Jerusalem: Israel Academy of Sciences and Humanities, 1986–1993.

INTRODUCTION

E cclesiastes has been called the strangest book in the Bible. That may be the one thing most of its readers can agree on, for this small book may well have engendered more widely differing interpretations than any other book of the Bible. Its ability to disquiet and to generate controversy among its readers is glimpsed in its earliest interpretive history. Ancient rabbinic discussion in the centuries around the turn of the era preserves evidence of a debate about the status of Ecclesiastes as sacred scripture. As to the concerns involved, there is just enough information to pique curiosity. The internal contradictions of the book are mentioned, and there is concern that the endorsement of pleasure might encourage hedonism or an inclination to heresy (11:9 is at issue; it unabashedly encourages the young man to follow the ways of his heart). We cannot be sure of all the factors involved in the controversy, only that in the end it was the wisdom of tradition to include this discordant and perplexing book (see further Fox 2004, xiv–xv).

More than anything else, this book is about the human encounter with death. Qohelet returns to the fact of human mortality time after time—as if he cannot quite fathom it. The pervasiveness of this theme in his reflections has, quite understandably, led some readers to see the book as a dour if not morbid treatise, wafting "the smell of the tomb" (Robinson 1946, 258). Indeed, it is true that a constant preoccupation with coming death may issue only in immobilizing anxiety, rage, or despair. There is, however, a long tradition of thought in which the encounter with death is seen as a potentially redemptive confrontation. I propose that the book of Ecclesiastes stands in that tradition. Reflection on human finitude and, more specifically, its import for the question of meaning in human existence, is as old as human culture itself. It finds its expression in what might be termed *boundary myths*—stories in which heroes and heroines in one way or another butt up against the limitations that define being human. It is striking how often the protagonists of such tales are not *mere* humans, but rather of some semidivine or quasi-superhuman nature. Thus people are asked to contemplate not just the average specimen, but the very best that humanity has to offer; it is humanity as close to the divine as is humanly possible. The failure of even such a hero as this reinforces the distinct boundary—the ultimately unbreachable divide—between god and human. In this way such stories underline the inevitability of mortality for *everyone*, encouraging listeners to come to terms with this absolute of human existence.

In modernity the theme of human finitude permeates the thinking of a strand of philosophy termed *existentialism*. Though the label represents a wide and varied spectrum of viewpoints, certain themes recur among the philosophers, novelists, and theologians included in this category. For existentialist thinkers, the fact of death is central to diagnosing the nature of the human plight. We must, each of us, die. This given of human existence is concomitant with other givens of the human situation: our existence is fragile and utterly contingent (entirely dependent on factors beyond our control), we are ultimately alone, and our faculties of reason can take us only so far when it comes to the depths of existence. It is with just such limits that Qohelet travails.

Title of the Book

"Ecclesiastes" is taken from the ancient Greek translation of the book's Hebrew title, *Qohelet*, a designation of the book's spokesperson. Though the origin of the Hebrew word is of some dispute, it is most commonly related to the word for "assembly" or "congregation" (an interpretation also reflected in the ancient witnesses), thus suggesting the meaning "one who assembles." The specific form is a verbal noun, a grammatical form sometimes used as a professional title or to designate an office. One may well ask, however, just what role *qohelet* designates, as the term is not attested elsewhere. Hence interpreters ancient and modern have differed on whether it refers to Qohelet's function as one who convened the people to teach them (reflected in the traditional rendition of "Preacher"), or to his collecting and arranging of proverbs and wisdom. Interestingly the tribute of the epilogist at the end of the book is suggestive of both roles, remembering Qohelet as one who "taught the people knowledge, weighing and studying and arranging many proverbs" (12:9). The NRSV translation "Teacher" seems to be based on this reference to Qohelet's pedagogical activity. In the following commentary, Qohelet will be referred to by his Hebrew title, and Ecclesiastes will be used to refer to the book itself.

Setting and Audience

It is seldom the case that the date of a biblical book can be established beyond doubt. The date of Ecclesiastes is also debated, but fortunately there is some evidence to help us establish a probable time frame, even if the precise period remains in dispute. The Hebrew of Ecclesiastes, both its vocabulary and grammatical forms, reflects a later stage in the development of the language, a period some time after the Babylonian exile (597–538 BCE). In fact the presence of Persian loanwords in the text indicates that it is most likely dated after the rise of the Persian emperor Cyrus, who defeated Babylon and allowed the Jewish exiles to return to Jerusalem in 538 BCE. On the other hand, a *terminus ante quem* (date before which it must have been written) is established by evidence from the Dead Sea scrolls; fragments of the book found in Cave 4 date to the mid–second century BCE. This endmost boundary for composition is corroborated by the work of Sirach, a late wisdom book composed around 180 BCE, that reflects familiarity with the text of Ecclesiastes.

During the time frame in question (538 BCE to about 200 BCE), Judah lives under Persian rule until 332 BCE, at which time the conquests of Alexander the Great end Persian dominance in the Middle East. At this point Greek cultural influence begins to assert itself in the region. After Alexander's death in 323 Judah is under the control of the Ptolemaic Egyptian ruling family until a series of wars in the mid-third to late second century, during which Israel rotates between Ptolemaic and Seleucid rule. It is some time in this broad period of foreign domination that the book of Ecclesiastes is composed.

Scholarly opinion is divided as to whether Ecclesiastes was written in the Persian or the Hellenistic era. While arguments for the Hellenistic period have sometimes been predicated on theories of direct contact between the author and specific philosophical sources within Hellenism (such as the Stoics or Epicureans [for a proposal on the former, see Rudman 2001]), such theories have generally not gained consensus. More often arguments for a Hellenistic origin have been made on more general grounds, appealing to a kind of influence by osmosis: the sage's intent quest to find "what is good for mortals to do the numbered days of their lives" (2:3, AT) is seen against the background of the central preoccupation of Hellenistic philosophy—namely the achievement of individual happiness by means of human reason. Scholars taking this position maintain that Qohelet is evidently influenced by the spirit of his times but also allow that the manner in which such influence is mediated is difficult to track (e.g., Murphy 1992; Fox 1999; Bartholomew 2009; cf. Krüger 2004). Several other scholars subscribing to the theory of Hellenistic origin base their assessment primarily on sociohistorical evidence rather than on parallels with Greek philosophical thought or language (e.g., Whybray 1989; Krüger 2004; Harrison 1991).

The most persuasive and influential argument for origin in the Persian period has been mounted by C. L. Seow. Among other warrants for this date—including a constellation of thematic links with the socioeconomic world of the Persian period (see further Seow 2008)—Seow has adduced important evidence on the basis of linguistic evidence. So, for example, he has examined the book's vocabulary in comparison with Aramaic words attested in economic and legal texts of the fifth and fourth century BCE (see *JBL* 1996, 643–66). A few unusual expressions in Ecclesiastes are paralleled by their Aramaic cognate forms in these Persian period texts. Three such terms—"profit," "deficit," and "calculation/sum"—are in fact unique to the book of Ecclesiastes in the Bible. Though the surviving documentary evidence is too scant to decide a date by this means alone, the extant data are intriguing, in that Qohelet's employment of these terms coheres with their use in these Aramaic legal contexts. A term of particular interest is the verbal root *šlt*, "to have right, power." The word occurs in Aramaic legal documents of the Persian period in a specialized usage referring to transferable rights over property. This technical meaning seems to be at play at a few points in Ecclesiastes (2:19; 5:19 [Heb. 18]; and 6:2). This evidence is striking since Aramaic economic texts from the Hellenistic period, which are ample, show no such correspondences in terms of shared vocabulary and usage.

Scholars arguing for a Persian date also point out the absence of Greek vocabulary in the book. Still it may be countered that other biblical books of clear Hellenistic origin, such as the book Sirach, lack Grecisms as well.

The question of a Hellenistic versus Persian provenance remains a lively debate (for a recent review see Bartholomew 2009, 43–59); it is unlikely that it will be resolved on the basis of linguistic arguments alone. A further problem one faces in establishing a date for Ecclesiastes is that it contains no explicit references to historical events or persons, at least as far as we can tell. Some scholars have seen allusions to contemporary events in such passages as 4:13-16 (a reference to a foolish king and a poor youth who replaces him on the throne) and 9:13-16 (a reference to a great king's military siege of a small city). However, it is also possible that Qohelet was describing or illustrating typical happenings, not current affairs. In any case, these passages lack sufficient detail to allow any certain identification with historical events or persons, despite a great many attempts to the contrary.

Still the book of Ecclesiastes does contain clues as to its social environment. Qohelet's numerous references to money, wealth, and issues of inheritance and property are quite striking. They suggest a situation in which financial concerns are paramount (Seow 2008, 189–217; Kugel 1981, 32–49). Several examples and allusions indicate a volatile economy in which fortunes may be both made and lost (5:13-17; 11:1-2; cf. 7:14; 9:11-12). Other passages hint at a social and political instability that corroborates this economic profile (Qohelet speaks, for instance, of an abrupt reversal of status for slaves and princes [10:6-7; cf. 4:13-14; 10:16-17]). The social status of those to whom Qohelet addresses his thoughts cannot be determined with certainty, but by most indications they are persons of some means, whose resources exceed subsistence level needs; in short they have certain economic options (e.g., 4:4, 6-8; 5:10, 11, 13). This status is further supported by the fact that Qohelet refers to relationships with one's servants (7:21) and to concerns about inheritance (2:21; 4:8; 5:13-17; 6:2), and he speaks of oppression as something observed rather than experienced (4:1-3; 5:8). Moreover, he assumes that his listeners might have access to the governing elite and serve in some official capacity (8:2-5; 10:4). Qohelet's own status is a matter of some debate, though it is apparent he sympathizes with the concerns of his constituency. Wherever he himself is situated on the social ladder, he shows himself to be acutely aware of hierarchical structures. His advice to any who find themselves in the presence of authority or power is uniformly conservative: he advises caution and diplomacy (8:2-5; 10:4; cf. 10:20). In several instances Qohelet intimates a wary if not critical attitude toward governing powers (4:1; 5:8; 8:9; 10:5,16-19).

Unfortunately, this sketch of the setting of Qohelet's composition does not necessarily advance the debate concerning a Persian versus Hellenistic origin in that these two periods share a few salient characteristics in common. In both cases Judah lives under foreign domination but is granted a certain level of political autonomy (at least up through the Ptolemaic period), with governance coming both from within Judah's own aristocracy and from those representing the imperial power. Both periods see the implementation of aggressive taxation measures (which exerts pressure for production), and both see substantial increases in trade (which bring with them both opportunity and risk for the inhabitants of Palestine). For the time being the debate over the specific dating of Ecclesiastes is not resolved. In any event this profile of audience and setting serves to corroborate the broader boundaries given us by the linguistic and other external literary evidence just discussed. On the basis of these considerations this commentary allows for broad parameters with respect to the date of composition, assuming only that the book was written sometime after the second half of the fifth century, and sometime before the mid-third century BCE (anytime before the second half of the fifth is doubtful given the presence of Persian loanwords, and anytime after the mid-third is unlikely since the book shows no sign of the instability brought on by the series of Seleucid wars beginning at that time).

Ecclesiastes and Wisdom

Despite some ambiguity with respect to its historical setting, the book's intellectual context is not in dispute. Ecclesiastes belongs to what scholars have long regarded as the wisdom tradition, also represented in the Hebrew Bible by Proverbs and the book of Job, and in the Apocrypha by Sirach and the Wisdom of Solomon. Proverbs, Job, and Ecclesiastes are somewhat distinctive among the traditions of the Hebrew Bible. Perhaps their most salient feature is an omission: they make no reference to the national themes of salvation history and covenant, such as the exodus, election of a people, and conquest of the land. The focus of these wisdom books is instead on the realm of day-to-day living, and on the individual in relation to God, society, and the world. In the wisdom perspective, God is first and foremost creator God, the one who has ordered the structures of cosmos and society. The wisdom authors seek to impart awareness and understanding of these divinely ordered structures so that humans can live in a state of harmony and well-being with the world around them. By such wisdom humans may navigate the complexities of life and find well-being and success.

That Qohelet shares the foundations and presuppositions of wisdom is evident. He places his attention squarely on the question of individual well-being, seeking to discover what is good for humans to do (2:3b). His lexicon is that of the wisdom tradition (*wisdom* and *knowledge* are common in his vocabulary, and he employs such typical contrasts as wise/foolish and righteous/wicked), and he draws upon the distinctive literary forms employed by the sages in their pedagogical instruction—such as sayings, admonitions, and example stories. Yet one need not read far into the book to see that Qohelet uses the methods of wisdom to take a hard look at some of its central claims. In response to the claim of Proverbs that the possessor of wisdom obtains "life" (e.g., Prov 11:19; 12:28; 13:14), Qohelet, while allowing wisdom's practical benefits and bonuses, states emphatically that wisdom cannot secure one from death. Every human dies. And this means that the wise meet the same fate as the foolish. Moreover, the insistent claim of wisdom that the good will prosper and the unrighteous will be punished (e.g., Prov 11:21; 14:14; 22:4; 28:18) is not borne out by life. Qohelet observes the exceptions and is deeply troubled by these contradictions of what his tradition teaches. In addition, wisdom is vulnerable: its accomplishments are quickly forgotten, and its progress or advantage easily nullified by just a small measure of folly (wisdom is far from foolproof). Such recognitions highlight the vulnerability of human existence, and the fact that our lives are not under our power.

Qohelet's insistent probing of the assumptions of wisdom is sometimes understood as a thoroughgoing polemic against his legacy or as a move to jettison the entire tradition. This misses the nature of Qohelet's relationship with his forebears. His critique comes from one who stands *within* the tradition. As Roland Murphy has observed, Qohelet is engaged in dialogue, not polemical assault (Murphy 1992, lxi–lxiv). Qohelet values wisdom deeply. One sees this in his repeated use of the means of wisdom to attain his goals. Notably, Qohelet's criticisms never lead him to prefer folly to wisdom. In fact the relationship of wisdom to folly is described as that of light to darkness (2:13). The disillusionment Qohelet expresses has less to do with wisdom per se and more to do with its object of inquiry (see also Fox 1999, 91–92). Yes, Qohelet laments the fact that the powers of human intelligence are not equal to the task of comprehending the world, or a rationale for life's events. However, this is due less to the limits of human intellectual capacity than it is to a God who has created barriers to human insight. When Qohelet speaks of the failure of human comprehension, he does so in the context of a God who has withheld information, who has stacked the deck, so to speak, against humanity (1:12-15; 3:11,14; 6:10-12; 7:13-14).

STRUCTURE AND TONALITY

If way to the Better there be, it exacts a full look at the Worst.
Thomas Hardy, "In Tenebris"

I'm not afraid of death. I just don't want to be there when it happens.
Woody Allen

It is not hard to understand why many readers have seen the book of Ecclesiastes as bearing a message of unrelieved pessimism. Qohelet not only questions the meaning of all those experiences and endeavors in which people find value, such as work, personal achievement, fame, and prosperity. He also challenges the belief structures that underpin and give order to human existence: there is no necessary relationship between actions and consequences; people do not know what will happen in the future, much less control what befalls them; and they do not discern a coherent design or pattern to such happenings. God's actions are enigmatic, God's will inscrutable, and divine sovereignty trumps human capacity to secure outcomes. For Qohelet there is one certainty in life: death for everyone.

If these were the only thematic elements of the book, there would be little debate about its tonality! However, Qohelet interlaces these probing critiques with a series of affirmations of joy in certain elemental pleasures—in food, in drink, in work, in companionship (2:24-26; 3:12-13, 22; 5:18-20; 8:15; 9:7-10; 11:9-10). These two strains of thought create a kind of irreducible tension, and the question of tonality comes to hinge primarily on how one perceives their relationship to one another and where one places the weight of emphasis.

The problem is that the author has given the reader few cues as to the relative importance attached to these themes, hence opening the book to widely divergent interpretations. Had the writer provided more formal clues in the way of design or hierarchy of passages, the interpretive dilemma would be helped. However, as most readers of Ecclesiastes will testify, the book does not give the impression of a systematic or even organized presentation. Qohelet moves from one topic to the next and back again, without apparent plan, at times verging on a stream-of-consciousness mode. This absence of evident order has led some scholars to view the book as a loose collection of separate units, or even as a relatively haphazard collection of reflections and sayings. For others it has proved a tempting lure to discover the code or key that would pull back the veil and expose the hidden logic of arrangement. Few such proposals have received widespread acceptance.

Though it is true that the book betrays little evidence of a thoroughgoing design, there are suggestions of organization on a broad level. A poetic prelude and postlude introduce and close the reflections of Qohelet (1:3-11; 12:2-7), and the thematic statement on the pervasiveness of "vapor" (NRSV "vanity") brackets these two poems. As noted, on either side of this frame is a narrating voice, the first presenting Qohelet's words and the second assessing them.

Beyond this framework, however, there are few clear signs of detailed organization. This is not to say that the book of Ecclesiastes is without coherence. As Michael Fox has observed, cohesiveness and unity are achieved through the vehicle of a single narrating voice. All of the book's reflections are filtered through this consciousness (2004, xvi–vii). In contrast to other wisdom books in which the author or speaker remains in the background, here the author is constantly in evidence to the reader. All we read comes through this subjective narrating "I." To show just how crucial this subjective feature is to reading Qohelet, Fox has rendered Qohelet's opening words of 1:12-14 in an impersonal mode (xvii): "Studying and probing with wisdom all that happens under the sun is an unhappy business, which God gave men to be concerned with! All the happenings beneath the sun are futile and pursuit of wind" (based on NJPS).

Compare this with the text as it stands: "I, Koheleth, was king in Jerusalem over Israel. I set my mind to study and to probe with wisdom all that happens under the sun. —An unhappy business, that, which God gave men to be concerned with! I observed all the happenings beneath the sun, and I found that all is futile and a pursuit of wind" (NJPS). The comparison shows the ramifications of the choice for a subjective narrating presence. A significant effect is to create a reader-hospitable environment, one that quite naturally fosters a certain receptivity and involvement on the part of the listener. Rather than being handed conclusions about life and meaning, we are invited to listen in on a process of discernment and reflection. Moreover, in the chapters to come Qohelet's thoughts are repeatedly marked by such locutions as "I said to myself," "I saw," and "I perceived." Thus the listener is never allowed to forget either this subjective narrating presence or this dynamic of process. To elaborate on the latter, Qohelet's reflections are presented as a journey. The reader is, by implication, invited to be a fellow traveler on the circuitous and serpentine routes he has traveled.

Qohelet set out to discover "what was good for mortals do under heaven during the few days of their life" (2:3b). He is asking the fundamental questions of existence. Human labor receives no truly meaningful recompense; any achievement, no matter how grandiose, is tenuous and ultimately utterly forgotten; sometimes the good and the innocent suffer while the wicked flourish. To grow in wisdom means only to gain a more acute sense of these shortfalls and inequities, including the fact that the wise and the foolish both die just the same. Human existence is so fragile. We are hemmed in by limits on all sides—limits in knowledge and comprehension, and the ultimate limit of death. Yet at the very points at which Qohelet voices these criticisms most profoundly, he offers his exhortations to make merry.

What is one to make of this? One way to view the relationship of these two components of Qohelet's thought is to understand the positive affirmations in the mood of simple resignation—that is, all that is *left* to do once we have perceived the bleakness of human existence, our helplessness before life, and our inevitable death. If that is all there is, we might as well take what we can, when we can, as consolation prize for an irremediably flawed world. This is certainly one plausible reading of the text (in support one may point out, for instance, that the book culminates in a long meditation on death, not on celebrative living).

There is, however, an alternative reading that draws upon a tradition of thinking about human finitude that is as old as civilization itself. Within this tradition life and death are understood as inextricably entwined. Death is a part of our very identity as physical creatures; the process of dying begins the day we are born. In that sense there is no *true* escape from the knowledge of death, for it lodges in our bones. The paradox understood by such ancient thinkers and their modern counterparts is that to avoid the fact of death leaves us in thrall to the terror of it. Because life and death are interdependent, we cannot avoid confronting death without in some fashion severely attenuating our experience of life. It is only by coming to direct terms with death as a part of life that we can participate fully and authentically in the joys and goods that also belong to this mortal state.

This particular sensibility of the nature of human finitude and its implications for existence are explored in virtually every period of human history, in modes both philosophical and imaginative. As an initial step toward elucidating the thought of Qohelet, I turn to one story in particular, the Epic of Gilgamesh.

KING GILGAMESH AND THE PERENNIAL QUEST

The tale of King Gilgamesh is of ancient origins. The historical figure behind the tale, ruler of the Mesopotamian city of Uruk (on the northern bank of the Euphrates), is believed to have assumed the throne around 2600 BCE! Beyond this we have little historical record of him. Yet something about this personage caught the imagination of subsequent generations of storytellers. Tales of his exploits were circulated orally and eventually written down in Sumerian (ca. 2000 BCE). Then around 1700 BCE a Babylonian author writing in Akkadian drew creatively on these various tales to compose an epic story of this king's efforts to thwart mortality and achieve eternal life (known as the Old Babylonian version). Though the remains of this epic are fragmentary, they point to the existence of an integrated epic (see the assessment in George 1999, xxi; Tigay 1982, 42–54). A few centuries later this epic was reworked and enlarged (tradition ascribes this work to a priest in Uruk [George 1999, xxiv]). It is this expanded edition (the Standard Babylonian) that has survived in most complete form, primarily in sources coming from the seventh century BCE (for differences between the two versions, Tigay 1982, 39–109; Moran 1987, 557–60; Jacobsen 1990, 231–49).

Scholars have long recognized specific textual parallels between the Gilgamesh epic and the book of Ecclesiastes. However, the affinities between the two compositions are more substantive than two or three instances of shared phraseology.

I suggest that the story of Gilgamesh is deeply etched in Qohelet's imagination (see Jones 1990, 349–79; Brown 2000,
3–7 and *passim*). As a step toward illuminating the tonality of
Ecclesiastes, I will summarize this older tale of quest after
meaning. Quotations are from the translation of Maureen Kovacs (Kovacs 1989) unless otherwise noted.

The epic opens with a majestic vision of the king: Gilgamesh
is unequaled in strength, beauty, and grand achievement. Indeed, he is no mere human—he is two-thirds divine. But as
the narrative action commences we learn that Gilgamesh's ex-
ceptional strength is causing trouble for the ordinary humans
who are his subjects. Coercing the young men of the city into
contests of strength and tournaments, Gilgamesh plays too
rough for them. The cry of Uruk's harassed inhabitants rises to
the gods, who determine that Gilgamesh needs a companion,
a peer who can be a match for him at his own singular level
of proficiency. Thus the gods commission the creation of a
counterpart, Enkidu.

A primitive born and reared in the wilderness, Enkidu
roams wild with the animals, causing trouble for hunters by
freeing their prey from traps. One day a trapper spots him in
the herd and sends a harlot from Uruk to seduce him. Thus begins Enkidu's entry into human culture. After an extended sex-
ual encounter, Enkidu attempts to rejoin the animals. But they
now dart away in fear, and he finds he can no longer keep pace
with them. Enkidu returns to sit at the feet of the harlot, and
she further inducts him into human ways—clothing him and
leading him to a shepherd's camp, where he learns to eat bread,
drink beer, bathe, and groom himself. Enkidu is city bound.

As Enkidu is led by the harlot through the streets of Uruk,
the people gather to gape at this splendid figure who bears an
uncanny resemblance to the lordly Gilgamesh. Enkidu and
King Gilgamesh meet up in the town square and engage in a
colossal wrestling match, sending tremors throughout the city.
Though it is unclear who wins, the result of the conflict is mutual admiration. Deeply drawn to one another, Gilgamesh and

Enkidu embrace and become devoted friends from that moment onward.

For a time the two lead a contented life in Uruk. But it is not long before Enkidu becomes anxious that the good life is making him soft. In response Gilgamesh proposes a perilous expedition across the wilderness to the sacred Cedar Forest. There they will conquer its divinely appointed guardian, the mighty Humbaba. Enkidu, the one better acquainted with the terrors of this ogre of the forest, balks at the treacherous mission. In a telling passage, Gilgamesh rebukes him for his reluctance: "[Only] the gods can dwell forever with Shamash [the sun god]. As for human beings, their days are numbered, and whatever they keep trying to achieve is but wind! . . . Should I fall, I will have established my fame. [They will say]: 'It was *Gilgamesh* who locked in battle with Humbaba the Terrible!'" (Kovacs 1989, 20). Gilgamesh's philosophy of life is encapsulated here. He lives by the warrior ethic. Since all humans must die, what counts is to have an honorable death against a worthy foe, thus ensuring one will live on in reputation. But Gilgamesh's hero ideology is to be challenged by one cataclysmic event.

Despite the great odds against them, Enkidu and Gilgamesh slay the terrible Humbaba and fell the sacred Cedar. Back in Uruk, bathed and groomed after his triumphal return, Gilgamesh attracts the attention of the goddess Ishtar. She proposes marriage but Gilgamesh declines, noting the unhappy fates of her previous lovers. Incensed, Ishtar unleashes the terrible Bull of Heaven on the city. The Bull wreaks destruction on Uruk and its inhabitants, blowing giant pits in the ground with each titanic snort. Nonetheless Enkidu and Gilgamesh are able to defeat the Bull with some strategic teamwork. The enraged Ishtar pronounces a curse on Gilgamesh, and Enkidu responds by ripping off the shank of the bull and flinging it at her. As Ishtar and her women mourn, Enkidu and Gilgamesh celebrate their victory, hailed by the women of the palace in a chorus of praise.

Gilgamesh and Enkidu are at the top of their game. But they have encroached on divine territory, and there will be consequences. That same night in a dream Enkidu sees the gods deliberate in council and then rule that he must bear the punishment. Enkidu falls ill, and Gilgamesh can only watch helplessly as he deteriorates day by day. On the twelfth day Enkidu dies. Grief-stricken, Gilgamesh circles the body frantically, tearing out his hair and stripping off his finery. He then clings to the corpse for so long that physical decay sets in.

Gilgamesh has had a taste of death. He is inconsolable for the loss of his beloved friend, but that is not the only consequence. The sight of death in its concrete reality has brought Gilgamesh face-to-face with his own mortality: "I am going to die—am I not like Enkidu?! Deep sadness penetrates my core" (Kovacs 1989, 75). Henceforth Gilgamesh is obsessed. He must, at any cost, find a way to avoid this dreaded fate. He determines to search out the only human ever known to have attained immortal status, the flood hero Utnapishtim. In ancient times this king survived the great deluge and was then by divine decree exempted from the fate of humankind. Gilgamesh will make his way to the dwelling of the flood hero at the far end of the earth and wrest his secret from him.

Dressed in animal skins, foraging for his food, digging wells for water, Gilgamesh traverses the steppe in a stupor of grief and fear. Those he encounters try to dissuade him from his futile quest. But Gilgamesh is undeterred. When the sun god, fearing for his well-being, implores him to desist from roaming, Gilgamesh replies that there will be rest aplenty in the grave. At long last Gilgamesh comes to the edge of the earth. If he is to reach the dwelling of Utnapishtim, he must first cross the ocean that surrounds it and then cross the lethal waters of death. It is then that he encounters Siduri, the wise keeper of the tavern at the ocean's edge. Seeing his dishevelment, she takes him for a hunter or some rough type and bars her door. Assuring her he is indeed the renowned king, brought to such a state by the loss of his comrade, Gilgamesh beseeches her for help:

Enkidu, whom I love so dearly,
who went with me in all hardships,
has now gone to the fate of humankind.

Days and nights I wept over him.
I would not give him up for burial,
as if he would rise up to me at my cry,
seven days and seven nights,
until a maggot fell down from his nose.
Since his passing I have not found life;
I have roamed like a hunter in the midst of the wild.

O tavern-keeper, now that I have seen your face,
Let me not see the death that I ever dread. (AT)

Siduri, chiding gently, replies:

Gilgamesh, where are you going?

The life you pursue you will not find.
When the gods made humankind,
Death they assigned to humankind,
Life they kept in their own hands.

You, Gilgamesh, let your stomach be full.
Day and night enjoy yourself,
Of each day make a festival,
Dance and play, day and night.
Let your garments be sparkling fresh,
Bathe your head, may you wash yourself in water.
Look on the little one holding your hand,
Let the wife in your embrace have pleasure time and again.

This is the task of [humankind]. (AT)

In response to Gilgamesh's inconsolable grief over the de-
parted, Siduri urges him to turn to the living. In response to his
abject terror of death, she urges him to accept it as a given and
drink deeply of life and its pleasures, making *each* day a feast
day (see discussion of Eccl 9:1-12 for further comments on the
message of Siduri).

But Gilgamesh cannot hear her counsel. He can see only the "death that [he] ever dread[s]." With the guidance of Siduri, he locates the ferryman who will take him the final stage of his journey. At long last he reaches the flood hero. Utnapishtim replies to Gilgamesh's stricken appeal with a lengthy rumination on the inevitability of death. It renders all human effort and action transient: "For how long do we build a household? For how long do we seal a document? For how long do brothers share the inheritance?" (Kovacs 1989, 93). Utnapishtim ends with reiteration of Siduri's assurance: the gods have decreed death as the lot of humans; no exceptions apply.

To be noted in particular is the opening of Utnapishtim's speech, which responds specifically to the incessant questing of Gilgamesh in his attempt to avoid the inevitable. Here Utnapishtim draws out a particular irony in the situation of the hero. Noting wryly that the village idiot also dresses poorly and eats bad food, he says: "You have toiled without cease, what have you got? Through toil you are wearing [yourself] out, you are filling your body with grief, *you are bringing forward the end of your days*" (Lambert 1980, 55; emphasis added). The irony is that the denial of death is life-sapping. Gilgamesh, in his frantic efforts to ward off the inevitable, "[brings] forward the end of his days."

Siduri the barmaid, in her address to Gilgamesh, has referred to the actions she has advocated as the "task" of humanity. I suggest that these words hearken back to her initial assertion: when the gods made humans, they kept one destiny for themselves and assigned humans another. Her ensuing call to Gilgamesh to feast, to celebrate, to love with affection and passion, becomes, in effect, an amplification on mortal status. It is a description of what *is* properly the human domain. Gilgamesh has wished to transcend his mortal nature. In response Siduri assures him he cannot. But she points out those other things that also belong to that status. In seeking to avoid death, the defining mark of his humanity, Gilgamesh has also missed out on those *goods* that are a constituent part of humanness. It is noteworthy that before Siduri offers Gilgamesh a *modus vivendi,* she asserts the certainty of death for every human. Implicit in this sequencing is a recognition that before Gilgamesh may reenter life he must come to terms with the inevitability of death. He must accept death before he can begin to live.

Drawing masterfully from the ancient lore surrounding this mighty warrior legend, the author of this tale has composed a kind of anti-epic. The heroic postures by which people seek to thwart death are exposed as illusory. The story asserts the very real limitation of death on human existence but at the same time affirms the sweetness of the goods and blessings that are part and parcel of that finite existence. As we will see, the thought of Qohelet is imbued with such themes.

ECCLESIASTES 1:1-2

Making Introductions: The Speaker and His Theme

1:1 Introducing Qohelet

The book of Ecclesiastes begins with two important pieces of information—an identification of its author and an encapsulation of its contents—yet each does more to pique curiosity than to satisfy it.

Qohelet (NRSV "Teacher" [see introduction]) is introduced as speaker of the words to follow. He is further identified in a way that suggests a royal identity, and a specific one at that. Though the patronymic "son of David" might refer to any descendant in David's line, Qohelet's own self-announcement in verse 12 points to the figure of Solomon, and the ensuing first-person report is reminiscent of the biblical image of that king (1:12–2:11). Still, the text of 1:1 stops short of naming the name. This is noteworthy, for no such restraint is seen in the ascriptions of the books of Proverbs and Song of Songs, which include explicit attributions to Solomon. In fact, the name Solomon is found nowhere in the book of Ecclesiastes. More to the point, the royal identity adopted here does not seem to play a role after the first two chapters. In the remainder of the book Qohelet speaks from the perspective of a subject, not a ruler (e.g., 4:1; 8:2-4; 10:4, 16-17), and at the conclusion of the book, where he is once again spoken of in the third person, he is eulogized as a wise man, not a king (12:9-10). These factors suggest that the royal identity sketched at the opening of the book is a kind of guise adopted for rhetorical effect—Qohelet plays a role to argue a point—which is then shed after it has served its purpose in the opening two chapters (see 1:12–2:26).[1]

1:2 All Is Vapor!

Verse 2 offers a motto or summary of Qohelet's teaching in the form of a quotation. The theme word here, Hebrew *hebel*, traditionally translated as "vanity," occurs thirty-eight times within the book of Ecclesiastes. These attestations account for over half the word's occurrences in the entire Old Testament! The literal meaning of the Hebrew word is "mist, vapor, breath." Strikingly, however, it is used in its concrete sense in just one instance (see Isa 57:13). Otherwise the word is most often used metaphorically throughout the Old Testament, with connotations that derive in some fashion from the physical properties of vapor.

The fact that this word is chosen to exemplify Qohelet's central motif is most intriguing. It does not seem to have a precise significance that the book's ancient audience would easily recognize, at least so far as the biblical evidence will take us. While the term in context often has negative connotations, such as futility and even deception (presumably drawing upon vapor's insubstantial properties), it can also matter-of-factly refer to the impermanence of things and the transient nature of human existence (see Excursus). The malleability of the term is one reason commentators have come to such markedly different conclusions about the tonality of the book (see introduction).

---

1. For alternative conceptions of the role and function of the royal identity in Ecclesiastes, see, e.g., Perdue 1994, 194–201; Longman III 1998, esp. 15–20; Koh 2006; Barbour 2012.

As for its first occurrence here in the prelude to the book, the status of *vapor* as theme word is heralded with a fivefold repetition. The construction of the Hebrew phrase is a superlative and might be rendered, "Utter vapor . . . utter vapor. All is vapor." This motto is repeated almost verbatim at the conclusion of Qohelet's words (12:8), thus serving as a frame for them. Yet, as noted, the import of the declaration "All is vapor" is far from self-evident! Thus the statement functions as a tantalizing lure, urging the reader further into the contents of the book.

Excursus: *Vapor* in the Old Testament and in Ecclesiastes

Vapor in the Old Testament

Vapor is predominantly used as a metaphor in the Old Testament. Its connotations may be, broadly speaking, divided into two categories: that which is insubstantial and that which is transient, though the division is somewhat artificial in some instances (see Miller 1998, 445–48).

Vapor *as Insubstantiality in the Old Testament*

Miller has characterized this category as "a matter of expectation versus reality" (1998, 446). This quality leads to such connotations as *ineffective* and *useless*, as in Isaiah 30:7, where Egypt's military assistance for Judah is pronounced "[vapor] and empty." In a similar vein it is used to connote futile exertion, as in Isaiah 49:4: "I said, for emptiness I have labored, for nothing and *vapor* I have spent my strength" (AT; see Job 9:29;

Ps 39:6 [Heb. 7]). In a meaning that is related to the sense of inefficacy, the word can suggest deception, something illusory, as in Job 21:34: "How then will you comfort me with [*vapor*]? There is nothing left of your answers but falsehood" (cf. Zech 10:2). *Vapor* is employed in several places as an epithet for false gods (e.g., Deut 32:21; Jer 8:19; 16:19), a use that derives from its associations with inefficacy and that which is illusory or deceptive.

Vapor *as Transience in the Old Testament*

This dimension is seen in a few passages, primarily from the Psalms, where the term is used to connote the transience of human existence. The psalmist prays: "You have made my days a few handbreadths, and my lifetime is as nothing in your sight. Surely everyone stands as a mere breath [*vapor*]" (Ps 39:5 [Heb. 6]). The image of humans as vapor—a mere breath—is a means of expressing the definitive demarcation between creator and creature, divine and mortal. In Psalm 144:3-4 the poet exclaims: "O Lord, what are humans that you regard them, or mortals that you think of them? They are like a breath [*vapor*]; their days are like a passing shadow." In these and similar meditations *vapor* is part of a matrix of images (such as "breath," "cloud," and "shadow") that convey the condition of human finitude (see further Pss 39:11; 62:9 [Heb. 10]; Job 7:16).

Vapor in Ecclesiastes

In keeping with biblical convention, Qohelet, too, employs the term metaphorically. But Qohelet is quite unique in one respect. In other biblical contexts the connotations of the term are constant within a given literary setting. By contrast Qohelet may employ the term with differing connotations within a given passage; the question of which is at play is informed by the immediate context in which it is found. The malleability of the image is demonstrated in chapter 11.

In verse 8 *vapor* is associated with the state of death: "Even if a man lives many years, let him rejoice in them all. Let him remember that the days of darkness will be many. All that comes is *vapor*" (AT). In verse 10, however, it is applied to the days of youth. Here a young man is addressed and urgently encouraged to savor life to the fullest, for (translating literally) "youth and dawn are *vapor*." Obviously *vapor* cannot carry the same import in these two instances. In the latter case the reference is to the fleeting nature of youth. In the case of 11:8, however, *vapor* appears to function as an elaboration on "the days of darkness," hence it is the shadowy, obscuring qualities of vapor that are at play. Thus we see that within the span of a few verses Qohelet employs the image with different connotations, though both are in some way related to the qualities of *vapor* (see also 6:11-12).

Qohelet's use of the metaphor shares common ground with other biblical tradents in that he often uses it to connote transience and insubstantiality. Yet, as is evident from 11:8 (where *vapor* is related to the days of darkness, or death), Qohelet is also exploiting other inherent possibilities for the metaphor. *Vapor* is, in fact, a versatile image for Qohelet, thus presenting a challenge for interpreters as its meaning must be gleaned from clues in the context.

It is helpful to begin, however, with some examples that follow more typical biblical usage.

Vapor *as Insubstantiality in Ecclesiastes*

In some passages Qohelet uses *vapor* to convey that which is insubstantial. In this domain *vapor* can refer to things or actions that are ineffectual, futile, trivial, or ultimately lacking in any satisfactory result. In chapter 5 *vapor* characterizes the talk of a fool: "As a host of vaporous dreams, so are many words; instead fear God" (5:7 [emended]). In chapter 6 it applies to superfluous speech in general: "The more words, the more [*vapor*], so how is one the better?" (6:11).

Vapor *as Transience in Ecclesiastes*

In other passages vapor's impermanence and transience are at play, as seen in 11:10, where the young man is encouraged to enjoy life while there is still time. This aspect is evident in 6:4, where *vapor* conveys the ephemeral existence of a stillborn child: "For it comes in *vapor* and goes into darkness, and in darkness its name is covered" (based on NRSV). In 6:12 it characterizes the fleeting nature of human existence in general: "For who knows what is good for mortals while they live the numbered days of their *vapor* lives, which they pass like a shadow?" (based on NRSV). Compare also 7:15 and 9:9.

The Ambiguity of Vapor *in Ecclesiastes*

There are, however, other places in Ecclesiastes where the nuances of *vapor* are outside of the associations typically found elsewhere in the Old Testament (see Seow, "Beyond Mortal Grasp: The Usage of *Hebel* in Ecclesiastes," *ABR* 48 [2000]: 10–14). To make matters more challenging, Qohelet most often applies *vapor* to situations, or a constellation of circumstances. Because the *vapor* assessment is applied to scenarios, the precise target of the evaluation may be in question, a matter that impacts the question of vapor's nuance: "Again, I saw *vapor* under the sun: one man, and no companion; nor does he have a son or a brother. And there is no end to all his toil. Moreover his eyes are not satisfied with wealth. 'For whom am I toiling,' he asks, 'and depriving myself of pleasure?' This also is *vapor* and an unhappy business" (4:7-8, AT). What is the *vapor* of this scenario? Is it the desolate solitude of the man (cf. 4:9), the absence of any heir (cf. 2:18-19), the fact that he toils compulsively (cf. 2:11), the unquenchable desire for more (5:10 and 6:7), or the sum of all these? Does *vapor* convey a hollow existence, futile striving, the illusion of wealth as a means of fulfillment, or all of the above? The passage well illustrates the inherent ambiguity in the metaphor, as well as in Qohelet's application of the vapor assessment. There is in fact a riddle-like quality to *vapor* in Ecclesiastes. We as readers are exercised to ponder the image in its relationship to the situations put before us.

The NRSV follows the King James Version in rendering *vapor* with the abstract term "vanity." The consistent translation of *vapor* with a single abstract term is not unique to the NRSV and King James Version; this is in fact the most common route taken in translations and commentaries. Proposals offered have included "meaninglessness," "futility," "transience," and "incomprehensibility," to name a few. Yet due to the pliant nature of the image in Ecclesiastes, such terms founder at one point or another when they are inserted for every occurrence of *vapor*. No single word fits all occurrences of *vapor* in Ecclesiastes. The problem, however, is not just with the constricting nature of a single term, but with the constriction inherent in the use of an abstract term for a poetic image: as with any key poetic image, it cannot be glossed without losing a *play* of meaning. Throughout his discourse Qohelet wields words with a poet's sensibility; his use of *vapor* is no exception (see Miller 1998, 444–45). It is best to allow *vapor* to stand as is, as a poetic image or metaphor in which various qualities or dimensions of the entities *vapor/breath* shift and move to the fore, depending upon the literary context (compare Miller 1998, 437–54).

Even at this, we may suggest that Qohelet's repetition of the word in a wide array of settings pushes at the bounds of its metaphorical possibilities, suggesting the status of a coded term—a word that draws on traditional usage, but for which Qohelet is forging additional ramifications. When Qohelet considers that humans and animals both share the fate of death, he deems this *vapor* (3:19-21). One cannot take this simply as a matter-of-fact observation on creaturely transience, for when Qohelet dwells upon this shared essence between humans and animals without acknowledging any distinction at all, he is countering biblical traditions on the orders of creation (compare, e.g., Ps 8:3-9 and Gen 1:27-31). Moreover his sense of affront is palpable. He dwells at length on the fact, stating it first one way, and then another, as if he cannot quite fathom it: "They all have the same breath, and humans have no advantage whatsoever over the animals; indeed all is *vapor*. For both go to one place; both are from dust, and both turn to dust again" (3:19b-20, AT).

A similar tone is found in his comparison of wisdom to folly in 2:12-16. Qohelet acknowledges wisdom's relative advantage over foolishness—"The wise have eyes in their head, but fools walk in darkness" (2:14)—but is aghast at the fact that both suffer the same fate of death and moreover are consigned to oblivion: "Then I said to myself, 'What happens to the fool will happen to me also; why then have I been so very wise?' And I said to myself that this also is [*vapor*]"(2:15). Again in chapter 8, Qohelet's indignation is at its height as he observes that sometimes it is in fact the righteous who meet an untimely end and the wicked who enjoy long days (8:14; cf. 12-13). The situation presented is an affront to the most fundamental of wisdom principles: that the righteous and the wicked will ultimately receive their due justice from God (Prov 10:27; 11:4; 13:9, etc.). That such an inversion should occur is beyond comprehension, something Qohelet cannot "get his head around," so to speak. Qohelet underscores the *vapor* of this situation by hemming it round with the verdict: "There is a *vapor* that takes place on earth . . . I said that this also is *vapor*."

The passages cited have to do with a fundamental dissonance between who a person is and what befalls him or her. Too often things are not as they should be. Qohelet covers the gamut of disappointments in his observations on life, from that of corrupt persons accorded public recognition and honors at their death (8:10) to the individual who toils earnestly with skill and wisdom, only to lose all to one who has done nothing to deserve it (2:21). Speaking broadly, the refrain of *vapor* in Ecclesiastes becomes a kind of cipher for disillusionment—the fundamental disparity between human hopes and expectations for what life should be, and life as it is. Such disparities boggle the mind of the sage steeped in traditional wisdom teachings. To speak of these as disappointments is not adequate. The effect is one of profound disorientation, a disorientation that Qohelet allows the readers to see (see introduction).

While allowing that the various translations proposed for *vapor* offer illumination at one point or another, it should be reiterated that to translate all occurrences with any single abstract term will invariably prove a misfit at one point or another, given its nature as metaphor. The ultimate effect of translating the metaphor with a single abstract term is to reduce the variegated shades of this work to a monochromatic tone. Given the nature of *vapor* as a metaphor, which clearly encompasses multiple valences for Qohelet, the concrete term should be preserved. It may be argued, moreover, that the widely favored and long venerated translation of "vanity" is particularly unhelpful. In modern English usage the word conveys something without value, or emptiness as well as futility (something done "in vain"). Also included is the meaning *self-conceit*, a more common connotation in popular usage, perhaps the first that comes to mind for the average reader.

Reading Ecclesiastes with "vanity" as the theme word has had undue influence on popular interpretations of the book. In general such a reading tends to locate the source of the flawed world observed by Qohelet in the shortcomings of humanity. Though Qohelet does indeed bemoan the misdirected strivings of humans (e.g., 4:7-8; 5:10-11, 13-17) as well as (more rarely) the role of self-conceit and pride in human effort (e.g., 2:4-9; 4:4), these are minor concerns as compared with his larger preoccupation—that is with the way in which human desire for meaning and coherence is thwarted at most every turn. Qohelet's musings are not, then, in the vein of pious chidings from above. His sympathy is squarely cast with his fellow earthlings, who thirst for meaning and understanding in the face of divinely set limitations.

The Legacy of Amnesia

The opening two verses of the book have introduced Qohelet and announced the theme statement of vapor. In verse 3 a poem begins. Qohelet's reflections will also conclude with a poem (12:2-7), which will in turn be followed by a repetition of the vapor statement in 1:2.

Literary Analysis

A question initiates the passage: What do people gain from all their toil in life? The ensuing poem displays a world of incessant movement: the tramp, tramp of generations, the perpetual movement of the sun, the unremitting cycle of the wind, the coursing of the world's water sources. And yet, as soon becomes apparent, all this energy belies an inertia at the heart of things.

The poet has employed certain formal devices to convey this sense of ceaseless and pointless movement. The abundant use of participles conveys a mood of continuous activity and busy-ness (going, coming, rising, rounding). At the same time the monotony and tedium of these activities are highlighted by a repetitive style. For instance, the verb *to go* appears six times in verses 4-7, and the verb *to go round* appears three times in verse 6 alone. Moreover, instead of using pronouns for subjects already stated (e.g., the sun rises, and *it* sets) the poet repeats the subject: a "generation . . . a generation" (v. 4); the "sun . . .

the sun" (v. 5); the "wind . . . the wind" (v. 6); the "sea . . . the sea" (v. 7). These devices create an aura of monotony and weariness.

After pondering the succession of generations and the constant and recurring movements of elements of nature, Qohelet turns to the realm of human activity (v. 8). The manner in which these images cohere with one another and relate to the larger theme of the poem is explained in different ways, but it can be said broadly that they reinforce the theme of constant movement without attainment of any goal or sense of fulfillment. Verse 9 states the theme that unifies the images of verses 4-8: "What has been is what will be, and what has been done is what will be done; there is nothing new under the sun." Verses 10 and 11, written in a more prosaic style, elaborate on the theme of "nothing new under the sun." Verse 11, in its allusion to the succession of generations, harks back to the initial image of verse 4, forming a frame with it.

Exegetical Analysis

1:3 Toil and Gain

"What do people gain from all the toil at which they toil under the sun?" With this question Qohelet initiates his investigation into the nature of human life and experience. "Toil" is an apt rendering of the Hebrew term, which carries connotations of drudgery and arduous labor for Qohelet (4:8; 5:15; 6:7). As one reads further in the book it becomes evident that Qohelet also employs the word to encompass human activity and experience in general—it is the toil inherent in human existence (e.g., 3:9; 4:9; 8:17; compare Job 3:10; 5:7).

The term "gain" (*yitrôn*) is unique to Ecclesiastes in the Old Testament. The verb means "to surpass, to exceed, be additional." Hence the noun may, on the one hand, be used comparatively to indicate an advantage (this meaning is clear in 2:13, for instance). Alternatively it can indicate a surplus or gain. In fact, taken within the context of the number of other economic terms employed by Qohelet, such as "inheritance," "salary," and "money" as well as such words as "account" and "deficit" (see Seow 1997, 22), the term might be translated as "profit" (2:11; 3:9; 5:9, 16). The issue of toil and its profit (or lack thereof) will preoccupy the sage, particularly in the first half of the book (2:11; 2:22; 3:9; 5:16 [Heb. 5:15]). It is as if Qohelet adopts the status of an accountant, examining life as one might the columns of a ledger sheet. The implied scenario belies the poignancy of the subject matter; Qohelet's opening query speaks to the heart of human desire for meaning.

1:4-11

An epoch is but a swing of the pendulum; and each generation thinks the world is progressing because it is always moving.
George Bernard Shaw, *Man and Superman: A Comedy and a Philosophy*

I put a dollar in a change machine. Nothing changed.
George Carlin

Beginning with the steady march of generations, the first line of the poem evokes the ever-constant cycle of death and birth. This opening line is often read as a contrast between the transience of humanity on the one hand, and the stability and permanence of the natural realm on the other. While this is a viable interpretation, it is difficult to support within the immediate context of the poem, since this theme is not developed. The Hebrew word for "earth" is not limited to the physical earth but may also be inclusive of humanity—in other words, the world. In that case the point of verse 4 is that despite the continual turnover of the generations the world continues on as ever (NRSV "forever"). In this reading the world in its relationship to the generations is not unlike the sea in its relationship to the rivers (v. 7). Just as the sea remains unaffected by the incessant flow of the channels, so the world remains unchanged by the constant cycling of the generations. All this activity leaves no mark in its wake.

The vocabulary of this opening verse merits further attention. In the poetry of the Old Testament, the phrase "generation to generation" in conjunction with "forever" is expressive of an idea of continuation or continuity, as in Psalm 79:13: "Then we your people, the flock of your pasture, will give thanks to you forever; from generation to generation we will recount your praise" (Seow 1999, 106; see also Exod 3:15; Deut 32:7; Pss 45:17, 89:1 [Heb. 89:2]; 100:5; Isa 51:8). Qohelet's invocation of this idea in a wisdom context carries additional connotations. Wisdom tradition emphasizes the imparting of wisdom through generational channels. The present generation can learn from the previous generation, which has learned from the generation preceding it (Prov 4:1-4; Job 8:8-10; Sir 8:9). Such a view of history, with its supposition of a fund of knowledge held in common, is inherently optimistic. Qohelet's vocabulary in these two lines is evocative not only of the poetic language of continuity cited in the examples above but, within the specific context of wisdom discourse, this optimistic lens on history. However the actual content of verse 4 creates a dissonance with this idea. Qohelet's language is more that of discontinuity than continuity: one generation departs, another arrives, and nothing comes of this succession. The world goes on as ever (see Brown 1996, 123–25).

The focus shifts to elements of nature—sun, wind, and water. The sun's twenty-four-hour journey ultimately brings it back to where it began. The exertion of the trek is conveyed by the nuance of its hastening or, better, panting to its starting point (see Isa 42:14, where the verb describes the gasping of a woman in labor). The portrayal contrasts with Psalm 19, where the sun "comes out like a bridegroom from his wedding canopy, and like a strong man runs its course with joy" (v. 5). The image is one of virility and brimming vigor; bursting forth on the horizon, the sun skims across the sky like a mighty warrior running his course. By contrast the sun in Qohelet's portrayal is almost decrepit. Taxed by its course, it huffs to its destination, only to have to start again.

Verse 6 commences with a heaping up of verbs—*going, rounding, rounding, rounding, going*—with the subject of all this activity withheld until the end of the third poetic line (a delay not evident in most English translations). This strategy momentarily focuses the reader's attention on the activity itself. The repetition of the participles conveys an energetic movement that verges on frenetic. The wind, like the sun, is confined to a circuit. Despite great expenditure of energy, the wind can only come round to its starting place, again and again. There is much activity but no progress, no achievement, no goal attained.

With the image of the flowing rivers (v. 7) Qohelet conveys this theme of movement without progress by a different dynamic. All streams flow to the sea and do so repeatedly, and yet the sea does not fill up. Thus the image of futile activity, conveyed by the image of a cycle in the case of the sun and the wind, is here expressed as the constant activity of one entity upon another, with no change to show for it (compare v. 4).

Certain stylistic shifts highlight verse 8 and mark it off from what has preceded. The verse consists of four concise declarative statements, each with its own subject. The participle form of the verb is no longer employed and repetition is minimal. The lament that "all things are weary [NRSV wearisome]; more than one can express" is an apt response to the view of the grand elements of nature toiling along to no avail. It is intriguing, however, that the Hebrew word translated "things" can also mean *words*. Thus the line may alternatively be translated: "All *words* are weary [or: worn out]; a person is unable to speak." The reference to speech and its inefficacy is, in fact, in continuity with the images of frustrated seeing and hearing that follow: "The eye is not satisfied with seeing, or the ear filled with hearing."

In this latter interpretation Qohelet has, with the first clause of verse 8, turned his focus to the human realm, which mirrors the cosmos in its courses of futility. Though commentators

14

usually align themselves with one reading or another—reading either "all things" (v. 8ab is a response to the comprehensive vision of futility in verses 4-7) or "all words" (v. 8ab signifies a shift to the human realm, and the meaning of the first line is only fully discerned after reading further), it is possible that the poetic ambiguity should be maintained: verse 8ab is a caesura that momentarily positions the reader before the view of the weary, unfulfilled cosmos before shifting the reader's attention to the analogous human situation.

With the sweeping assertion that "what has been is what will be, and what has been done is what will be done; there is nothing new under the sun," Qohelet states the unifying theme of the depiction of the natural elements: sun, wind, and water can do what only they have already done. The pronouncement also embroiders further on the unsatisfying nature of human expression and perception: words, sights, sounds—it has all been said, seen, and heard before.

In verse 10 Qohelet anticipates an objection to the claim: If there is nothing new under the sun, how is it that people have the sensation of novelty—of new discoveries and unprecedented achievements? The response to this is played out in the closing lines of the poem. In short, any experience of newness (hence achievement or progress) is an illusion, created by the fact that humans are confined to a limited perspective. Verse 11 merits a closer look, as translations of it differ. According to the NRSV translation it is "people" who are not remembered. Though Qohelet would heartily agree with the statement that all persons are eventually forgotten by subsequent generations (and will lament this fact in the chapters to come), this idea is a non sequitur in the immediate context of the poem. The underlying Hebrew terms for "people of long ago," and "people yet to come" may alternatively refer more generally to events: "There is no remembrance of things past, nor of things yet to come will there be remembrance among those who come still later" (Fox 1999, 164). Happenings and events of history seem new only because of human forgetfulness. The concluding line of verse 11 is key: "Nor of the things yet to come will there be remembrance *among those who come still later*" (Fox 1999, 164). The final clause is a subtle masterstroke. As observed, the opening image of the poem in its reference to generation following generation evokes a sense of continuity and, implicitly, development. But it does so only to bring the worldview behind such images into question by subsequently presenting a cosmos where things can only repeat themselves and no progress is made. The image of successive generations would normally imply continuity and, within the wisdom context in particular, the concomitant idea of the handing on of knowledge from one generation to another. Here in verse 11 Qohelet once again alludes to this idea only to subvert it: the thing that is "passed on" from one generation to the next is not knowledge, but *forgetfulness*. Just as one age has no remembrance of things prior to it, so the subsequent age will have no knowledge of things prior to it. Though the ongoing succession of generations should offer the potential of a shared fund of human wisdom and understanding, there is no such data bank.

The reflections in verses 4-11 help to frame and define the initial question posed in verse 3. On the face of it, the question about toil and its profit pertains to an individual's life and work, probing the possibility of meaning from a more individualistic standpoint. Qohelet will indeed explore the question from this perspective. But here at the beginning of the book Qohelet has contextualized the question of life's meaning in a particular way, by stepping back and pondering the world and the flow of time at a remove. The question of "profit" for a person in his or her own life and work is immediately held up to this grand-scale canvas. The question of meaningful existence and action has a slightly different hue in this context, where all of history, past and future, is assayed. The cosmos presented here is characterized by much industrious labor, but this grand play of light and movement is exposed as a phantasmagoria. This is a world where things can only repeat themselves, and no progress is made. So it is with the human realm, despite the perpetual toil of humanity. History is not progress. It is repetition.

Humans will never achieve a novel thing, attain a new goal, or reach uncharted territory.

Theological and Ethical Analysis

Weariness comes at the end of the acts of a mechanical life.
Albert Camus, *The Myth of Sisyphus*

It was in the midst of the Nazi occupation of France that the French-Algerian author Albert Camus wrote his most noted essay, *The Myth of Sisyphus* (published in 1942). As with Qohelet, Camus was asking fundamental questions about life and its meaning. For him these questions were pressed to urgency by his belief that people could no longer take refuge in the idea of a world governed by a sovereign God or in a life beyond the grave. These were myths whose day had passed. He thus sought to address what he perceived as the fundamental disorientation arising from a ground shift in cultural and religious assumptions, in which humans found themselves alone "in a universe suddenly divested of illusions and lights" (Camus 1955, 5).

Camus's account of the wearisome workaday grind of everyday life carries resonances of the opening poem of Ecclesiastes: "Rising, streetcar, four hours in the office or the factory, meal, streetcar, four hours of work, meal, sleep, and Monday Tuesday Wednesday Thursday Friday and Saturday according to the same rhythm—this path is easily followed most of the time" (Camus 1955, 10). The routines of our lives bear us along and absorb us, keeping us occupied with that next task or that next goal just ahead, even as we come round to where we started. Yet . . . sometimes it happens that an event, or an experience, interrupts us in our accustomed round. It might be a story in the news, a tragic accident we witness, news of a schoolmate's death, a parent's sudden infirmity, or an event quite insignificant on the face of it. We are brought up short and we ask, "What is it all for?" It is such a moment that interests Camus—that moment when "the habit of living" is called into question: "But one day the 'why' arises and everything begins in that weariness tinged with amazement" (Camus 1955, 10).

This capacity to step back from our lives and to ponder our existence at a remove is unique to human beings. It is the quality that sets us apart from all other living creatures. We alone have the ability to ask: Is there value and meaning to what I do? What is the point of it all? Is this all that there is to living? One may well question whether we are to be envied for such a capacity. Would it not be more merciful to be as the worker bees or the ants that know their tasks and follow their instincts unburdened by reflection? As Camus acknowledges, confrontation with the limits of our existence brings pain, fatigue, and a metaphysical disorientation. Camus even allows that such awareness may bring a despair that ends in suicide. One may in all earnestness ask why consciousness is worth the risk.

For Camus, however, the alternative—to remain in oblivion, or to revert to that state—is itself a kind of death. To deny the conditions of our human existence prohibits us from truly claiming our lives. It is only through an honest and full address of the limits of our existence that we gain access to ourselves as we truly are in this world and are thus able to lay claim to our lives with clarity and authenticity. So Camus advocates, for all its hazards, the route of confrontation over that of oblivion, the route of honesty over self-deception.

As for Qohelet, the starting point for his thought is not as stark as that of Camus. For Camus God is entirely absent from the world, leaving humans to make their way in an indifferent universe. Qohelet holds to belief in a sovereign creator. Nonetheless there are strong affinities between the two thinkers. Though Qohelet never questions the existence of his God, or his God's sovereign status, he does find this God enigmatic in actions toward humans, distant and inscrutable for all practical purposes. Moreover Qohelet offers no respite from life's harsh realities in the notion of a life beyond death (3:19-22). Though Camus and Qohelet may articulate the plight of humans after different assumptions, for both death is the ultimate boundary. For both as well, confrontation with the limits of being human is requisite to any subsequent process of making or discovering meaning.

Qohelet's opening poem is trenchant testimony to that moment of metaphysical vertigo in which a person steps back and views his or her life, work, and aspirations against the larger vista of planet and history—glimpsing humans for the small and finite creatures they are. "Weariness comes at the end of the acts of a mechanical life," writes Camus, "but at the same time it inaugurates the impulse of consciousness" (Camus 1955, 10). The poem of Ecclesiastes 1, standing at the brink of Qohelet's journey, reflects such an inauguration.

The Royal Quest: When All You've Ever Wanted Isn't Enough

With verse 12 of chapter 1 the book shifts from the impersonal mode to the autobiographical style that will dominate until 12:8. In verses 1-2 of this chapter the words of Qohelet were mediated to us as if by a third party. Now Qohelet himself steps forward in his own voice, introducing himself and his project. Yet in this initial phase of the book he chooses to speak under an assumed identity—the royal guise of king.

Literary Analysis

The development of thought in these two chapters is not easily tracked, as can be seen in the diverse ways in which commentators have catalogued and tagged their components and transitions. It seems that, for whatever reason, the writer has not been intent on presenting a highly structured or even logically organized argument in this opening section. Any identification of discrete segments and topics is somewhat artificial and fails at one point or another to take account of some part of this multileveled rumination. The identification of segments and topics presented here is provisional and is intended to serve more as a heuristic guide to a discourse that is, at points, more akin to a stream-of-consciousness reflection. I propose three major parts to this section, followed by a conclusion in 2:24-26. The initial segment, comprising 1:12-18, is an introduction and summary of the author's quest to comprehend his world. In the ensuing segments of 2:1-11 and 2:12-23 he fills in the content of his search for understanding and meaning. In 2:1-11 he explores the possibility of fulfillment through pleasure as well as ambitious work—grandiose ventures in building and acquisition fit for a king. In 2:12-23 he ponders the value of wisdom in the context of death (2:12-17), and from there he turns again to the issue of dedicated toil and its shortfalls (2:18-23)—also in the light of death. The recognition that *all* human accomplishment is expunged by death is, in fact, the place to which all Qohelet's reflections have been moving. The closing reflection in verses 24-26 is offered in the light of this recognition.

An understanding of cultural context is highly illuminating for this introductory section. In features of both language and style it imitates the royal inscription, a genre amply attested in other cultures of the ancient Near East (Seow 1995, 275–82). Such inscriptions, often written in the voice of the king himself, commemorate the grandeur of his achievements, detailing his great wealth and possessions, his triumphs in war, and his grand-scale architectural works. In addition to such material accomplishments these records often vaunt the king's vast learning and wisdom. So the Babylonian king Nabonidus alleges: "I am wise, I know [all], I see hidden things" (cited in Seow 1995, 281). Notably, the authors of such inscriptions are not content to proclaim the king's uncontested success in all these arenas. A prominent motif in these compositions is that this king did it *better* than any king before him. The claim is succinctly conveyed by Kulamuwa, "the king of Sam'al," in the ninth century: "But I am Kulamuwa, son of *TML*—what I achieved [my] predecessors had not achieved" (*COS* II, 147, lines 4–5).

Needless to say, hyperbole is the stock-in-trade of such records. Their purpose is to exalt the king and to memorialize his achievements for posterity. In this introductory segment of Ecclesiastes one sees Qohelet's familiarity with such inscriptions, both in the various types of accomplishments he has tabulated and in the general style of the passage (note, for instance, his repeated assertion that he has outclassed all his predecessors: 1:16; 2:7, 9). But Qohelet has turned this form to an opposite purpose. Borrowing from a genre that parades colossal success, Qohelet dramatizes his colossal failure. The sage's accomplished inversion of the formula is a preview of the erudition, ingenuity, and mordant wit that characterize the reflections to come.

The royal persona that Qohelet assumes is none other than King Solomon (1:12; cf. 1:1), the Israelite monarch distinguished as the sage-king par excellence in biblical tradition (1 Kgs 3–11). In response to Solomon's request for understanding and discernment at Gibeon (1 Kgs 3:5-14), God grants him wisdom that surpasses even that of foreign peoples renowned for their wisdom (1 Kgs 4:29-31 [Heb. 5:9-14]). But Solomon receives more than wisdom. God also grants him riches and honor (1 Kgs 3:13), the two rewards attendant on wisdom in sapiential tradition (Prov 3:16; 22:4). Solomon acquires staggering wealth and achieves legendary success in all his undertakings. Qohelet capitalizes on this apotheosis of the wisdom "success story," chronicling how wisdom and its accompanying wealth and achievements are relativized by death, the fate that overtakes every human.

Exegetical Analysis

1:12-18 Preliminary Findings

These verses serve as introduction and summary of the quest Qohelet embarked on. Verses 12-15 outline his undertaking and preview his conclusion, while verses 16-18 amplify on the process and reiterate its disappointing outcome. The two subsections are akin to one another in structure, with each ending in a judgment of *vapor* and/or *chase of wind*, followed by a proverbial saying.

The author now introduces himself. As noted, this opening section of the book imitates the style of ancient royal inscriptions that boast of the king's accomplishments. Such records are typically headed by such designations as: "I am Yehawmilk, king of Byblos" (cited in Seow 1997,144). Qohelet's indebtedness to the genre is evident in the style of verse 12, which may be translated: "I am Qohelet. I have been king over Israel in Jerusalem" (Seow 1997, 144). Here additional information about the speaker is added to that of the heading of 1:1, in that the jurisdiction of this king in Jerusalem is identified as Israel, the name for the united kingdom before its division into north and south. Solomon is the only king who answers to the description "son of David who ruled Israel," and so the reader is given further indication that the royal voice heard is none other than that of the consummate sage-king.

The speaker begins by defining his enterprise and his method of inquiry (v. 13a). His quest, intimidating in its magnitude, was nothing less than to understand all worldly phenomena in some integrated way. More specifically, Qohelet identifies the object of his inquiry as all that is done "under heaven." Throughout the book Qohelet will identify the realm of his inquiry as that which is done "under heaven" or, more commonly, "under the sun" (as in v. 14). This particular way of delineating his focal point has led some readers of the book to assume that Qohelet's focus (and judgments) are confined specifically to *human* pursuits and activities. Yet his use of these phrases elsewhere makes clear that they refer not only to what humans do (e.g., 4:1, 3), but also to those happenings that are the result of divine activity and decree (e.g., 2:17; 9:3). A particularly illuminating passage is found in chapter 8. There, as here, Qohelet ponders frustrated human attempts to comprehend the world: "Then I saw all the work of God, that no one can find out what is happening under the sun" (8:17a). Here what happens "under the sun" clearly denotes the divine activity in the world. (The synonymy of "the work of God" and "what is happening under the sun" is yet more evident in the Hebrew: "Then I saw all the *deed* [*ma ʿăśēh*] of God—that no one is able to find out the *deed* [*ma ʿăśēh*] that is *being done* [*na ʿăśāh*] under the sun.")

Qohelet's investigation into all that happens under heaven yielded no satisfying results. Having outlined the task he assayed, he moves directly to his sweepingly negative verdict: the business of humans is an unhappy one (v. 13b). Qohelet's pronouncement should be interpreted with due attention to context. The business of humans is not a generalized reference to the things that people do and pursue; rather the statement refers directly to the endeavor to *comprehend* the world (v. 13a). It is this undertaking that is deemed unhappy (see 3:10-11; 8:16-17). One cannot help but notice that the information gap between Qohelet's announcement of intent and his despondent conclusion is considerable. It is the proverbial saying of verse 15 that intones the source of Qohelet's disillusionment: "What is crooked cannot be made straight, and what is lacking cannot be counted." The implication is that any attempt to comprehend the world (v. 13a) is thwarted by the nature of the object of inquiry. Something about this world defies and resists explanation. In chapter 7 Qohelet enlarges on this assessment, explicitly identifying the crookedness as the divine doing: "Consider the work of God; who can make straight what he has made crooked?" (v. 13). The reference to "crookedness" in these two passages resonates with an Egyptian wisdom text that suggests an analogy between a crooked stick and a resistant pupil ("Instruction of Any," *COS* I:114). Perhaps a stock image for a student unamenable to instruction is now used to convey a *world* unamenable to comprehension.

Verses 16-18 elaborate on the venture heralded in the first segment. Verses 16 and 17 affirm that Qohelet acquired wisdom in abundance, exceeding all his royal predecessors. The puzzling inclusion of "madness and folly" (v. 17) under the purview of his pursuit of understanding is not justified or explained but would seem to be a way of conveying the thorough and comprehensive nature of his investigation (compare 2:12). In fact the Hebrew text exhibits a balanced parallelism and is more accurately translated: "I applied my mind to know wisdom *and knowledge*/madness and folly." In other words, Qohelet explores the totality of human experience as evinced by these polarities.

Qohelet's success in acquiring wisdom is considerable (v. 16). Why then does he once again register a judgment of *unsatisfactory*, reckoning all his accomplishment but a "pursuit of wind" (v. 17; see Excursus: "Chasing after Wind"). As with the first unit, the verdict leaves an information gap that is once again filled in by the ensuing proverb: "For in much wisdom is much vexation," concludes Qohelet, "and those who increase knowledge increase sorrow" (v. 18). The second proverb is thus is entailed in the first: a world that resists comprehension means that acquiring wisdom can bring only a more acute sense of its limits.

The subversive nature of Qohelet's claim should not be missed. In response to wisdom teaching that obtainment of wisdom brings well-being and happiness, Qohelet contends that it brings only "vexation" and "sorrow." His choice of terms is extremely canny. In proverbial wisdom "vexation" is a state that plagues the fool (Job 5:2; Prov 12:16; Eccl 7:9). Now Qohelet associates it with the lot of the diligent sage. There is also a wry turn in his choice of "sorrow." This particular Hebrew term is usually employed in the context of divine chastisement for wrongdoing (!), as in Lamentations 1:18: "The LORD is in the right, for I have rebelled against his word; but hear, all you peoples, and behold my *suffering*; my young women and young men have gone into captivity" (see further Ps 32:10; Isa 53:3-4; Jer 30:15; Lam 1:12). The prick to tradition is subtle but unmistakable to any familiar with wisdom teaching, for the sages exhort their young pupils to embrace reproof and punitive measures as necessary goads for keeping them on the path to knowledge (e.g., Prov 3:11-13; 6:20-23; 12:1; 13:1). Qohelet's pithy improvisation of 1:18 puts a perverse spin on this "no pain, no gain" approach to the acquisition of wisdom.

Now the pain *is* the gain. Period. With this ironic probe, Qohelet intimates the question that will come to distinct articulation in 2:12 and the ensuing reflections: Just what is the advantage of the wise person over the fool?

In order to discern the tonality of this initial section we should return to verse 13, where Qohelet speaks of the business God has assigned to human beings. As observed above, readers have sometimes interpreted this business to refer very generally to human affairs and endeavors, which are then deemed *vapor* in verse 14. Though Qohelet would agree with such an assessment, it is important to see that the central thrust of his opening foray is *not* a lesson on the vanity of all human pursuits, nor an exhortation to wonder and humility before a scheme too grand for human comprehension. These are simply not the terms in which he chooses to express the problem of human finitude. The business of human beings is specifically the quest for comprehension introduced in verses 12-13: "I . . . applied my mind to seek and to search out by wisdom all that is done under heaven" (compare 3:10-11; 8:16-17). This task Qohelet deems unhappy. As observed above, with the proverb of 1:15 Qohelet locates the reason for such frustration in the nature of the thing investigated, not in the limitation of the examiner.

2:1-11 The Pursuit of Satisfaction on a Royal Scale

Having set the stage with summary comments on his quest for understanding, Qohelet recounts the journey in more detail. The question the sage-king puts to himself is just this: What is the beneficial and fulfilling thing humans might do in their limited days on earth? (2:3). In his quest for fulfillment Qohelet will try out pleasurable indulgences as well as test the rewards of devoting his toil to grand achievements. The two are not presented as entirely discrete categories. Still it would appear that there are two phases to the king's trial (both introduced by the summary statement and advance judgment of 2:1-2): one in which he experiments with more hedonistic pleasures, and one in which he seeks to gratify himself with grand achievements.

The first phase is described in compressed fashion in verse 3 ("I searched with my mind how to cheer my body") and the second in verses 4-11 ("I made great works"). In fact the latter phase is distinguished by the bracketing phrase "my works" (vv. 4, 11), a telling feature that has been omitted in most English translations.

It may strike readers as strange to have two such different avenues to fulfillment depicted side by side. But when seen in the light of the central dynamic of the passage—a confrontation with death—there is a compelling psychological authenticity to this juxtaposition. These two phases portray two common routes by which people attempt to cope with the fact of inevitable death. In the first case we seek to avoid it by losing ourselves in activities that bring instant gratification. In his book *Living with Death*, Helmut Thielicke speaks of the life of "dissipation," drawing simultaneously on the word's reference to intemperate living and on its root meaning of the dispersion of something (Thielicke 1983, 25–27). The life of dissipation is ultimately a dispersing or scattering of attentions and energies, an attempt to flee the inevitable through diminished awareness. In the second case we seek to circumvent death by projecting our identity onto something or someone who will survive us—a fortune, a reputation, a descendant. Qohelet's probing commentary in verses 4-11 (and indeed throughout this whole opening section) bears the imprint of a realization that any such transference is a fiction. It is the self that is extinguished at death, and this cannot be transferred to another entity.

In describing his phase of industrious work and monument making, Qohelet lists a panoply of activities (vv. 4-9). A striking aspect of this varied litany is that all of these accomplishments are attested in royal inscriptions from neighboring cultures of the Near East, right down to the acquisition of male and female singers. The building and orchard construction, reservoir development, and accrual of assets (slaves, livestock, silver, gold) are typical of those things listed in the royal boasts of kings (Seow 1995, 282–83). So, too, is the claim to have surpassed all one's predecessors (1:16; 2:7, 9). And yet Solomon has only one! The point is worth highlighting. The very irrelevance of the claim points to Qohelet's real interest, which is in evoking the genre itself, and thus its attendant assumptions. The purpose of such royal inscriptions was to memorialize the king and his achievements for future generations. The intent is nicely encapsulated in the words of Assyrian king Esarhaddon, who described his sedulous preservation of his achievements on documents of silver, gold, lapis lazuli, and other such durable materials, proclaiming: "The might of the great warrior Marduk, the deeds which I had achieved, my works of my hand I wrote thereon and placed them into the foundations. *I left them to eternity*" (cited in Seow 1995, 284; emphasis added).

Barring the possibility of actual immortality, the royal inscription is the next best thing—a continuation in one's reputation. Qohelet is intent on showing the futility of such an endeavor, indeed of all human endeavors, to overcome mortality.

Commentators have long puzzled over the contradictions in the book of Ecclesiastes. One of the most bedeviling of these occurs in the final two verses of this unit. Initially Qohelet appears to have found a measure of satisfaction in all his efforts: "For my heart found pleasure in all my toil, and this was my reward for all my toil" (v. 10b). Yet this is followed by a verdict of *vapor* and a reprisal of the somber pronouncement of 1:3: "There is no profit under the sun" (v. 11b, AT). What has transpired between? The only clue provided is in the brief notation of verse 11a: "Then I considered all [my works] that my hands had done and the toil I had spent in doing it." And yet Qohelet has just proclaimed that his heart found pleasure in his toil, and that this pleasure provided a certain satisfaction—a "reward." The Hebrew word *ḥeleq* is perhaps best translated as "portion" in Ecclesiastes. Elsewhere in the Old Testament this word refers to an inheritance (Gen 31:14), including the tract of land that is assigned or bequeathed to a family line, tribe, or nation (e.g., Deut 10:9; Josh 15:13; 19:9; Micah 2:4; compare Deut 32:8-9). Such a meaning is discernable in Qohelet's complaint of 2:21: "For though a person toils with wisdom and knowledge and skill, he has to give the portion over to someone who did not toil for it" (trans. Murphy 1992, 24).

The meaning of *ḥeleq* in Ecclesiastes, which occurs six more times in the book (3:22; 5:18 [Heb. 17]; 5:19 [Heb. 18]; 9:6, 9; 11:2), is perhaps best understood in relation to the word *profit* (*yitrôn*) in Ecclesiastes (see discussion of Eccl 1:3). For Qohelet, a portion is something that humans might reasonably hope to have and experience (see 3:22; 5:18; 9:6). This is as opposed to profit, which is not possible to realize, and the pursuit of which can only end in frustration. The distinction is prominent in an illustration from chapter 5. Qohelet tells of a wealthy man who hoarded his money to his own detriment, losing it all in one bad venture (5:13-18). The man ends his days in anger and gnawing regret. Qohelet judges this to be a grievous ill: "Just as he came, so shall he go, and what profit does he have from toiling for wind?" (AT). In the wake of this portrait of misdirected energies Qohelet enjoins his reader to a different orientation: "This is what I have seen to be good: it is fitting to eat and drink and find enjoyment in all the toil with which one toils under the sun the few days of the life God gives us; for this is our [*portion* or *ḥeleq*]" (5:18). Qohelet's admonition is an oblique comment on the case of the ruined man and what he finds tragic in it: the man did not partake of what was his in the moment. As opposed to pursuing the chimera of profit, says Qohelet, mortals should experience and take pleasure in what is theirs in the moment—savoring the modest daily satisfactions of food, drink, and work (work for its own sake, and not only as a means to an end; see further 5:10–6:9).

The connotations of *portion* and *profit* in the book give some insight into the contradiction embodied in verses 10 and 11. Initially the sage-king finds a pleasure *in* his toil—in the very process, it would seem, of his ardent labors. This pleasure is his *portion* (NRSV "reward"). But then he takes a step back and makes a more panoramic assessment of his accomplishments. Upon survey of all his works the product does not seem to justify the toil and labor spent. Once the measure of profitable outcome is introduced, the return that he assesses cannot be said to justify the effort expended. Even at this, we have not gotten to the heart of Qohelet's protest in verse 11. The nub of his complaint remains to be stated and explored in the ensuing segment: it is death. The place to which Qohelet's rumination is moving is presaged by his employment of the royal inscription form, a literary vehicle dedicated to preserving the monarch's name for posterity. A rhetorical feature in verses 4-9 elucidates the impetus behind all the king's energetic endeavors: the expression "for myself" occurs no fewer than eight times in these verses. This phrase is consistently attached to the verbs of production and acquisition that pepper verses 4-9 (Fox 1999, 176). Moreover the summary statement introducing all this is "I made [my] great works," a telling detail routinely omitted in translations (v. 4). The king's assiduous land and building development, his indefatigable expansion of royal holdings—these things do not spring from a sense of civic duty or communal obligation. They are all directed to one purpose, the gratification of the ego. More than palaces or conservatories or reservoirs, the king has wished to build himself a name that would endure. But (Qohelet will go on to say) no such attempts to circumvent mortality can succeed. The sage has set up his king for failure.

2:12-23 "So I Turned to Consider Wisdom"

Royal endeavors to gain fulfillment through pleasure and industrious labor have proven unsuccessful. Qohelet turns his attention to the question of wisdom weighed against madness and folly. His assessment is interrupted by an interjection: "For what can the one do who comes after the king? Only what has already been done" (v. 12). The Hebrew text of this line is not intact and various translations have been offered. The proposal offered here (which follows the rendition of the NRSV) is that Qohelet now critiques the claim to unprecedented success and achievement that is the motif of royal inscriptions (1:16; 2:7, 9). This is now deemed an illusion. Successors can do only what their predecessors have done. The aspirations of the Solomonic king are now viewed from the perspective of the introductory poem: "Is there a thing of which it is said, 'See, this is new'? It has already been, in the ages before us" (1:10). The successor to the king can only repeat history.

In verses 12-14 Qohelet weighs wisdom against folly. In doing so he articulates a question that was intimated in the second part of his opening segment (1:16-18). There he ended his reflection on his acquisition of wisdom by concluding that much wisdom brings much pain. Does Qohelet then believe that "ignorance is bliss"? More to the point, *does* the wise man have any advantage over the fool? Such questions are latent in the tart adage of 1:18, and he answers them here in no uncertain terms: the advantage of wisdom over folly is described in terms that are polar opposites—as that of light to darkness. He follows his affirmation of wisdom's value with a proverbial illustration: the wise man sees where he is going while the fool stumbles around in ignorance. Thus Qohelet does affirm that, in spite of all, it is better to have knowledge than to be the fool. Still we have not yet reached the clincher in his series of observations. As clearly as he sees that wisdom is superior to folly, he also sees that the fool and the wise man will meet the same fate (v. 14b). With this assertion he challenges the rhetoric of the sages, who repeatedly draw a stark contrast between the fate of the foolish and the wise, as in Proverbs 11:19: "Whoever is steadfast in righteousness will live, but whoever pursues evil will die" (see, e.g., Prov 1:32-33; 2:21-22; 10:27; 12:21).

It is important to see that, with Qohelet's assertion of death for the wise and foolish alike, the proverb of verse 14a acquires another dimension, if only implicitly. When first read in relation to the preceding verse, the wise man's sight versus the fool's daze is quite obviously a positive elaboration on the wisdom/light versus folly/darkness equation. But in view of his ensuing statement about the ultimate destination of both (v. 14b), one cannot miss that the wise man's vision affords him the knowledge . . . that he dies (presumably knowledge the fool is spared). Thus, once again, Qohelet affirms that in the world he has observed wisdom brings with it a more acute sense of

31

human limits (1:15; 1:18). Is the assertion of universal death intended to wholly negate his affirmation of wisdom's superiority? It is not. Despite ambivalence about its rewards, Qohelet clearly holds wisdom superior to folly, for he never entertains the latter as an option (see also 7:2-5; 10:2, 12). In the final analysis Qohelet prefers seeing to not seeing, even when that clarity brings painful information (see especially 7:2-4). Indeed, the searching journey he records embodies his choice.

The fact remains that Qohelet finds the discourse of traditional wisdom on retributive justice gravely deficient or, one might say, grave deficient. There are two dynamics at play in his protests here. First, as a corrective to the rhetoric of the sages, he registers the *universality* of death (even when retributive justice runs its proper course and the fool dies young, the wise man is ultimately headed for the same place). Second, Qohelet asserts the *physical* reality of death as a counterweight to "death" as a metaphor in the wisdom tradition (e.g., Prov 8:35-36; 10:2; 11:4; 13:14; 14:27; 15:24).

Qohelet's rumination on the universality of death is no detached philosophical disquisition; so much is clear from the terms in which he states the application of his perception in verse 15: "What happens to the fool will happen to *me* also" (emphasis added; the grammatical construction of the Hebrew is emphatic here). There is a world of difference between intellectual assent to the dictum *All humans are mortal* and the realization of this fact for oneself. Qohelet has had this realization. Neither wisdom, nor any other power, can rescue him from this fate. With his next remark in verse 16 he anticipates a consolation offered by tradition—a person can live on in one's good reputation. Such assurance is offered in the compressed contrast of Proverbs 10:7: "The memory [*zeker*] of the righteous is a blessing; but the name of the wicked will rot" (compare Sir 41:11-13). But Qohelet avows that there is no enduring remembrance of either the fool *or* the wise. *Zikkārôn*, the Hebrew word translated as "remembrance" in the NRSV, is most often used concretely to refer to a memorial symbol or token (e.g., Exod 28:12; Num 16:40 [Heb. 17:5]; Josh 4:7; Zech 6:14). In opting for the more concrete image, Qohelet's denial of any enduring "memorial" for the wise man becomes at the same time a fuller exposition of the royal discontent voiced in the concluding evaluation of 2:11: "Then I considered all that my hands had done . . . and there was no gain" (AT). As observed, the monument building of the wise king is ultimately directed to one purpose—the perpetuation of a legacy. Qohelet's consignment of every person to oblivion applies to the aspirations of his great king as well as his wise man. Death has the final word. Any semblance of a continuance beyond it is illusory.

Commentators tend to identify a shift in topic, hence a new unit, at 2:18 when Qohelet revisits the topic of toil (vv. 18-23; cf. 2:1-11). Perhaps, however, it is the underlying continuity of his thought that should be stressed. With verse 14 Qohelet has identified death as the gravamen of his complaint of *vapor*. What follows in the ensuing verses is his exploration of the repercussions of this condition for all human effort and aspiration.

Qohelet does not ponder the example of just any toiler; rather it is the *wise, skilled* toiler he describes (in the background are the wise king's exertions). One might speculate that the sage's vested interest in the problem is reflected here—the specific situation he describes is also his own. It is also the case that, in offering an example of the man who has used his *wisdom* to obtain success, he offers us the world at its best. Arguably this is the ideal vision of the proverbial literature: those who labor with wisdom, knowledge, and skill will flourish. But for Qohelet the crude fact of death mocks the ardent labor and refined skill of the wise person. No matter how one acquires one's gains, no matter how justly they are deserved, death comes all the same, and those gains devolve to another.

In the process of ruminating on this, Qohelet ponders another asymmetry between effort and outcome: the fruit of one's diligent, skilled labor may be passed on to one who has done nothing to merit it (2:19, 21). Qohelet's lament on this count should not be taken to mean he would be satisfied if one could know that the product of one's work would go to a deserving recipient. This might in some small way ameliorate the situation, but the real sticking point for Qohelet is the fact of death. The underlying theme of verses 18-23 is the demise of all human accomplishment in death. This acknowledgment is in fact the place to which all his reflections have been moving. The closing verses of 24-26 are offered in light of this recognition.

2:24-26 Simple Pleasures

The observation of verse 24 sounds a theme that will occur six more times in the book, reaching its most complete expression in chapter 9: Qohelet commends eating, drinking, and enjoyment in life (3:12-13, 22; 5:18-20; 8:15; 9:7-10; 11:9-10). Although the refrain itself is expressed in variant forms, there is some consistency with respect to the context in which this theme is expressed: typically it is in the context of a confrontation with the limits on human existence. As we have seen, the subcurrent of 2:1-23 is the way in which death encroaches on all human endeavor and accomplishment, rendering it unsatisfying in the end. In the wake of this encounter with mortality, Qohelet offers a modest response. Profit may not be possible, but eating, drinking, and experiencing joy amidst one's toil are within human reach. These things are commended not as a means to any end, but for their own intrinsic merits.

Qohelet's observation that these things are "from the hand of God" (v. 24b) has two facets. On the one hand it reflects an awareness that God is the benefactor behind such good gifts; on the other it carries a recognition that such goods are ultimately dependent on the divine disposition (see 3:13 [NJPS]; 5:19; 9:7b, where similar recognitions occur in the enjoyment refrain). It is the latter idea that is amplified in verse 26, where Qohelet contrasts the lot of the one who pleases God with that of the one who displeases God. The Hebrew word ḥôṭe usually means "sinner" (so translated in the NRSV). In that case Qohelet would describe a situation of due rewards: the one pleasing God receiving good things, and the sinner hurrying and scurrying, only to lose out to the God pleaser. But the capping judgment of *vapor* at the end of verse 26 brings this reading into question. If the *ḥôṭe* were indeed a wrongdoer, Qohelet would not assess the scenario in this way; on the contrary the offender's fate would be a laudable instance of justice. These considerations suggest that the terms "pleasing to God" and "offender" are not moral categories (see also 7:26; cf. 10:4); rather Qohelet uses them to convey a wry comment on the mystery of the divine disposition; the sovereign God gives blessings to some and withholds from others, and humans do not know the divine rationale.

The fact that Qohelet ends on a downbeat should not obscure the significance of his conclusion—an affirmation of food, drink, and the enjoyment of life as undeniable goods. His final assessment on this count would seem to be at odds with certain judgments that have preceded it. Notably at the beginning of chapter 2 Qohelet has concluded that revelry and pleasure are inane and of no use. However the observation at the end of chapter 2 is presented on the other side of consciousness: that is, not as one of the avoidance routes for death, but in the very wake of a gradual internalization of this reality. From this vantage point the affirmation of eating, drinking, and enjoyment is of a different substance entirely. The same activities that were symptomatic of the stance of *flight* from death (death avoidance) now reflect an orientation that is distilled out of a profound realization of that truth.

Theological and Ethical Analysis

The truth of human death comes to light only when I can speak in the first person—"I die"—so that I understand the death to be mine, to belong to me.

Helmut Thielicke, *Living with Death*

It is only in the face of death that man's self is born.

Attributed to Augustine

Death as a fact of life is something we become acquainted with early on. Whether we suffer the devastating loss of someone dear to us or are fortunate enough in our early years to be spared all but a distant awareness of death, eventually we learn that all living creatures must die. Yet acknowledgment of this reality and the realization that we ourselves will die, that our own breath will cease, are two different things. We know that we die, and yet we do not know. The terror of death and the inconceivability of our own dissolution spur us to find ways to distance it or keep it abstract. The psychic drive to distance ourselves from death is portrayed in a brief scene from Leo Tolstoy's *The Death of Ivan Ilych*. Ivan's acquaintance and colleague, Peter Ivanovich, ponders the final anguished days of Ivan's life:

> "Three days of frightful suffering and then death! Why, that might suddenly, at any time, happen to me," he thought, and for a moment felt terrified. But—he did not himself know how—the customary reflection at once occurred to him that this had happened to Ivan Ilych and not to him, and that it should not and could not happen to him. . . . After which reflection Peter Ivanovich felt reassured, and began to ask with interest about the details of Ivan Ilych's death, as though death was an accident natural to Ivan Ilych but certainly not to himself. (Tolstoy 1967, 253)

The stratagems by which we seek to distance death from ourselves are indeed numerous and inventive. We generalize its application as Peter Ivanovich does (*others* die); we put it away from our sight in hospitals, hospices, and funeral parlors; we engage in frenetic amusements to stave off awareness; and we attempt to displace our identity onto something that is not our self—our name, our achievements, our possessions, our progeny. All of these are means by which we avoid speaking in the first person when it comes to death. Thielicke points to a parable from the Gospel of Luke, which trenchantly interrogates the dynamics of death denial (Luke 12:16-21). Jesus tells the story of a rich man who thinks himself set for life because he has packed his barns with an abundant harvest. But God responds with the news that he will die that very night—"And the things you have prepared, whose will they be?" (Luke 12:20). The impingement of death consciousness on the farmer's self-satisfied conversation with himself surfaces the question of the personal nature of dying. As Thielicke observes, it is the fact of death, like no other fact, that strips us of the illusory idea that we can hide among our possessions. In such a moment, the self is nakedly exposed, and the question of identity is posed to us (Thielicke 1983,15–16).

These opening segments of Ecclesiastes are a searching contemplation of this mortal condition. There is a sense in which this passage invites a gradual absorption of the fact of death. As Qohelet examines the question of human desire, aspiration, endeavor, and accomplishment—from this angle and from that— he breaks the news to us. We do not survive in our accomplishments, our name, or our possessions, says Qohelet. In short, he tells us that we cannot send a proxy to death.

This is a dread-inspiring realization. And yet it is potentially redemptive. As Thielicke suggests, "Only when the death at issue is mine does it cease to be a general and half true phenomenon and become a personal experience *in which I know the mystery of my being*" (Thielicke 1983, 10; emphasis added). The paradox of death awareness is that even as it inspires dread, it affords an opportunity that is ours through this route alone. The realization of the personal nature of dying— *I die*—offers me a chance to meet myself: to confront the question of my identity—who I am apart from the possessions, endeavors, ambitions, and accomplishments that so readily and subtly become synonymous with who I am. "The mystery of death is none other than the mystery of this I" (Thielicke 1983, 11). In confronting the knowledge that it is myself that is expunged in death, I may come upon the self that is noninterchangeable.

Excursus: "Chasing after Wind" in Ecclesiastes

The expression "chase of wind" or "pursuit of wind" is a catchphrase in the first half of Ecclesiastes, occurring nine times within the first six chapters. In seven of these occurrences it serves as complement to the vapor pronouncement, as seen in its first appearance in 1:14: "I saw all the deeds that are done under the sun, and see, all is *vapor* and a *chasing after wind*" (NRSV, modified). While the Hebrew underlying the translation "chase" is actually two different Hebrew words—*rĕ'ût* and *ra'yôn*—the two variant forms of the phrase appear to function with the same meaning in Ecclesiastes. These occur in 1:14; 2:11, 17, 26; 4:4, 6; and 6:9 (*rĕ'ût*); 1:17 and 4:16 (*ra'yôn*). Both terms appear to be related to an Aramaic word meaning "pleasure, will, ambition, desire." A similar Aramaic root has the meaning "to feed, to graze, to shepherd." Hence, in the first case the meaning would be to desire or pursue the wind, and in the second to guide or direct the wind. In either case the image conveys an impossible task—the attempt to obtain or control something elusive. One who engages in such is sure to find frustration and disappointment.

The phrase first occurs in Qohelet's introduction of his comprehensive quest to make sense of the world and human experience (1:12-18). His assessment of this undertaking is twice pronounced to be *vapor* and/or *a chase of wind* (1:14, 17). In each case the rationale for his verdict is presented in the form of a proverb. In the first instance the attempt to understand the world is foiled by the nature of the object under investigation: the world is "crooked" and hence resists comprehension (1:15). Verses 16-18 expand on the quest presented in verses 12-15. Significantly King Qohelet does not deny that he gained *great* wisdom, surpassing all those who ruled before him! Why then the judgment that all this was but a chasing after wind? Once again the explanation comes in the ensuing proverb: "For in much wisdom is much vexation, and those who increase knowledge increase sorrow" (1:18). The second proverb is thus entailed in the first: a world that resists comprehension means that acquiring much wisdom can only bring a keener sense of wisdom's limits. The image of chasing wind (here used without *vapor*) conveys frustration and disillusionment at a venture that does not repay the effort (see further 2:11, 17, 26).

In these instances, the emphasis is on the futile nature of the endeavor in question. Yet the figure of *chasing wind* retains a certain flexibility in terms of emphasis (or nuance), as seen in its occurrence in a sequence of proverbs evaluating various aspects of work and income. In 4:6 (the second instance in which the phrase occurs without *vapor*), Qohelet weighs the value of hard toil for higher return against the merits of moderate toil for lower yield. Not surprisingly he finds in favor of the latter: "For better is one handful with rest, than two fistfuls with toil and a *chase after wind*" (AT). Since Qohelet is not denying that one can indeed obtain *more* with more effort, the thrust of the image is not futility. In this case it is more the wearying nature of pursuing wind that is at play. In appending the familiar phrase Qohelet effectively reinforces the point of the saying: less gained in repose and quiet is better than twice that amount gained with exertion and strain. Possibly verse 4 of this passage carries similar connotations. Here Qohelet declares "all toil and all skill in work" to spring from a single source—envy. Notably Qohelet does not question the positive end product of the competitive urge—proficiency and excellence. Nonetheless he pronounces this scrambling, get-ahead mentality "a chasing after wind." Implicit here may be recognition of the toll such ambitious striving takes.

In at least one instance (4:13-16) the referent of the image of *chasing wind*, and hence its import, is more ambiguous. The passage initially begins with a reflection on the value of wise rule, describing a scenario in which a young but wise commoner is able to succeed an old but foolish king (v. 13). But from here the passage moves in a somewhat unexpected direction, with Qohelet's ruminations turning to the unstable nature of political power and the capricious nature of popular acclaim (vv. 15-16) as he describes a scenario in which one ruler is replaced by another in seemingly arbitrary fashion, with all the populace following the man of the hour. The passage concludes with a contrast between the teeming throng of supporters for the ruler of the moment, and the future generations who will have no use for him. The import of the *vapor* and *chase of wind* declaration here is not self-evident, since human effort is not the theme of the passage. While the lesson of this passage is far from clear (a difficult Hebrew text compounds the issue), it is possible to read it as a reflection on the relative value and limits of wisdom. While wisdom can be effective, it cannot be depended upon to secure its advantage/gains (see 9:13-18 for similar reflections on the value and limits of wisdom). The use of the *chase of wind* expression in such a context suggests it can be used with the broader connotation of a frustrating or disappointing state of affairs.

The Mystery of the Times

Literary Analysis

Chapter 3 commences with one of the most familiar and oft-quoted texts from Ecclesiastes: the poem on a season for all things. The poem is followed by a prose addendum in verses 10-15, a kind of literary coda that is crucial to understanding the meaning of verses 1-8. A rhetorical question placed as conclusion to the poem functions as a transition between the two major parts (v. 9).

The poetic segment of 3:1-8 consists of an introductory heading (v. 1) stating the thesis of the poem: there is a right time for everything. The idea is developed in a series of balanced pairs describing various experiences and activities in human existence, for example, loving/hating and weeping/laughing. The stately cadence of the poem is created by the repetition of "time" at the beginning of each phrase. This repetition, in conjunction with the compressed expression of complementary opposites, conveys a sense of gentle ebb and flow: "A time to weep, and a time to laugh; a time to mourn, and a time to dance" (3:4).

The word "time" in these verses does not refer to a specific date or hour, but rather to occasions in a human life. The listing of pairs is intended to be representative of all that occurs within the frame of human existence; this is seen in the thesis line of verse 1 ("*every* thing"/"*every* matter") and in the lead pair of events that place all that follows within the framework of birth and death (3:2a). In these ways the poem illustrates and reiterates that there is indeed a proper time for every human activity and experience. The poem is linked to the ensuing prose reflection by a question (v. 9) that, while familiar (cf. 1:3), is somewhat enigmatic in the immediate context: What profit has the worker in his/her toil? The ensuing commentary consists of three subunits. The initial comment states the core of the passage (vv. 10-11): the mysterious oscillation of "times," good and bad, is identified to be in the hands of God; humans know only enough to know that they cannot discern or comprehend the larger scheme of things. The next unit responds to this condition of limits: the constraints so heavily enunciated in the preceding verses lead Qohelet to state with equal conviction and verve that life and the pleasures it affords should be enjoyed with gusto (vv. 12-13). The concluding verses (14-15) are obscure on several points and difficult to interpret; in sum, however, they reiterate the theme of sovereign control and human limitation propounded in verses 10-11.

The poem bears little trace of Qohelet's style and vocabulary except perhaps for the expression "under heaven" at the end of the opening line. It is with verse 9 that Qohelet's distinctive style and concerns emerge. Such differences in style, vocabulary, and tone between the poetic and prose sections suggest the possibility that the poetic segment reflects an existing composition that Qohelet adapts and reframes for his own purposes (compare Whybray 1989, 66–70).

Exegetical Analysis

3:1-8

The thesis statement of the poem (v. 1) affirms that for every affair under heaven there is an appropriate moment. A sequence of occasions illustrating such matters will follow, with fourteen pairs of events that occur in the course of human life. Significantly it is headed by the two events that bound human existence: birth and death. The continuation of the poem in verses 2b-8 describes the various events that occur within these two boundaries of birth and death. Speaking broadly, the events may be categorized as constructive versus destructive actions (e.g., building up/breaking down, v. 3b), or desirable versus undesirable things (e.g., laughing and weeping, v. 4a). The pairs of opposites illustrate that each event or activity has its right time, even the unfortunate and destructive events.

Despite efforts to identify some intricate structure in this sequence, none has been convincingly demonstrated. The most salient formal feature is the repetition of "time" at the head of every phrase, along with the series of twenty-eight items occurring in fourteen pairs (vv. 2-8). R. N. Whybray has proposed that these formal characteristics suggest comparison to the genre of the catalogue, a compilation of items arranged by kind (such as trees or species of animals) used to instruct or to illustrate a point (1991, 469–82). Such lists, which are amply attested in the traditional literature of Egypt and Mesopotamia, reflect a perception of the cosmos as ordered in its categories and subcategories (cf. 1 Kgs 4:33; Prov 30:18-31). Viewed through this lens, the poem of chapter 3 constitutes a catalogue of "times"—occasions illustrating the principle of a right time for every happening.

The notion of a right time for everything is a theme woven throughout the teachings of conventional wisdom. For the sages, timing is everything, as demonstrated in such sayings as Proverbs 15:23: "To make an apt answer is a joy to anyone; and a word in [its *time*], how good it is!" (cf. Prov 25:11; Sir 1:23-24; 4:20, 23). It is the task of the sage to discern the propitious moment for acting and speaking, or refraining from such as the case may be (Prov 26:4-5). Qohelet refers to this wisdom theme in the context of advising counselors in the royal court: "Whoever obeys a command will meet no harm, and the wise mind will know the *time* and way" (8:5). This theme in wisdom, in addition to the traditional form of the poem as catalogue, suggests the possibility that Qohelet has adapted a composition that originally concerned the wisdom topic of discernment of the "right time."

3:9-15

The prose reflection in these verses molds (or remolds) the impression of the poem. The initial question posed in verse 9 about *profit* (NRSV "gain") to the worker in his toil takes up a familiar concern from Qohelet, with familiar vocabulary (cf. 1:3; 2:22; 5:16 [Heb. v. 17]), and yet there is a riddle-like quality to it in its current context. It is an odd characterization of the activities that have preceded it, most of which are not toil per se; one may ask, moreover, what is meant by *profit* in such a context as this. The conjunction of meaning between this question and the poem is simply not clear; it remains to be elucidated by what follows.

With verses 10 and 11 Qohelet resumes his language of personal reflection ("I saw," 1:14; 3:16; 4:1, etc.). While the poem has identified no agent behind the various times enumerated, Qohelet now identifies God as the one who makes everything happen in its *time*. Though some interpreters see an allusion to the creation acts in Genesis 1, both the context (the poetic description of life's events) and the reference to timing suggest that this refers to God's ongoing activity in the world vis-à-vis the events of human life. That it is God who controls events is Qohelet's main point. God's making, or "doing" as it is also translated (cf. NJPS: "brought to pass"), is virtually a refrain in this segment, occurring again in verse 11b ("God has done") and twice more in verse 14 ("God does"; "God has done"). The concentration of the phrase in these verses underlines Qohelet's message. Moreover verse 11a states that God does *everything*. With this evocation of the theme line of the poem—"To *everything* a season"—God is identified as the one who is behind the properly timed occurrence of things.

The rhythms of our lives are not in our control; it is God who brings events to pass. Qohelet has yet to delineate the most frustrating aspect of the human status. Verse 11b states that God has "put a sense of past and future into [persons'] minds, yet they cannot find out what God has done from the beginning to the end." The phrase "sense of past and future" reflects Hebrew *'ōlām*, a word that means *eternity* or, more precisely, "virtually unlimited time, past or future" (Provan 1999, 210). Other suggestions emend the text to read "toil" or explain the existing term to mean *obscurity*. However, the emphases of the passage weigh in favor of *'ōlām*. The statement exposes an irony in the human situation, one that has been engineered by the deity. God has placed within the human consciousness some sense of the larger scope of time and cosmos. Still, this awareness is sufficient only to tell us what we do not know. In fact it is our capacity to be aware of our "selves" as beings in time that also makes us aware of the contingencies that such a condition places on us. We know enough to know that we do not grasp the course of human affairs—what God has done, from start to finish. We are enlightened enough to know we are ultimately benighted—"caught between self-transcendence and stifling ignorance" (Brown 2000, 43). Qohelet's characterization of God's timing as "fitting" (v. 11a; NRSV "suitable") cannot be read apart from these divinely imposed limitations on human knowledge. The suitability claimed for God's timing is not within the purview of humans, who catch only glimpses of a larger vista. God's action is fitting, in *God's* time. In Derek Kidner's expressive analogy, humans are "like the desperately near-sighted, inching their way along some great tapestry or fresco in the attempt to take it in" (1976, 39).

Thus the "business" that God has conferred on humans to preoccupy them (v. 10) is identified as the endeavor to comprehend the work of God, a pursuit destined for failure (see 1:13-15, where the God-given business is similarly that of making sense of all that happens in the world; compare 8:16-17). To return to the query posed in verse 9—What is the profit to humans in their toil?—one may ask if it is not in this vein that it is to be read. Most interpreters take *toil* to be a figure for the various activities in the poem (weeping, dancing, building, etc.). The characterization does not quite fit, but one may allow for poetic license. In the understanding proposed here, toil refers not to the activities themselves but to the human effort to comprehend the scheme of things (compare 8:16-17, where *toil* also denotes the human effort to grasp the scope of God's work).

However one understands the referent of *toil* in the query of verse 9, the accent of verses 9-15 falls on the impotence of humans to identify the moment for acting. It is remarkable then that Qohelet does in fact enjoin a response to this implacable fact of human existence. In verses 12-13 he speaks again of the possibility of enjoyment (see 2:24-26), this time voicing his commendation in the first person ("I know"): humans should rejoice and enjoy themselves while they are alive. The context in which this is said should be weighed carefully. His statement, far from being glib or callow, is made in the very wake of a recognition that we are not the agents of our destinies. We cannot simply *will* only the good for ourselves. Times of joy and sorrow are inevitable. In this setting his perception is an invitation to recognize the good occasion when it comes and to be fully present to it (see further Theological and Ethical Analysis).

This good is identified in the elemental blessings of food, drink, and one's work (v. 13). Qohelet's manner of phrasing the second part of his conclusion is significant (translated more literally): "And for any person to eat and drink and experience pleasure in all his or her toil—this is a gift of God" (based on Fox 1999, 192). There is a kind of Janus face to this statement. It is, on the one side, a distinct affirmation of God as the source of the good things of this life; hence enjoyment of them comes with divine approval. It is, on the other, a reminder that God may dispense *or* withhold such blessings. The latter reminder is in keeping with the matter-of-fact observations of the poem and commentary: life is constituted of moments of weal and woe, dearth and abundance, joy and loss, all of which come from God (compare discussion at 7:14). Humans cannot predict the events of their lives, much less shape them; we *are* free to choose in what manner we will receive them.

Qohelet concludes by stating a further implication of divine control and human limits. These final verses are difficult and commentators disagree about how to interpret them. The theme that comes through clearly, despite the disputed nuances, is that of divine alterity. God is God; humans are mortal and limited. In keeping with the preceding declarations, the point is made with specific reference to the divine action. That which God *does* is abiding. Qohelet's elaboration on this (v. 14b) draws on a formula from the book of Deuteronomy. There similar words guarding Mosaic Law convey its authority and its sufficiency as a guide for the Israelite people (see Deut 4:2; 12:32). The implication of the reference in Ecclesiastes is open to interpretation, as can be seen from the spectrum of viewpoints in the commentaries. The context suggests that his allusion reinforces the authoritative nature of divine doing: when it comes to the divine ordinances, humans are not able to alter or revise their course. The assertion reinforces the theme of a God who has timed everything fittingly but leaves humans in the dark with respect to the grand course of things. Thus we cannot know whether any given undertaking is in sync with the time God has made for it.

The divine intent Qohelet ascribes to this austere governance is that humans should "fear" God (v. 14c). The "fear of the Lord" is a central theme in the wisdom literature with rich connotations. It encompasses both right action and a proper disposition toward God. Entailed in the concept is an awareness of the distance between God and humans (e.g., Prov 20:24; 21:30-31; Job 11:7-8). In Ecclesiastes this awareness is keen. In fact, the contexts in which Qohelet speaks of God-fearing tend to reflect an acute cognition of God's transcendent otherness, a God who cannot be predicted or manipulated (see discussion at 5:1-7 and 7:15-18). This accent suggests that, while his use of the concept retains some continuity with that of Proverbs, Job, and other traditional wisdom literature, it is not limited to the conventional understanding (compare Lee 2005, 85). As

Roland Murphy remarks (1992, lxvi): "Qohelet's understanding of what it means to fear God seems to flow from the mystery and incomprehensibility of God. If one cannot understand what God is doing (3:11; 8:17, 11:6) . . . reverential fear is in order (cf. 3:14; 5:6)."

Qohelet's concluding remark to his meditation on human existence and divine governance has the aura of a conundrum: "That which is, already has been; that which is to be, already is" (v. 15a). Similarly, the final half of the verse—"and God seeks the pursued" (NJPS)—is enigmatic. Perhaps it reflects a popular saying whose meaning is now lost to us. The first half of the thought plays upon a key passage from the poem of chapter 1: "What has been is what will be, and what has been done is what will be done" (1:9a). There, however, the focus was human activity, and the futility of such to accomplish anything new ("There is nothing new under the sun," 1:9b). Here in 3:15 the context is *divine* action. Hence the play upon 1:9 may imply a contrast between human attempts to achieve gain or make progress and God's decisive ordination of times.

Theological and Ethical Analysis

The poem on the times from Ecclesiastes 3 is the most familiar passage from the book and the most often quoted. Its quotation and recitation in a wide variety of settings attests to a fascinating dimension of the composition, namely its interpretive ambiguity. Its terse, unelaborated quality makes it amenable to a variety of readings; context, inflection, and subtle adjustments make all the difference in how it is heard (Borg 2001, 167). Pete Seeger's folk adaptation "Turn, Turn, Turn (To Everything There Is a Season)" demonstrates this well. The lyrics of the song follow the biblical text quite closely (King James Version), though with some rearrangement of sequence. The main change comes in the final line: "A time for war and a time for peace." Here in the final stanza "a time for war" has been omitted and an exclamation added: "A time for peace, *I swear it's not too late.*" This seemingly minor emendation shifts the tenor of the poem in a particular direction. The effect is more far-reaching than to commend peace over war. The addition suggests by implication that within all the preceding oppositions there is a right action and a wrong, a good choice and a bad choice. Thus the song introduces (or reintroduces!) the element of human agency into the various "times" of the poem. Seeger's other notable revision of the biblical text might in subtle fashion bolster such an impression. The addition of the refrain "Turn, turn, turn" is, of course, a patent allusion to the perpetually changing seasons of life (3:1a), yet read in conjunction with the hortatory embellishment of verse 8—"I swear it's not too late!"—it yields another possible dimension: it may also be understood as a *summons* to turn from one course of action to another. In this way Seeger has, by relatively small adjustments, shifted the tone of the poem toward the prescriptive, a move that has in turn influenced other popular interpretations of the poem as well.

Qohelet, too, has contextualized this poem to give it a particular significance and tonality. With his postscript in verses 10-15 he emphasizes that these times are in no way under human sway. For Qohelet the poem's kaleidoscopic vista of sorrow and celebration, loss and recovery, repair and ruin describes rather than prescribes. It is simply what *is*. Human discernment is not a factor here. Mortals are not in a position to alter or otherwise amend this inevitable revolution of human affairs. All things are the work of God, and that divine doing remains opaque to human comprehension.

Qohelet does perceive, however, in no uncertain terms, *a space* for human action, even if limited in nature: humans should "be happy and enjoy themselves as long as they live" (v. 12). As observed, in its current setting his statement cannot be seen as an optimistic invitation to, in modern self-help parlance, "create your reality," for it is not within our power to circumvent the misfortune, sorrow, and loss that come into our lives. Nor is it, I believe, a recommendation to accept the bad with the good in serene equanimity, as is the path in some Eastern philosophies. Qohelet's perception, containing within it a keen awareness of the evanescence of all moments, is instead an invitation to recognize specifically the good occasion when it comes and be fully present to its joy.

A fuller exposition of the tenor of his counsel is found in chapter 7. The passage comes as the climax to a series of proverbs that reflect not only on wisdom's potential, but on its limits. "Consider the work of God; who can make straight what he has made crooked? In the day of good, enjoy, and in the day of misfortune, consider: God has set the one next to the other, so that humans will not know what happens next" (7:13-14 AT). In a sense these brief lines are a concentrated distillation of all of 3:1-15. In this abridged contemplation of God's inscrutable work and human ineffectiveness Qohelet directs his focus to the question of human response. The rhetorical details of this instruction merit further attention. On the bad day one is to *reflect*. Times of suffering, by their nature, call for some critical distance or perspective. But on the good day the only mandate is to *be joyful*. The human capacity to look ahead and behind, to know that a time to weep comes as surely as a time to laugh, a time of mourning as a time of dancing, can stall us on the brink of *this* moment's proffered happiness; knowing it cannot last, we fear to plunge in. Strikingly, the literal translation of the Hebrew is "Be *in good*" (the expression is without exact parallel elsewhere in the Old Testament). Times of good, by their nature, beckon full immersion. This is the wisdom Qohelet offers in the face of human limits.

Injustices Lamented

Literary Analysis

With verse 16 of chapter 3, Qohelet moves to the topic of human injustice. It is the first reference to such in the book, though not the last (e.g., 4:1-3; 5:8; 8:9-11). Qohelet responds to his observation of rampant injustice in two parts, each presented in the form of self-dialogue: "I said in my heart." His first response is to affirm that judgment is ultimately in God's hands (3:17). This is followed by a second, more extended reflection in which Qohelet ponders the fact that humans and animals share a common fate (3:18-21). Interpretation of this puzzling transition is complicated by the fact that the translation of verse 18 is highly uncertain (compare, e.g., the NRSV and NJPS). One may speculate that Qohelet's thoughts, moving from injustice to divine redress, lead him to the ultimate injustice, the fact that a death sentence awaits everyone (compare 2:12-17; 9:1-3). Whatever the process by which Qohelet moves from one topic to the next, the effect of his prolonged reflection on the common destiny of animals and people is to underscore the finite nature of humanity. In the matter of death, we are no different from God's other creatures. In verse 22 Qohelet offers the conclusion to these thoughts ("So I saw . . ."): Humans should take joy in their work.

While 4:1-3 is often seen to belong with the following section (4:4-16), the subject of these verses returns to that of the opening segment (3:16-17), suggesting an inclusio movement (see 9:1-12 for a similar structure). Verse 1 unfolds in a manner akin to 3:16: once again Qohelet observes something under the sun, and once again that something is human injustice ("all the oppressions that are practiced"). This time, however, such thoughts do not lead to an affirmation of divine judgment, but to a sober contemplation of the relative merits of life and nonexistence.

Exegetical Analysis

3:16-17 The System Gone Awry: Human Injustice Observed

Qohelet's opening observation is expressed in highly charged fashion through a condensed couplet: "In the place of justice, there was wickedness! In the place of righteousness, there was wickedness!" (AT). The places of justice/righteousness referred to here are courts of law and other locales of legal proceeding. Qohelet witnesses injustice, and in the very places where one might hope for its redress. The repetition of "there was wickedness" from one line to the next conveys the ubiquity of such miscarriages and reinforces Qohelet's sense of affront at such (compare the repetition at 4:1).

The next statement is a response to this dire situation, made to himself ("I said in my heart"): "God will judge the righteous and the wicked." It is important to discern where the emphasis of this statement lies. It is not a simplistic affirmation that all will be made right (hence it need not be seen as the work of a pious interpolator, as has sometimes been suggested). Still, Qohelet does open up a possibility for closing the disparity between what *is* (namely what he has seen) and what should be. The statement first of all asserts that it is *God* (not humans) who is ultimately judge of everyone. Second, it allows for the possibility that divine judgment has been deferred to some future time. The latter idea is expanded upon in the ensuing clause, where

Qohelet bolsters his proposition of coming judgment with a reminder that there is a "time for every matter," thus hearkening back to the theme line of the poem on the times (3:1b). In the course of 3:1-15, Qohelet asserted that it is God and God alone who governs the timing of events under the sun. By adverting to the theme of this sequence, Qohelet reminds the reader that what a human is able to observe may not be the whole story. At the same time one cannot help but be reminded of the rub: the divine timing is inscrutable to humans.

To expand further on the quandary underlying Qohelet's self-dialogue in these two verses, note that it is a given for him that judgment is in God's hands; he does not dispute this assumption of Israelite tradition (e.g., 8:12-13; 11:9). As this passage unfolds he reminds himself, then, that the *timing* of such is also God's (cf. 3:11a, "He has made everything suitable for its time"). As R. N. Whybray puts it, "God has, as it were, 'a time to judge and a time to refrain from judging'" (1989, 78). In this way Qohelet addresses the tension between his tradition (God is righteous judge) and what he observes (injustice often prevails). That Qohelet does not find this response entirely satisfactory is suggested by his concluding reflections in 4:1-3 (compare 8:10-14).

3:18-22 The Common Fate of All the Living

Although parts of verse 18 are obscure, the gist of it is evident: God in some way demonstrates to humans that they are like animals. Qohelet then elaborates on the comparison. The import of this sequence is best appreciated in light of Psalm 8:3-5, another Israelite tradition that meditates on the place of humans vis-à-vis other creatures:

> When I look at your heavens, the work of your fingers,
>   The moon and the stars that you have established;
> What are human beings that you are mindful of them,
>   mortals that you care for them?
> Yet you have made them a little lower than God,
>   and crowned them with glory and honor.

The psalmist continues this ecstatic discourse on human status by describing their divinely granted authority over all other creatures (beasts, birds, sea creatures, etc.) and expresses awe that humans, while created beings, are not categorically the same as other created life. The passage is closely related to the creation story of Genesis 1, as seen in Genesis 1:27-28, where the statement that humans are made in God's image is followed by God granting them dominion over other creatures. Both passages exude solemn, awestruck wonder before the majesty and splendor of God the creator; it is precisely within this awed awareness that they celebrate the marvel of human status in its demarcation from the rest of all created beings.

Qohelet's comments in 3:18-21 pose a dramatic counterpoint to these traditions. The sage shifts the focal point to the matter of mortality. Humans and beasts share the same origins and destiny; they come from dust, and they turn back to dust (v. 20). What they hold in common, he underlines, is nothing less than their finite existence. True, Qohelet does not bring up for challenge the human vocation of *governance* over all other created life. And yet the import of his comments is that the realities of death and finitude render this hierarchy moot, and perhaps even invest it with a kind of irony: humans, the climax and crown of creation in Genesis 1, are not substantively different from the creatures over which they are elevated and made sovereign. This is compellingly expressed by the closing thought of verse 19, where Qohelet states that humans have no advantage *whatsoever* over animals (the Hebrew syntax expresses emphasis).

Qohelet's implicit suggestion in these verses is that whatever theological speculations one might engage in regarding human vocation and destiny, certain realities impinge. Humans and animals alike are born and decompose (v. 20b). This is something we know because we can see it. Qohelet's query about what happens to the human spirit after death is spoken in this vein (v. 21). That is, Qohelet does not here entertain hope in a continuing existence; rather he emphasizes a decisive limit on knowledge ("Who knows?") that tends to deprive the matter of practical significance.

Verse 22 is Qohelet's response to these conditions on human existence ("So I saw"). Once again Qohelet speaks of the possibility of enjoyment in response to his observations on the limits on human existence (2:24-25, 3:12), this time naming work as the locus of that potential. Enjoyment in our activities (the Hebrew word is plural) is something at hand, in the here and now, which is authentically ours to take hold of—our "portion" (NRSV "lot"). Here he calls upon a familiar term (*ḥēleq*) that is at certain other points used in tension with the concept of "profit" (*yitrôn*): while profit is not within human reach, a portion is (see 2:10). Now here at the end of chapter 3 another unattainable—knowledge of what happens beyond the grave—is the context for Qohelet's defining of humanity's portion. Death is a wall we do not see over. The thought is reiterated by his closing rhetorical question: there is no one who can show us what happens beyond the grave (in context, "after them" is shorthand for *after their death*). Thus Qohelet's affirmation of enjoyment is encircled by agnosticism about what happens beyond the parameters of this existence; the impossible environs the possible, bringing it into sharp relief.

4:1-3 Human Injustice Revisited

In 4:1 Qohelet returns to the subject broached in 3:16-17. Here, however, Qohelet moves from a wide spectrum view of miscarriages of justice to a tighter lens—the distress of the victim of injustice: "Look, the tears of the oppressed." One might say that Qohelet intensifies the questions asked in 3:16-17 by narrativizing them. The victims are utterly bereft of solace (twice he deplores the absence of any comforter for them), and power is concentrated in the hands of their abusers.

This shift in focus—that is, his close-up contemplation of suffering—evokes a different response from that of 3:17 (an avowal of God as ultimate judge). Instead he asks a question about the relative merits of life versus death. Such a question is radical within Israelite thought and is entertained only rarely in the Old Testament, where it is assumed that the state of life is preferable to the state of death. The specific setting here should not be overlooked: whereas at later points in the book Qohelet will pronounce life preferable to the nothingness of the grave (compare, e.g., 9:4-6, 10), for this moment he stands in the presence of evil in the form of callous exploitation of the defenseless. It is in this specific context that Qohelet deems the dead "more fortunate than the living" (4:2). In fact, Qohelet reckons those who have never been born more fortunate still (4:3). What both have in common is that they do not have to look upon such a travesty. Qohelet is not making a literal distinction between the dead and the unborn, since "the dead know nothing" (9:5). The move is rhetorical. Qohelet invokes these two categories as a means of conveying, and reinforcing, his central point: in a world such as this, oblivion is preferable to a state of consciousness.

Thus Qohelet closes this segment as he has begun it, by contemplating the problem of evil. In this second case, however, he does not invoke divine intervention in response to suffering. Earlier he responded by saying, "God will judge." And yet such judgment is at some point in the future, at a time humans do not know and may not see. Meanwhile, there is the incontrovertible *fact* of human anguish. Qohelet, the sage observer, looks on this and is troubled.

Theological and Ethical Analysis

Ecclesiastes 3:16–4:3 is framed by a troubled contemplation of the most vexing of theological questions: the problem of evil. If God is indeed just and righteous, how is it that injustice happens? If God is God—*both* powerful and good—how is it that unspeakable atrocities occur and the perpetrators continue unchecked? The passage reflects the conflict between those things that the sage has been taught, and those to which he has been witness. The complexity of the issue for Qohelet is demonstrated in that, even as he moves to reconcile these things ("God will judge"), his language reveals the deficiency of the answer. By saying there is "a time for every matter" he alludes to the problem stated in the preceding sequence: God will judge, yes, but in God's time, and humans are in no way privy to this. The sage's dissatisfaction with this answer is evident in the closing segment of the passage where he returns to the problem. As remarked before, Qohelet's restatement of the problem moves from a wide-spectrum view of injustices (3:16) to a tighter, more vividly imagined lens—the actual suffering of individuals who are the victims of such inversions of justice (4:1). Qohelet's response in this section is surprising. His earlier reminder of a divine reckoning to come is conspicuously absent (3:17). One might expect the sage to engage in a defense of God or God's ways in the world, or at least to strain for some resolution. But here, in this context, Qohelet does none of these things. Rather, in the presence of such anguish, he can only commend the respite of oblivion. A question inherent in the interplay between these two passages is whether Qohelet's outcry of chapter 4 in some way supersedes his affirmation of a divine justice that will set things right. In fact, his writings offer no final word on the matter; these two dimensions of his thought coexist and constitute an ongoing tension (compare, e.g., 7:17; 8:12-13; 11:9 with, e.g., 7:15; 8:14; 9:1, 11). The one thing that *is* clear from his vexed response to the sight of suffering is his refusal to offer facile responses. For Qohelet the problem of evil and unjust suffering remains intractable.

Within this frame (3:16-17 and 4:1-3) Qohelet contemplates the limits of human existence. Humans have a beginning and an end; they come from dust and they return to dust (3:20). Elsewhere in the Old Testament "dust," as applied to humans, often signifies the great divide between mortals and God (Gen 18:27; Pss 104:29; Job 10:9; 34:15). So, too, with this passage. Here the gulf between human and divine is further expressed by emphasizing the *sameness* of humans and animals, which are both constituted of finite material and die. Qohelet even goes so far as to say that humans have no advantage at all over animals (3:19). This is a potentially devastating remark on the human prospect. Is Qohelet in fact saying that humans might as well be animals? Is there nothing to differentiate humans from animals? Interestingly it is precisely on this point that a self-contradiction, embedded in the text, emerges. In his very engagement of the question, Qohelet has demonstrated precisely that element in humanity that marks us off from the other creatures: our ability to be conscious of our "selves." Humans, unlike animals, have the unique ability to think beyond the moment, in terms of both a past and a future, and to do so in terms of "self." This means, therefore, that we are capable of envisioning our own death, something that is both awful and awe-inspiring. The advantage of such a capacity may be questioned. Still, it confers on humans a dignity that is not granted to other creatures. As Helmut Thielicke suggests, the ability to conceive one's end, while potentially incapacitating, also holds the promise of transcendence. If one comes to terms with one's death one is freed to live, rather than be forever in flight from, or denial of, that which is inescapable. Realization of one's own death affords one the opportunity of self-actualization (Thielicke 1983, 13).

Thus the heart of this passage constitutes an exquisite irony. The sage, in the process of propounding that definitive thing that unites animals and humans (death), engages in that very thing that distinguishes them (human ability to confront death). Qohelet's judgments on the "identity" of humans and animals are deconstructed by the consciousness that makes them possible.

Of Earnings and Yearnings: Relocating Value

Literary Analysis

This sequence comprises four units treating topics of toil, human relationships, and political power: 4:4-6; 4:7-8; 4:9-12; 4:13-16. Two of these segments are rounded off with a proverbial saying (4:6, 12), and two with the *vapor* pronouncement (4:8, 16). A unifying rhetorical feature in this sequence is the "better than" saying, a wisdom form that compares two entities or situations and pronounces one to be superior to the other. Proverbs 28:6 nicely illustrates the device: "Better to be poor and walk in integrity than to be crooked in one's ways even though rich." In this passage the "better than" form occurs in the first unit (v. 6) and in the third and fourth units (v. 9 and v. 13). A second unifying feature is the theme word "two" or "second," which, beginning in verse 8, occurs throughout the passage (see verses 9, 10, 11, 12, 15). Although the individual units of this sequence are not tightly related, each section connects to the following in a way that suggests that the grouping is not entirely arbitrary.

Exegetical Analysis

4:4-6 Toil and Rest

Toil is the unifying theme of these three verses. Qohelet begins by probing its motivation, identifying the impetus behind all toil as envy. Never one to simplify, Qohelet does not disregard the potentially positive end product of the competitive urge—proficiency and excellence (NRSV "skill in work"). It is all the more noteworthy then that this in no way alters his judgment. Drawing on his familiar image of *vapor* he deems such contentious striving as futile and self-defeating.

The image of competitive industry evoked in verse 4 is followed by a proverbial portrait of laziness. The meaning of the reference to folding one's hands is evident from its use in Proverbs, where it conveys idleness: "A little sleep, a little slumber, a little folding of the hands to rest, and poverty will come upon you like a robber, and want, like an armed warrior" (6:10; 24:33). As Qohelet observes, it is the fool who opts for this self-destructive route.

The third component in this sequence, also expressed proverbially, draws a conclusion to these two scenarios, expressed in the form of a comparison (v. 6). It is crafted to interact in nuanced fashion with what has preceded it. The first element of the comparison picks up on the connotations of idleness evoked by the folding of hands: "Better a single palm full of rest . . ." (AT). Already in these few words Qohelet signals a third position, one that at once differentiates itself from the ambitious scrambling of the climber *and* from the easy equation of repose with sloth. The reader's attention is captured. In the completion of the comparison Qohelet exploits a double meaning for the Hebrew word 'āmāl, a term that often connotes "toil" in his vocabulary, but that on occasion refers to the product of toil—one's earnings (e.g., 2:19): "Better a single palm full of rest, than two handfuls of *toil/earnings*, and a chase after wind" (AT). In the preceding two verses Qohelet has juxtaposed the two extremes of workaholism and indolence. Now he offers his view of the proper balance of toil and rest. He can give no measure but a relative one, yet it is a vividly drawn expression of his values. If the choice is between less gained in repose and quiet and twice that amount gained in toil-full strife, choose less. As elsewhere, Qohelet indicates a law of diminishing returns where toiling to accumulate wealth is concerned (compare 5:10-12 [Heb. 9-11]).

4:7-8 Toiling Alone

The thematic thread of excessive work and its futility continues from the previous unit, though now it is viewed in the context of human relationship. The toiler characterized here (the Hebrew subject is in the singular) is consumed by his work, yet never satisfied with the dividends. For Qohelet such toiling is futile in any case (compare 5:10-11 [Heb. 9-10], where it is also pronounced to be *vapor*). But in this case the absurdity of the situation is compounded by the fact that this person is bereft of human connection. The "case of solitary individuals" is more literally rendered "There is one and not a *second*." This might refer to a spouse, but more likely the point is that there is no companion of any sort (see 4:9-12). Moreover there is no blood kin, neither son nor brother. The man has no one to leave his earnings to, and no one to share them with. The abrupt interjection of a first person speaker in verse 8b (the Hebrew text does not identify a speaker, contra NRSV)—"And for whom am I toiling and depriving myself of the good thing?"— has prompted speculation. Perhaps Qohelet asks the question that the toiler does not have the imagination to formulate for himself. Or perhaps his use of the first person betrays his own identification with the man's plight. In any case the question captures the reader's attention by suddenly and starkly encapsulating "what the man's whole life is saying" (Kidner 1976, 46). Tellingly, the question centers not only on purpose (or absence thereof) but on cost: the man's single-minded toiling for wealth has meant the divestiture of all joy.

4:9-12 Two Are Better Than One

Having reflected on the plight of the lone toiler, Qohelet now puts forth the advantages of companionship. In the saying that begins this unit, two are pronounced better than one because they receive a good wage for their toil. In speaking of the advantage of two in terms of toil, Qohelet not only dialogues with the sad case of the solitary man toiling alone (vv. 7-8), he also makes an implicit response to the opening reflection on envy as the motive behind all such toil (v. 4): inherent in verse 9 is the proposal that there is benefit to viewing the "other" as partner rather than competitor.

Qohelet supports his assessment by outlining situations in which partners may provide mutual aid and assistance. The illustrations he chooses suggest the setting of a perilous journey: the reference to falling, to being at the mercy of the elements, and to threat of ambush or attack. Qohelet gives his illustrations a punch by ending each with a device for emphasis: a woe saying ("But woe to one who is alone"), a rhetorical question ("But how can one keep warm alone?"), and a proverb ("A threefold cord is not quickly broken" (see Raymond Johnson, "The Rhetorical Question as a Literary Device in Ecclesiastes," cited in Miller 2010, 85). These rhetorical markers add emphasis. Qohelet is not simply observing what is (as is the case in vv. 7-8). He wishes to persuade. Two are better than one! Significantly, this segment does not end with a declaration of vapor (Miller 2010, 85).

The saying about the strength of a three-ply cord rounding off the unit reflects a very ancient proverb. A fragment of the adage appears to be preserved in the Epic of Gilgamesh, and a fuller quotation with more context appears in an even older Sumerian story about Gilgamesh. Here Gilgamesh admonishes his comrade Enkidu about the advantages of two over one: "Stop, Enkidu. Two men will not die; the towed boat will not sink, a towrope of three strands cannot be cut. . . . You help me and I will help you, [and] what of ours can anyone carry off?" (Tigay 1982, 166, based on Shaffer 1967, 247).

The context of this scene is an imminent battle with Humbaba, the monster guardian of the Cedar Forest. In the face of daunting odds Gilgamesh seeks to encourage Enkidu by reminding him of the effectiveness of teamwork. Qohelet's own use of the proverb suggests he may well have been familiar with this ancient story, for in both cases the *three*-ply rope is used for the specific (and not necessarily obvious) purpose of illustrating the advantage of a twosome. More broadly, Qohelet's evocation of a journey—with fellow travelers affording one another protection and aid against assault—would seem to tribute this older narrative (see also Shaffer 1967, 247–50 and 1969, 159–60). In promoting the advantage of two over one, of partnership over "every man for himself," Qohelet alludes to the two valiant comrades par excellence (for the influence of the story of Gilgamesh on Ecclesiastes, see introduction and 9:7-10).

4:13-16 The Value and Limits of Wisdom

This segment is only loosely related to the preceding units in content, but it is connected to the larger sequence on the formal level by the "better than" proverb (4:13) and by the use of *second* (v. 15b; see below). The ensuing scenario of verses 14-16 may be an example story (an illustration created for didactic purposes; compare 5:13-17 and 9:13-16). On the other hand, the specificity of certain references, such as that of a man emerging from prison to take the throne, has led to speculation that Qohelet had historical events or figures in mind. No identifications have achieved consensus, however, as there are no known situations that perfectly fit the events described. It is nonetheless possible that Qohelet's narrative vignette was prompted by some historical event, now no longer recoverable. Weighing in favor of this view is the fact that the passage is not a particularly tidy illustration. One might expect an example story to be more obvious in its lessons.

The Hebrew text of this passage is very difficult. In particular, the syntax of verses 14-16 is ambiguous, and the subjects of some verbs are unclear, making it difficult to ascertain the events described and the actors involved. Any interpretation must therefore be tentative.

As a proverb, verse 13 is understandable on its own terms. On one side of the equation Qohelet places age and royalty, two things that normally occasion reverence and honor. On the other he places poverty and youth, two things that normally do not. In formulating the contrast in just this way he dramatically underscores the value of wisdom. It is wisdom that is decisive to the assessment of the better option. Where wisdom is, *there* is advantage, for wisdom outweighs status, power, and age. Qohelet's elaboration on the character of the old king as one who will no longer take advice suggests the issue to be that of able governance (see, e.g., Prov 11:14). The one who comes forth from prison to reign (v. 14) is probably to be identified with the poor youth of the previous line (the Hebrew can be read: "He came forth from prison to reign"). Though there are several ways to read this verse in its details, in sum it suggests a rags-to-royalty theme in which a young, wise commoner is elevated to the throne.

Verse 15 refers to a "youth who replaced *him*" (NRSV "king" is not in the Hebrew text). Some take the youth here to refer to the commoner-become-king of the previous verses. This is quite possible, but the party is referred to as the *second* youth (see NRSV text note), suggesting that yet another youth has been introduced. In fact it is possible to take the rest of the unit as Qohelet's rumination on the predictable train of events to come (Crenshaw 1987, 113–14; Fox 1999, 226). The verse may be translated: "I saw all the living—those who go about under the sun—with the next young man who would arise in his place" (Fox 1999, 224). As James Crenshaw observes, the passage then illustrates "the endless recurrence of events" (1987, 114); that is, one king will always be succeeded by another, no matter how wise that king, no matter how meteoric his rise. One notices that the vast number of the next young king's allegiants is underscored (those "moving about under the sun" is a way of saying, "every person living"; cf.

7:11). And yet, Qohelet continues, *this* king's great popular appeal will also wane. The Hebrew of verse 16 sets up a kind of antithesis between the teeming throng that he leads (the ones he is *before*—used spatially) and the future generations ("the *after* ones"—used temporally) who will not "rejoice in him." To say that this king will not be celebrated by future generations could mean that his reputation falls into disfavor. More likely, however, this is Qohelet's way of saying it is consigned to oblivion (see 2:13-16). Either way, the king's popular acclaim eventually gives way to posterity's disregard.

Although Qohelet begins verses 13-16 with an anecdote that illustrates the value of wisdom, he elaborates on it in such a way as to illustrate its limits as well. As Michael Fox has observed, "The first transfer [of power] demonstrates the power of wisdom, the second its frailty" (1999, 228). The wise youth is soon followed by another, and the populace will all support his successor, whoever he might be. Thus, while it is better to have wisdom, even wisdom is not so durable as one might hope, perhaps especially when it comes to mass appeal (one thinks of the poor wise man who saved a whole city, yet was remembered by no one, 9:13-16). In the end Qohelet's reflection on the limited value of wisdom becomes a segue into a more generalized rumination on the unstable nature of human power and popular acclaim.

Theological and Ethical Analysis

Getting and spending, we lay waste our powers.
William Wordsworth, "The World Is Too Much With Us"

He who dies with the most toys wins.

Malcolm Forbes

Qohelet's deftly drawn vignettes of a get-ahead, materialist mentality strike close to home. "She works 24/7," we say, though not with concern or sympathy but a begrudging admiration.

Even as the avenues from poverty into the middle class seem to be narrowing, the story of individual effort and personal determination rewarded by wealth compels. We love the rags-to-riches tale: the rugged individual who came to America with nothing but holes in his pockets, who, through dogged labor, made his millions. Above all we respect the one who pulls himself up by his own bootstraps, the one who made herself a success without help from anyone. In fact the "lone toiler" may enjoy a stature in American mythology unmatched elsewhere.

Qohelet regards all such frenzied activity as equally ephemeral. That one person is motivated by envy and another by honest pride in work, that one is skilled and another slapdash, that one achieves fame and power through effort and another remains obscure has no bearing on his conclusion: all is vapor. What escapes this pronouncement is worthy of notice, especially for those of us immersed in a culture that values feverish striving. The sharing of life—of toil and risk and harvest—this alone survives inspection, resolving into solidity even as the things that had seemed substantial—wealth, power, acclaim—turn out to be nothing but shadows.

In his book *The Dismal Science: How Thinking Like an Economist Undermines Community*, Stephen Marglin observes that the Amish do not buy insurance. When an Amish barn burns down, the community gathers to build it back up again. Hard work, skills, and good food are shared, the barn is rebuilt, but above all, community ties are strengthened. According to Marglin, the Amish "forbid insurance precisely because they understand that the market relationship between an individual and the insurance company undermines the mutual dependence of the individuals that forms the basis for community" (2008, 18–19).

Leaning on one another is not something with which we are comfortable. We have come to believe that our needs are only properly met at the convergence of our earning power and the marketplace. Like a nutrient that we have not even realized is missing from our diet, this insistence on going it alone, depending on money instead of one another, has left us starving for the sustaining by-product of mutual aid: community.

Reticence before God

Users of English translations may be puzzled by the fact that the versification does not agree with that of the Hebrew text. In fact, chapter and verse divisions in the Bible are not original; they were introduced into the text only from the thirteenth century CE onward. Therefore editors of modern versions must make judgments about whether or not to follow those divisions; such decisions are made largely on literary grounds. The chapter division followed by the NRSV and many other versions is justified in this case because the reference to the house of God in 5:1 (Heb. 4:17) signals a shift in topic. It is indeed a topic new to the book—appropriate behavior in the presence of God. This new focus is accompanied by a new style. For the first time Qohelet addresses the listener directly and in the imperative mood. Throughout the unit Qohelet will address the reader in the form of admonitions.

Literary Analysis

The opening command of 5:1 draws on a conventional figure from the discourse of wisdom in which one's "feet" connote the entirety of one's conduct (Prov 4:27; 6:18; Job 23:11; 31:5). This instruction to watch one's step forms a frame with the concluding imperative, "Fear God" (5:7b [Heb. 5:6b]). The series of warnings offered in between these brackets may be divided into three segments. Verse 5:1b (Heb. 4:17b) advocates listening obedience over sacrifice, and 5:2-3 (Heb. 5:1-2) and 5:4-7a (Heb. 5:3-6a) turn to the topic of speech before God, treating prayers and vows respectively. Each of these latter two segments concludes with a proverb-like reference to dreams and many words (5:3 [Heb. 5:2] and 5:7a [Heb. 5:6a]). The "fool" appears in each of the three segments and in each case serves the same function— to exemplify behavior to be avoided (5:1b, 3-4).

Qohelet counsels caution in the presence of God, "for God is in heaven, and you upon earth" (5:2). Qohelet posits a decisive gulf between God and earthlings. Humans are to be ever mindful of it. In chapter 3:18-21, Qohelet conveyed this same idea indirectly, through an extended reflection on what humans have in common with other creatures. Here it is stated directly. The mandate with which this passage concludes is a bottom-line summary of its message: fear God.

The passage as a whole reflects a distrust of wordiness, a common stance throughout wisdom literature, such as Proverbs 10:19: "When words are many, transgression is not lacking, but the prudent are restrained in speech" (also 13:3; 17:27; Sir 23:7-8). For the sages much talk is suspect, and it is such a view that is reflected throughout Qohelet's admonitions and proverbs in this passage. For instance, the listener is counseled to keep words to a minimum (5:2b) and told many words are the mark of the fool (5:3b). Moreover, in two instances words are in some fashion associated with dreams (5:3, 7a). The problem is that it is difficult to know the connotation of dreams in these sayings, since in both cases the text is difficult and the translation not obvious. Verse 5:7a may offer a clue by linking dreams with "vapors" (NRSV "With many dreams come vanities"). The first half of this verse is corrupt, but it is possible to construe dreams and vapors in a modifying relationship, hence "vaporous dreams" (Seow 1997, 197). With minor emendation the passage reads: "As a host of vaporous dreams, so are many words" (compare Fox 2004, 34). The remark is fitting preamble to Qohelet's final admonition: "Instead, fear God" (AT).

Such word associations as these—words and fools, words and dreams, words and vapors—convey the link between much talk and lack of substance. But it is one thing to acknowledge that speech can be hollow and vacuous, and another to say that words are harmless. The premise for Qohelet's admonitions is that one is responsible for one's words (note 5:4-6). The underlying assumption of the passage is not that words are without effect or repercussion; rather, inherent in Qohelet's warnings throughout the sequence is a sober recognition of the potential volatility of language, all the more serious when one is dealing with the supreme deity. Unconsidered speech can get one into serious trouble ("Do not let your mouth lead you into sin," 5:6).

Exegetical Analysis

5:1-3

Behave carefully, warns Qohelet, when going to the house of God. "House of God" most likely refers to the temple, since sacrifice is involved (for "house of God" as a term for Jerusalem's second temple, see Ezra 3:8; 6:22; 8:36). What is to be noted, in any case, is that one is to proceed with caution when coming into the presence of God. Qohelet's general guideline on behavior before God is followed by an appraisal of listening and sacrifice. Qohelet does not disparage sacrifice but relativizes its value in relationship to listening/obedience (the Hebrew word has both connotations; compare NJPS). His judgment echoes the values of the prophets (e.g., 1 Sam 15:22; Amos 5:2-24) as well as those of the wisdom tradition (Prov 15:8; 21:3, 27). Sacrifice cannot be substituted for right conduct: "To do righteousness and justice is more acceptable to the LORD than sacrifice" (Prov 21:3). Qohelet's identification of the sacrifice as that of "fools" does not imply that under some other circumstance sacrifice might indeed replace heedfulness! Rather the link with fools reflects an assumption about who is inclined to commit the folly of substituting sacrifice for obedience. The nature of the ensuing derogation is unclear in the Hebrew, which reads literally, "for they do not know to do evil." The text as it stands is ambiguous but suggests that the focus of the disparagement is more on the fools' limited intellectual capacity (cf. 10:15) than on their ineluctable urge to wrongdoing (NRSV). In fact, some take the phrase to mean that fools are ignorant of the wrong they commit; in that case it is translated "have no knowledge of doing evil" (compare Crenshaw 1987, 114; Seow 1997, 194; Bartholomew 2009, 201). Fools are so obtuse they are oblivious of wrongdoing when they approach God improperly. In any case the elaboration on the fool is parenthetical to the main idea: obedience is better than sacrifice.

Qohelet follows his high estimation of attentive listening by enjoining moderation in speech. Like the sages, Qohelet is keenly aware that one's mouth can get one into trouble (e.g., Prov 10:14, 19; 13:3). This is in fact a common trope in Egyptian wisdom literature. The recurrence of this theme in wisdom literature has led some to assume that Qohelet's caution of verse 2 refers to speech in general, but it is more directed than that. The context established in 5:1 is of going to the house of God, and the phrase "before God" in 5:2 confirms that this context continues (see also the continuation of the passage in 5:4-6, which assumes this same setting). Thus the passage treats the specific issue of speech in God's presence.

Qohelet exhorts his listeners not to be precipitate in their speech to God, encouraging thought before words (his reference to haste may anticipate the more specified warning against rash vows in vv. 4ff.). As noted, the rationale he gives for this caution should be carefully attended to: "For God is in heaven, and you upon earth" (5:2b). Qohelet's God is a transcendent God, one who is wholly other. Finite humans should beware. Acknowledgment of the vast distance between humans and God motivates a final warning to let words be few when speaking to God. The proverbial tag in verse 3 reinforces the point: many words are the mark of the heedless fool.

The exhortation to be brief in one's words before God has led some commentators to suggest an affinity between this text and a familiar text from the Sermon on the Mount. In Matthew 6:7-8 Jesus speaks about the appropriate way to pray: "When you are praying, do not heap up empty phrases as the Gentiles do; for they think that they will be heard because of their many words. Do not be like them, for your Father knows what you need before you ask him."

These two texts do in fact share certain similar assumptions about God's sovereign power and knowledge. In the sequence leading up to his words of guidance for prayer, Jesus encouraged his listeners not to be intent on performing prayers and almsgiving so that others will see. God knows when these things are done, and that is what matters; the implicit understanding is of a God who sees and knows all (Matt 6:1, 6, 18). Qohelet also assumes such a God, one surveying all from the lofty vantage point of heaven. But for Qohelet words should be few because of the great distance between God and humans. One should contrast this with the rationale provided by Matthew for few words in prayer: "For your Father knows what you need before you ask him." The emphasis there is not only on God's sovereign perspective, but on God's benevolent care; it is when one trusts to this that one allows one's words to be few. Hence the theological accent of the two passages is quite distinct. Qohelet is concerned his listener not transgress the divine/human boundary. To do so may place one in a precarious situation (see below, 5:6 [Heb. v. 5]).

5:4-7

Verses 4-7a continue the theme of language before God, turning more specifically to the subject of vows. At the temple or cultic location, worshippers could vow to make an offering to God. Such vows were pledged for various reasons, for instance to request God's aid or to express devotion (see, e.g., Lev 7:16-17; 22:18-23; 27:1-25).

Qohelet's guidelines, which draw closely upon the language of Deuteronomy 23:21-23 (Heb. vv. 22-24), emphasize the utmost seriousness of such a vow. Not only should one fulfill it, one should do so quickly. A vow to the deity is of such a serious nature that if there is possibility one might not fulfill it, it is better not to vow at all. Qohelet also foresees and preempts a possible means of retraction (a contingency not treated in the Deuteronomy passage). Once confronted for payment, a person cannot be released from a vow by calling it a "mistake" (in context the "messenger" appears to be a temple functionary who collects on unpaid vows, but there are no other biblical references to such an office). The Hebrew word underlying "mistake" refers to inadvertent sin and is employed almost exclusively in legal contexts (see Lev 4:2-35; Num 15:22-31). In such cases the guilty party may atone for such error through the means of a sacrifice offered by the priest. If this is in fact the background of Qohelet's reference, he pointedly excludes this legal recourse as an acceptable means of retraction. Qohelet's exclusion is in keeping with the principle stated at the outset: sacrifice is not to be substituted for obedience (5:1b). In sum, Qohelet's treatment of vows reinforces the binding nature of a promise to the powerful God in heaven (who will see through any subterfuge).

Qohelet states consequences for the default—divine anger and a severe form of garnishment, though, in keeping with his view of the erratic nature of retribution, he avoids stating the divine response in dogmatic or mechanistic terms. The admonition closes with two remarks, a proverb and a summary command (v. 7). The translators of the New Jewish Bible (NJPS) have rearranged the sequence of these two parts. Deeming the final injunction "Fear God" to be the logical follow-up to Qohelet's warning of divine penalty, it is relocated to the end of verse 6. But the sequence should remain intact. The intervening proverbial caption—"As a host of vaporous dreams, so are many words" (AT)—is, like so many proverbs, a brief but deftly drawn associative image, here conveying the emptiness and vanity of such excuses and temporizing before the sovereign deity (compare 6:10-11). It is a fitting prelude to Qohelet's final word on the matter: "Instead, fear God" (AT).

Theological and Ethical Analysis

The better part of this passage addresses the issue of speech before God. It is important to see, however, that it is far more than a simple reflection of Qohelet's view on vows and prayer. In the process of prescribing a certain attitude in one's speech before God, the sage limns an entire theological landscape. The fulcrum of the passage is to be found in 5:2: "For God is in heaven, and you upon earth." Qohelet's concern is specifically for the distance between divine and human. His prescriptions for the appropriate attitude and speech before God stem from an acute awareness of this divide (listen carefully; don't speak without thinking; keep your words to a minimum; don't shirk a vow by calling it an error). The opening and closing commands summarize this basic concern: "Approach God with due caution" and "Fear God."

While Qohelet's admonitions highlight the majesty, mystery, and transcendence of God, the passage is not, as some scholars would have it, offered in the vein of worshipful exhortation. Qohelet is less interested in edification than he is in practical orientation. His cautions offer practical guidance, a kind of survival manual, on how to behave before such a God.

The tone of the passage is consonant with the view reflected throughout the book. Qohelet's keen sense of creature/creator disparity weaves throughout his meditations. His God appoints a time for all matters but does not disclose such information to humans (3:1-11); no amount of strain or toil grants a person more than a glimpse of the grander scheme of events (3:11; 8:16-17). Humans cannot hope to remonstrate with such a being (6:10-11), much less alter or sway divine decrees (3:14-15; 7:13, etc.). Qohelet is by no means unique in his apprehension of the transcendence of the God of his people. Israel exudes a profound awareness of Yahweh's incomparable status and of the otherness of her God, as seen, for instance, in the limited nature of the theophany granted Moses in response to his request to see God's face (Exod 33:12-23), in the prohibitions against making an image of God (Deut 4:15-18), and in God's response to Job in the divine speeches at the climax of the book (38–41). The exilic prophet in the book of Isaiah expresses the divine/human gulf thus:

> For my thoughts are not your thoughts
>   nor are your ways my ways, says the LORD.
> For as the heavens are higher than the earth,
>   so are my ways higher than your ways
>   and my thoughts than your thoughts.
> (Isa 55:8-9)

Qohelet's distinctiveness with regard to the transcendence of his image of God inheres in the untempered, thoroughgoing nature of his view. As Roland Murphy has observed, "There is plenty of biblical precedent for the mystery of God; the difficulty is that Qohelet does not say anything else" (1992, lxviii). Qohelet's lofty God is not leavened with a God who comes down to mortals to commune with them, or who reveals the divine plans for humans (compare Jer 29:11). While this makes all the more striking Qohelet's unreserved avowal that God approves when humans avail themselves of life's pleasures (see especially 9:7), he claims no other insight into the mind of God. Indeed he repeatedly declares that humans cannot fathom divine actions and intentions (e.g., 3:11; 8:16-17) and moreover implies that God has orchestrated matters to obscure human insight (see especially 3:14; 7:14; compare 1:15; 3:11). Qohelet's reflections on the unpredictability of divine retribution are only further expression of the opaqueness of God's design (see especially 7:15-18; 9:1-2).

Qohelet's view of world and humans' place within it is, then, in many respects, quite stark. One sees little place in the book for the kind of intimate relationship with God that is more readily seen at other points in the biblical witness. Needless to say, Qohelet's message is not a word for all occasions. As with any biblical testimony, Qohelet should be heard among and in relationship to the concert of witnesses to Israel's relationship with God. Still, we lose much should we move too quickly to homogenize Qohelet's distinctive accent. Instead we might first explore what word it has for us as it stands, beginning with our own contemporary context in Western culture. Spirituality is currently a growth industry, with publications on the topic in no short supply. One need only visit the self-improvement section of any bookstore, browse the latest TED talks or PBS programming, or peruse the flood of blogs and websites devoted to spirituality and self-actualization to get a sense of the vast output of popular brands of spirituality. Although the emphases and paths on offer differ in various, often significant ways, a pervasive current many versions share challenges us to dispense with the concept of a distinction between God and humanity. God is the life force of the cosmos, and each of us possesses something of that energy. This idea of a unity between God and the human realm comes in a variety of expressions. Writer Elizabeth Gilbert, in an interview on *The Oprah Winfrey Show* in 2007, defined "God" as "the Perfection that absorbs all." When we rise to our highest self, we are absorbed in that perfection; we participate in the divine perfection. In a similar vein Wayne Dyer, author of *Manifest Your Destiny: Nine Spiritual Principles for Getting Everything You Want*, encourages us to trust ourselves as an extension of God: "I like to think of God as the ocean and myself as a glass. If I dip the glass into the ocean, I will have a glass full of God" (Dyer 2003, 25).

Needless to say, in such cosmologies as these, the power and wisdom of God are seen to be not only accessible but, in fact, residing in each one of us. The kernel of this insight is not new. Jesus himself suggested the presence of untapped, godlike power in each of us, dormant only for our lack of faith (Matt 17:20). Every spiritual insight comes with its own hazards, its potential for corruption. How can we awaken to the divine within ourselves without falling into the trap of identifying our own desires, biases, and prejudices with the divine will? If we allow the witness of Ecclesiastes to join the conversation, we may find in Qohelet's clear vision of a radically "other" God an essential and bracing corrective to philosophies that not only put the cosmic divine at human beck and call, but that, more ominously, court the risk of making God in the image of human desire and ideology.

Systems Failure
(Diagnosis and Prognosis)

I n this section Qohelet turns from the subject of speech and vows to a different topic, though not a new one. In chapter 4 Qohelet has offered a poignant reflection on the plight of the oppressed, wherein he lamented their abject vulnerability before those with power. In this section he returns to the topic of exploitation of the powerless, contemplating it within the context of hierarchies of power and systemic corruption. While this passage is not directly connected to the following section of 5:10–6:9, it serves well as a precursor to Qohelet's more extended reflections on the perennial nature of human appetite for gain.

Exegetical Analysis

Qohelet once again turns attention to human injustice (3:16-17; 8:10-11), this time explicitly identifying the exploitation of the poor (compare 4:1-3, where the vulnerable elements are identified as "the oppressed"). His advice not to be dismayed at such wrongdoing reflects his resignation to such situations of inequity (see 4:1-3). In this case he gives a reason for the predictable nature of such violations of justice, though the meaning of his explanation is open to interpretation. The "watching" of one high official over another might mean surveillance—a situation in which each official must act in accordance with the interests of his superior, and on up the ladder. Or "watch" might have a protective sense—"to watch out for" (the Hebrew verb allows for either meaning)—implying that the officials protect the interests of one another in a web of corruption. In this case the continuation of such practices is ensured by the mutual benefits shared within the bureaucracy. Either way, those on the bottom rung of society are left utterly vulnerable, having no recourse to a court of higher appeal, so to speak.

The Hebrew of verse 9 (Heb. 8) is obscure, and no proposed translation has garnered a consensus. Though even a literal translation cannot be agreed upon, verse 9 might be rendered: "But the profit of a land is for all; a king for a cultivated field." The meaning of this phrase is out of reach, but Proverbs 29:4 offers a relevant context in its reflection on the relationship of the "king" to the "land": "By justice a king gives stability to the land, but the one who makes heavy exactions ruins it."

Here the relationship of the king to the land and his subjects is spelled out. The proverb sets out two diametrically opposed scenarios. A king who executes justice ensures the building up of his kingdom, whereas practices that take a heavy toll on his subjects lead inevitably to the ruin of his kingdom. Policies that rest on the backs of the people are not just deplorable, they are a form of royal self-sabotage. Qohelet's own words in chapter 10 reflect similar assumptions about the necessity of responsible governance to a healthy state of affairs in the land (see commentary at 10:16-20). As William Brown puts it, "Justice in the land is not a luxury of royal policy, but its very basis" (2000, 59). If taken in this vein, 5:9 anticipates Qohelet's ensuing reflections on the pitfalls and sorrows awaiting those who make gain their only priority, pursuing it at the cost of all else (5:10–6:9).

Portion over Profit

Literary Analysis

If the world be worth thy winning, Think, O think it worth enjoying.
John Dryden, "Alexander's Feast"

Quite often commentators summarize this passage with a heading that focuses on money or wealth. But such rubrics define the passage too narrowly. The issue at the heart of this passage, which unites all the proverbs and small scenarios, is nothing less than human happiness—both its possibilities and its limits. It is true, however, that in the course of considering this question, Qohelet closely examines the role of material things.

The unit begins with a short series of proverbial sayings (5:10-12 [Heb. 9-11]) and proceeds to consider a specific case story (5:13-17 [Heb. 12-16]). The heart of the unit is found in the commendation of 5:18-20 (Heb. 17-19). This is followed by consideration of a second case story. The unit ends, as it has begun, with a short series of proverbs. An overview of the content of these segments follows.

In the opening proverbs and the ensuing example story Qohelet explores and critiques attitudes toward wealth and possessions. This material does not, on the face of it, present a tight unity. And yet running through it is a concerted argument: the one who makes money the purpose of life will never be satisfied (this is true whether one loses a fortune *or* amasses one!). This sequence issues in the passionate statement of 5:18-20. Here Qohelet earnestly promotes a course of action: people should take enjoyment in the day-to-day pleasures of their food, drink, and work. These goods are the gift of God.

The second specific example (6:1-6) marks a move from the positive affirmation of 5:19 (Heb. 18), in which God is the giver, to a candid recognition of its negative counterpart—in some cases God withholds opportunity for enjoyment. The transition is abrupt, following as it does on Qohelet's passionate affirmation of the good in life. And yet the recognition is consonant with the realism of the sage, as seen also in previous commendations (2:24-26; 3:12-13, 22).

The unit concludes as it began, with three proverbial sayings. But the sayings of 6:7-9 contain ambiguities and are subject to significantly different interpretations. As opposed to the opening proverbs, a unifying theme is not immediately apparent.

Exegetical Analysis

5:10–6:9 Less Is More: Portion over Profit

The theme of these verses is that the pursuit of wealth will not bring fulfillment. The insight is all the more compelling in that the first three proverbs describe the best-case scenario: the lover of money obtains his dearest wish—more money! The result is not satisfaction, but dissatisfaction. Dissatisfaction and unrest (v. 12 [Heb. 11]). The problem is that the acquisitive urge is fueled by its very gratification; more begets desire for more (v. 10 [Heb. 9]). In addition, the more one has, the more one needs (v. 11 [Heb. 10]). Whether Qohelet's reference to more "eaters" refers to the expenses required to manage and sustain wealth or to swarms of hangers-on, the point is that wealth generates its own drains, illustrating the old adage that you can't get ahead. So what good is wealth to the wealthy? It exists primarily for their viewing pleasure (cf. 4:8) as they watch it pass through their hands. The net benefit of riches is limited. In verse 12 the satiety of the rich man, in view of its consequence—a troubled sleep—is often taken to mean overindulgence at dinner. This is the ostensible meaning, and Qohelet may in fact be alluding to a popular adage. Yet his observation on the blissful sleep of the worker, whether on little food *or* much, would seem to preclude this interpretation. Instead the proverb may enlarge on the theme of v. 11: since more requires more, the magnate is kept wakeful by his anxious striving to maintain and enhance his assets (cf. 2:22-23). No matter how one interprets these references, the salient contrast is between the blissful sleep of one who possesses little and the "rest-lessness" of one who has much. Prosperity is no guarantee of quality of life.

Qohelet does not leave the matter there. In verses 13-17 (Heb. 12-16) he elaborates on the pitfalls of wealth by presenting a particular case. A man of wealth (the Hebrew is a masculine singular) loses everything in one business venture. To compound the disaster, he has an heir to whom he now has nothing to bequeath. Qohelet's refrain in verses 15-16 [Heb. 14-15] does not in itself describe what is so grievous about this situation in particular, for the fact that humans depart the world as they come into it is recognized by Qohelet as a universal condition, albeit also bitterly lamented (e.g., 2:18). What compounds the tragedy of the universal situation for this man in particular is cued in the introductory line—he clung to his wealth. The scenario thus continues the theme of the preceding proverbs—attachment to money for money's sake or, put another way, resources viewed as capital versus portion (5:19; NRSV "lot"]). The dire consequence of the man's attitude is seen in his response to his financial loss, detailed in the final line of the unit (v. 17 [Heb. v. 16]): "Yes, all his days he eats in darkness, in much vexation, sickness and anger" (AT). This vividly describes one who has lost their very mainstay; the aftermath of the financial loss is an existence permeated by grief and resentment.

The significance of this final line for the message of the unit is liable to be overlooked because translations often introduce it by a conjunction ("Besides" or "Moreover") that gives it the ring of an afterthought. But the underlying Hebrew word may also be rendered emphatically ("Yes!" or "Indeed!"). In fact verses 16 and 17 both begin with this particle and may be read as presenting two concluding exclamations in a parallel grammatical structure: "Yes, this is a grievous ill, just as he came, so he goes" and "Yes, all his days he eats in darkness." The final sentence is no afterthought. The portrait it draws indicates the crux of the problem. Twice within the span of two verses Qohelet refers to the man's toiling and does so in relation to outcome—nothing/wind (vv. 15-16 [Heb. 14-15]); the point is that the man's energies and desires have been tragically misdirected.

In verses 18-20 (Heb. 17-19) Qohelet offers an alternative course to the futile pursuit of profit that ends in anxiety, agitation, and disillusionment. Once again he sounds the theme of enjoyment (2:24-26; 3:12-13, 22). His words are similar in content to the previous expressions but more emphatically stated. His introductory statement might be translated or paraphrased: "Pay attention: This is what I have seen to be good." The word "good" is an antonym to the word "ill"—the word that has twice summarized the case of the ruined man (5:13, 16 [Heb. 12, 15]). In other words Qohelet responds to this "ill" with a "good"—one that he can promote wholeheartedly. The actions of eating, drinking, and finding pleasure in one's toil take on added resonances in this particular literary setting. Here these evaluations of what is good respond to the tragedy of one who, for the prospect of some future gain, deferred pleasure. This is the grave ill of his situation, that he did not partake of what was his in the moment. For Qohelet, the time for enjoying the resources at hand is *now*.

The reminder that humanity's days are "few"—literally, numbered—in such a context is not parenthetical (v. 18). It is in fact the finitude of human existence that gives impetus for truly receiving and relishing the good things in life (see 11:7–12:8). In verse 20 (Heb. 19) Qohelet suggests that to live in such a mode has, in turn, its own beneficial effect on the human psyche, for such a person "will not dwell excessively on the days of his life" (AT). It should be noted that "days of his life" in verse 20 does not refer to a person's daily cares and concerns, as is sometimes assumed. Rather, in context, "days of his life" echoes "numbered days of his life" from verse 18 (AT). Here, as there, it signifies mortality. Hence Qohelet's insight is this: to live rooted in the present, immersed in the moment-by-moment blessings of existence, wards off immoderate preoccupation with death. To be sure Qohelet also adjures confrontation with death, as we have well seen (see especially 1:12–2:26; 9:1-12): to do so is potentially redemptive in that it can impel one to live life to the fullest, laying hold of its goods with gusto. In turn, occupation with the good things of the moment averts morbid *obsession* with death. For Qohelet, death-cognizance is a matter of balance (see discussion at 7:1-4).

A recurring element in Qohelet's theme of enjoyment is to take pleasure "in one's toil." The import of this phrase is debatable since the Hebrew allows for more than one interpretation. It could mean that one should take enjoyment *amidst* one's toil (in other words, despite its onerous nature). Alternatively, given the fact that the Hebrew word can refer not only to toil but to its compensations, it may be construed to encourage enjoyment of one's earnings (compare NJPS: "One should eat and drink and get pleasure with all the *gains* he makes"). Finally, it could mean simply that one should take pleasure *in* one's work—that is, in the very doing of it (a meaning implied by most English translations). The phrase as it is attested at other points in the book allows for each of these meanings at one point or another. In the current context of 5:10–6:9 the emphasis suggested is that work is an activity to be enjoyed in the very doing. The wealthy man forfeited happiness by toiling away for a result that never materialized (5:15-16 [Heb. 14-15]). Qohelet's curative for a product-oriented mentality is a process-oriented approach to one's work (see 3:22; 9:10). In this understanding work is a blessing in its own right, standing alongside the other gifts of food, drink, and rest (see Brown 2001, 271–84).

Qohelet's commendation in 5:19 emphasizes God as giver. As in previous occurrences of the theme, there is an interplay between divine determination and human agency (2:24-26; 3:13; compare 9:7): "Moreover, every person to whom God gives wealth and possessions, and whom he permits to enjoy them . . . this is a gift of God" (AT). Once again Qohelet recognizes God as the source of those things that allow for human happiness and—entailed on that—the divine prerogative to dispense or withhold. Yet, as implied in the very mood of Qohelet's address, namely that of exhortation, there is a place for human initiative, if only in the choice as to how to respond, should God bestow such bounty.

It is in 6:1-2 that Qohelet elaborates on the negative counterpart to the positive scenario of divine giving. The subject of 6:1-2 is the man who has everything. Nothing he might want is beyond his reach. But God does not grant the conditions that allow him to take enjoyment in these things; rather a stranger enjoys them. Qohelet does not spell out the factors involved, but the hypothetical case he presents in the ensuing verses (a man who lives a long life and has countless descendants) might suggest that it is untimely death, compounded by the tragedy of the absence of any heir (see 4:8 for a case where Qohelet acknowledges the misfortune of the latter). Qohelet does not shy from placing responsibility with God, or from deploring the situation as a sickening tragedy.

The ensuing verses of chapter 6 are best understood as an extended exclamation, drawing on hyperbole (vv. 3-6). The tragic instance of the man who is denied enjoyment moves Qohelet to state yet more emphatically its priority over all else. He ups the ante from wealth, possessions, and prestige, calling on those two things that epitomize a satisfying and rewarding existence in ancient Near Eastern culture: numerous offspring and a long life (Gen 24:60; Deut 11:21; Job 42:16-17; Ps 127:3-5; Prov 3:16). Even were a man to sire scores of children and live many years, his life is tragic if he has not experienced life's enjoyments. In an astonishing statement, Qohelet pronounces a stillborn to be better off than such a person (v. 3). He delays momentarily before reaching the rationale for his verdict in verse 6:5b. The effect of his initial comments is to foreground the *advantages* of the aged patriarch. As opposed to the man's great longevity the child has no life span at all (figured as a fleeting existence). As opposed to countless children who will carry on his line, the child does not even have a name (the word "name" in Hebrew refers not only to identity but to posterity).

With verse 5 Qohelet begins to approach his point. The child has no experience of consciousness (neither having "seen" or "known"). It is the child who has "rest." One may wonder at the choice of "rest" as the deciding factor. Qohelet's assessment reiterates his theme of the wearisome nature of existence where there is no satisfaction (e.g,. 2:22-23; 4:7-8; 5:15-17 [Heb. 14-16], cf. 1:1-11). That this is the point is seen in the poignant concluding question, "Do not all go to one place?" The patriarch and the stillborn are ultimately bound for the same destination. The listener supplies the implied: since both end up in Sheol, who is to be envied? The one of long life who experiences the frustrating, wearying existence of one who did not enjoy life's bounty, or the one mercifully enveloped in oblivion?

The reference to burial in verse 3 of this sequence has perplexed readers through the centuries. Many translations (including the NRSV) take this to be a further elaboration on the unhappy plight of the man: in addition to not having joy in life, he is deprived of appropriate burial rites upon his death. The reading is certainly plausible grammatically, though it is problematic in context. The emphasis of this sequence (indeed the theme underlying the entire unit) is that *nothing* can compensate for the absence of enjoyment in life. Even if it is granted that Qohelet has concern for proper burial (8:10), the introduction of such a consideration at this point would be anticlimactic. An alternative construal that better aligns with the pervasive tone of the section takes the denied burial to apply to the stillbirth (so NJPS, Crenshaw 1987, 126, and Murphy 1992, 48). In this case we have an anticipatory clause, in which the subject is not named until the second part: "Though it have no proper burial, I say the stillborn is better off than he" (AT).

The radical nature of Qohelet's comment in these four verses is not always appreciated. At the outset of the unit in 5:10-17 he has challenged the materialistic mind-set that assumes wealth brings happiness. Now he questions more deep-seated and dearly held cultural assumptions. Drawing on hyperbole, he holds up to view a man who has *the* circumstances that bespeak divine blessing—many descendants and a long life—and pronounces him no better off than a stillborn. The statement comes from his conviction that nothing is more important for humans than the experience of satisfaction and joy in one's day-to-day existence. Nothing can compensate for this lack.

6:7-9 Desire or Death?

Sheol and Abaddon are never satisfied,

And human eyes are never satisfied.

Proverbs 27:20

The conclusion to the unit mirrors the introduction of 5:10-12 in form with its short series of proverbial-type sayings. But the proverbs of these three verses contain ambiguities and are subject to significantly different interpretations. Such ambiguity is well demonstrated by the use of the catchword *nepeš*, which appears in the first and last saying (NRSV "appetite" [v. 7] and "desire" [v. 9]). The varied connotations of this word show it to be a fitting note on which to end the larger sequence. The Hebrew noun refers to the essential life force of a living creature, but it can also denote "appetite" or "desire," as it does in 6:7: "All the toil of a man is for his mouth, but the appetite is not satisfied" (AT). All human industry is devoted to the Sisyphean task of satisfying the unappeasable. Thus Qohelet harks back to the proverb that opens the entire passage in 5:10 and reiterates that human desire is never sated. The final saying of verse 9 refers to the "going" of such desire (there is no warrant for translating the verb in the particular sense of "to wander" as in the NRSV). But since *nepeš* can also refer to the animating life force, this final phrase might instead be an idiom for death (see below). The only certain thing here is that the "sight of the eyes" is deemed superior to this.

No satisfactory solution to the riddle of this section has been proposed. In particular, the overall progression of thought is unclear. While the first proverb is vivid in its statement on yawning human appetite and the futility of human efforts to satisfy it (cf. 5:10-12), its relationship to the ensuing interjections in verse 8 is not apparent. The two queries are in complaint mode, and in this context they may remark on the limited nature of wisdom given this state of human affairs. Wisdom (the accent here being on skill and diligent work; see 2:19, 21) affords one no advantage over the foolish (who are not known for their work ethic, 4:5), given the unquenchable nature of human desire. The reference to the "poor" man in verse 8b seems, in context, to function as a parallel term for the "wise man" (see 4:13-16 and 9:13-16 for scenarios that feature a poor, wise man whose wisdom ultimately brings no advantage). Hence the second line of the verse may repeat the sentiment of the first, describing the kind of discretion and practical knowledge (literally, "who know how to walk before the living") that *should* bring success and satisfaction.

The final saying is also problematic in its translation. As noted, the meaning of each part of the comparison is in question. That it is a comparison saying and thus states some relative good is clear. But what is better than what? While the most common understanding of "sight of the eyes" in this verse is that it refers to the pleasure one possesses in the moment, in Old Testament tradition the eye can stand for what one desires or covets (e.g., Num 15:39; Job 31:7; Prov 27:20; see Clifford, 1999, 240). Thus Job in establishing his innocence says, "I have made a covenant with my eyes; how then could I look upon a virgin?" (31:1). In Ecclesiastes this use of "eye" or "eyes" is evident in 2:10 and 4:8. It seems more likely that "sight of the eyes" refers to what one looks upon and wants, not what one possesses in the moment (compare 5:11 [Heb. 10]).

The interpretation of the second phrase is also in question. Though some commentators read the verb *halak* ("to walk," "go") with the meaning *wander* or *rove*, there is no justification for construing it in this particular sense. On the other hand, it has been pointed out that in several biblical passages it is used as a figure for the final departure—namely death (e.g., Job 14:20; Pss 39:13; 109:23)—a meaning found several times in Ecclesiastes (e.g., 1:4, 3:20, 5:14-15; 6:4, 6). The fact that *nepeš* can be translated either as "desire" or "life force" suggests the possibility of a double entendre. In this case the final proverb is a tart remark on human options (or the lack thereof). It has been said that there are two certainties in life: death and taxes. Qohelet's rendition tenders these options to be death and desire. Humans experience desire as long as they are alive. This is certainly not ideal, but then the only cure for this is death. When pressed to a choice, better to be in a state of desire than to have desire/life depart.

The passage concludes with the familiar pronouncement: this, too, is vapor and a chase of wind. While the antecedent of "this" is grammatically ambiguous (the assessment could refer to the final saying only [v. 9a]), most likely Qohelet's judgment sums up the situation of frustration and limitation reflected in the whole concluding set of proverbs (vv. 7-9).

Theological and Ethical Analysis

Oscar Wilde once wrote, "In this world there are only two tragedies. One is not getting what one wants, and the other is getting it." In this wry observation is the recognition that what people imagine makes for happiness and what in fact does make for happiness can be very different things. Ecclesiastes 5:10–6:9 may be seen as an expansion on this insight. Whatever else the examples and reflections of this passage accomplish, they effectively probe at assumptions people have about what will bring fulfillment.

Much of this passage is devoted to exploring the relationship between material goods and happiness. Qohelet does not suggest that material things are irrelevant for happiness. After all, in order to take pleasure in one's food and drink and work one must in fact have access to these basic resources. But he does say, "Possessor, beware." So quickly, so subtly, the situation turns, and it is goods that lay claim to owner. The process of acquisition has a momentum of its own. Too quickly obtaining becomes an end in itself. In contrast, Qohelet conveys a radically different orientation in which happiness consists of savoring the daily satisfactions of food, drink, work, and sleep. The interest accruing on a savings account has no bearing whatsoever on these pleasures.

As contemporary readers living in a period and culture far removed from that of Qohelet, we cannot know with certainty how this message engaged with the original context in which it was written. Nonetheless, as members of one of the most consumerist nations on the globe, we perceive its trenchant challenge to our own context. Qohelet's message to materialist culture is distinctive, and it is compelling. He does not promote detachment from material things so much as reattachment to our lives in the place where we live them. In that place, attitudes toward money and things are rehabilitated.

Prodding the Pupil

Literary Analysis

This segment comprises two subunits, 6:10-12 and 7:1-14. That 7:1 begins a new subunit can be seen in the shift in literary form to that of the proverb. For this reason, several commentators treat the prose segment of 6:10-12 as an independent section. It is true in fact that there is no tight organic relationship between these two units. The choice to assign 6:10-12 and 7:1-14 to the same exegetical unit is based on certain verbal and thematic connections between 6:10-12 and the final verses of chapter 7. Verses 13 and 14 of chapter 7 are in fact a reprise of ideas presented in 6:10-12.

Ecclesiastes 6:10-12 dwells on the limitations of humans. God is never explicitly named in the passage, but each assertion expresses a contrast between God's power and human finitude. This theme of human limitations and a powerful God who is beyond human reckoning is resumed in 7:13-14. Here God is explicitly named. God's work is described as a crooked thing that humans cannot make right. This crooked divine activity is seen in the oscillation of fortune and adversity in a human life. Such occurrences are beyond human control. A verbal echo in 7:14 further reinforces the thematic *inclusio* of human finitude in these frame passages: "God has made the one as well as the other, so that mortals [*'ādām*] may not find out anything that will come after them [*'aḥărāyw*]." In 6:12 Qohelet states a similar idea in the form of a question: "For who can tell them [*'ādām*] what will be after them [*'aḥărāyw*] under the sun?" The precise meaning of these two statements as they relate to their immediate context is in question. Nonetheless there is a discernable verbal play between them and, no matter how they are read in their specifics, both declare the problem of human ignorance in one form or another. For statements with similar wording and to similar effect, see 3:22 (humans cannot know what occurs beyond death), and 10:14 (humans do not know what will happen in the future).

Ecclesiastes 7:1-14 is the first of three collections of proverbs in the book (see also 9:17–10:4 and 10:8–11:4). A proverb is an artfully constructed literary vehicle for imparting instruction. As a literary form it may be highly compact—much is said in few words—creating a kind of riddle that stirs the reader into active reflection on its meaning. The proverb expresses some truth, entailed in which is a guideline for behavior. Nonetheless proverbs are not intended as universal truths or timeless absolutes. They have a limited applicability. A proverb that is appropriate in one situation may have no currency in another (thus one finds proverbs in the wisdom tradition that are in direct contradiction). It is useful to keep this general orientation in mind as one approaches the proverbs transmitted in these sections, some of which appear to cohere with Qohelet's broader ideas, and some of which do not.

The epilogist at the end of the book, in paying tribute to Qohelet the sage, gives an informative description of the responsibilities of the sage. Through his scrupulous study and conscious arrangement and presentation of the proverbs, the wise man is to teach the people (12:9). Thus, in including such a collection, Qohelet fulfills one of the sage's conventional duties.

In form the sayings are representative of the wisdom sayings of Proverbs (for instance they use parallelism, make use of contrasts between the wise and foolish, and are often linked by catchwords rather than by content). In content, however, these sayings represent an interesting intermingling of conventional and unconventional ideas. Scholars have suggested various scenarios that might account for this admixture. Some older studies on the subject explain it as a result of additions from other hands. These are representative of an earlier trend in scholarship that sought to harmonize the contradictions of the book by seeing the more conservative (traditional) statements as interpolations. More recently scholars have suggested that Qohelet is in dialogue with traditional wisdom and engaged in modifying or critiquing it. According to this argument Qohelet transmits conventional sayings and then challenges or problematizes these with another saying. An example cited in support of this is the sequence of sayings in 7:5-7, which, according to some interpretations, can be summarized to say: "Listen to the wise, not to the foolish; however this also is *vapor*, for the wise too may fail." Yet not all the clusters of proverbs show such a movement and countermovement (see, for instance, 7:11-12). There is no denying that this collection is made up of both conventional and unconventional ideas. But there is no clear or consistent pattern in the way the sage puts these together. In any case, Qohelet's overall perspective on the wisdom project of imparting guidance and instruction must be viewed in light of the fact that the proverbs of 7:1-12 are framed by assertions of human finitude with respect to knowledge. The meaning of the individual sayings in the collection can be debated, but by encasing these sayings in such declarations Qohelet affirms that the endeavors of the wise encounter certain definitive limits.

Exegetical Analysis

6:10-12 For God Is in Heaven and You Are on Earth (Eccl 5:2)

God is never explicitly named in Ecclesiastes 6:10-12, yet the divine power is ubiquitous in these verses. In the opening verse the passive verbs "named" and "known" refer to what *God* has named and what *God* knows. Qohelet goes on to assert that humans cannot dispute with God, who is so much stronger than they are (the Hebrew underlying "*those* who are stronger" [NRSV] is a grammatical singular and refers to God). Speech, the capacity that distinguishes humans from all other creatures, becomes a devalued currency—so much "air"—when the interlocutor is God (v. 11; cf. 5:7). In the pair of concluding questions in verse 12—"Who knows what is good for mortals?" and "Who can tell them what will be after them?"—the "who" is stated for rhetorical effect and means *No one*! Nonetheless, in this specific context, it puts the reader in mind of the one who could give crucial knowledge if so inclined. The contrast between all-encompassing divine power and knowledge on the one hand, and limited human capacities on the other, runs through the passage like a fissure.

Qohelet's question about what is good for humanity is couched in a recognition of the finite life span of humans (compare 2:3). The finitude of human existence puts a stake on the quest for what is good. It also presents the challenge. Mortals are confronted with choices at every turn, yet they have been given a handicap: they can in no way transcend the contingencies of human existence to gain the knowledge that would allow them to chart the optimal course (3:1-15). The theme of the transience of human existence weaves throughout verse 12. Life is vapor-like—that is, fleeting (not "vain" as translated in NRSV). Life span is compared to a shadow in its swift waning (as in Job 14:1-2: "A mortal . . . comes up like a flower and withers, flees like a shadow and does not last"; cf. Job 8:9; Ps 144:4). The precise meaning of the concluding question—"For who can tell them what will be after them?"—is not certain, though the modifying phrase "under the sun" limits the arena in question to events on earth (contrast 3:22). The ambiguity is due to the Hebrew underlying "after them" (literally "after him/it"). The phrase could be an ellipsis (a shorthand expression) for "after his death" (as in 3:22), but it is questionable how knowing what occurs on earth after one's death would help one make beneficial choices. More likely it reflects an idiom that means "afterward" or "in the future" (a sense supported by its occurrence in 10:14, where the preceding parallel line reads: "No one knows what is to happen"); in this case the problem is a person's inability to know what his or her future days hold. Whichever meaning one chooses, the problem is essentially the same. Inability to see into the future prohibits one from knowing with certainty what is good in one's day-to-day existence. In ending on this note, this section anticipates a theme that will be repeated with increasing frequency in the remaining six chapters, the opacity of the future to a human being (7:14; 8:7; 9:12; 10:14; 11:2, 5, 6).

7:1-4 Going to the House of Mourning

At their finest, proverbs, the instructional tool of the sages, possess a riddle-like quality that prods the listener into active engagement. The first proverb in this series nicely exemplifies this quality. The listener's attention is caught by its concluding line (v. 1b): in what way might the day of one's death be better than the day of one's birth? The meaning of the first line is more accessible. Qohelet's comparison of a good name to oil, a precious commodity to ancient peoples, is another way of saying that a good reputation is more valuable than wealth (Prov 22:1: "A good name is to be chosen rather than great riches; and favor is better than silver or gold"). The alliteration of this line, with its gliding sibilant sounds—*ṭôb šēm miššemen ṭôb*—exhibits yet another favored pedagogical tool of the sages (here reinforcing the contrast between a good name and fine oil). The specific choice of oil for comparison in this instance may refer to the practice of anointing bodies for burial. Perhaps this proverb was directed to those who could not afford fine oil for burial; better to be buried with a good reputation than with fine unguents (Murphy 1992, 63). An additional resonance may be discerned when one remembers that fine oil is by nature highly perishable (see 10:1). By contrast the testimony of biblical tradition is that a good name is durable—living on in the memory of one's children and one's community (Prov 10:7; Sir 41:11-13). If such a contrast is at play, the saying of verse

94

1a pairs something of lasting value (reputation) with something that is valuable, yet also unstable and liable to ruin (oil). It is this dimension of verse 1a that provides a cue for reading the second comparison of the couplet (Kugel 1981, 10). The day of death (when one's reputation is finally secure) as compared with the day of birth (the day on which one's reputation is not yet made, much less tested) is better. Though the progression of thought from the one saying to the next is not clear, such an understanding is evident in several ancient interpretations of this passage (e.g., the Aramaic version of the book, followed by medieval Jewish commentator Ibn Ezra). It may well be that Sirach has this passage in mind when he says: "Call no one happy before his death; by how he ends, a person becomes known" (Sir 11:28). A saying of the ancient rabbis, more starkly put, expresses a similar thought: "Do not believe in yourself until the day of your death" (*Mishnah Avot*, 2:4; cited in Davis 2000, 200).

The effect of the addition of the second line is that the sage puts a sting into the traditional idea expressed in the first: a good reputation is indeed more valuable than precious oil, but since it is secure at death, and only at death, that day is better than the day of birth. There is also a more subtle effect. A comment on the vulnerability of virtue is insinuated: don't count on an unvarnished name until the clods fall (compare verses 7-8 in this same sequence). In stating the advantages of death over life, verse 1b segues into verses 2-4. Qohelet has already commended attending the house of mourning over the house of feasting (v. 2). In verse 4 he makes the same point in a slightly different way: if you are wise, your heart is in the house of mourning; fools have their hearts in the house of mirth. The proverb in verse 3 is in keeping with the sober mood of the injunctions surrounding it. Qohelet suggests that sorrow is better than laughter. The rationale he gives for this, that a downcast face may gladden the heart, is given no elaboration. How might this be so? Verse 2b provides a helpful key to appreciating the sense of these three verses. The reason that attendance on the house of mourning is better than attendance on the house of feasting is that this is the ultimate destination of all humans. Thus there is a truth in the house of mourning that it behooves the living to ponder (the CEB translation "*should* take it to heart" as opposed to NRSV "*will* lay it to heart" better captures the sense of the final phrase; see also 11:8–12:1). Mirth and revelry should not obscure this reality. Taken as a whole, the tenor of verses 2-4 is that life is appropriately viewed from the vantage point of death. To the reader familiar with the themes of Ecclesiastes, the citation of these proverbs is not arbitrary, for the book is steeped in such a perspective (see especially 9:1-10; 11:9, 12:1).

Nonetheless, a closer examination is warranted if one is to do justice to the meaning of this passage as it relates to the larger context of the book. May one generalize from this passage that Qohelet "prizes death and sorrow over life and laughter"? (Longman 1998, 208). It is true that the proverbs of this section commend mourning and grief over feasting and mirth. The question is whether this is the sage's final word on the matter. In fact, the way in which the theme of this cluster of verses interacts with the environment of the book is a fine illustration of the limited application of the proverb, even as it is a study in the contradictions that Qohelet inhabits. Strikingly, at a later point in the book, he countermands the counsel of these verses, and in rather specific terms. In chapter 9, Qohelet voices one of his most extended and emphatic exhortations to take enjoyment in life. In addition to a more emphatic tone (the entire commendation is expressed in an imperative mood— "go," "eat," "drink"), certain new elements occur, including the encouragement to anoint one's head with oil and to wear fresh white garments. The significance of such activities is that they are specifically associated with feasting and celebration in the ancient Near East (see 9:1-12). It is not incidental that this passage in chapter 9 is both preceded and followed by serious and extended reflections on death as the inescapable fate of everyone. In response to unavoidable death, the sage enjoins his listeners to make *each* day a celebration (*at all times* let your garments be white, he says in 9:8a). One is tempted to summarize the tension embodied in these two segments of chapters 7 and 9 by saying that Qohelet commends going to the house of mourning but does not, in the end, suggest living there. As Thomas Hardy has written, "If way to the Better there be, it exacts a full look at the Worst." The sage who has recorded the saying, "Sorrow is better than laughter, for by sadness of countenance the heart is made glad," would no doubt concur.

7:5-7 The Wise and the Foolish

Qohelet once again poses a comparison: better to hear reproof from the wise than a song from the fool. The Hebrew word for "song" (*šîr*) may mean "praise" (Ps 149:1; Isa 42:10), thus providing the expected antonym for (wise) *reproof* (NRSV "rebuke"), or it may refer to revelry (cf. Amos 6:5), thus reminding that there is nothing of substance to be heard in the house of mirth (v. 4). The latter meaning is suggested by the elaborative aside on the grating sound of the fool's merriment (v. 6). The reference would appear to be the sharp crackling sound made by burning thorns. This is conveyed on the sensory level as well, as the Hebrew for "thorns under a pot" creates a hissing or lisping sound: *hassîrîm taḥat hassîr*. The ensuing vapor pronouncement is ambiguous in its application but may denote the emptiness of the fool's utterances. Whether they be odes of praise or drinking songs, they amount to naught.

Coming on the heels of his affirmation of wise reproof, Qohelet's suggestion that the wise may turn foolish is surprising (v. 7a). Qohelet has recognized and lamented the deleterious effects of oppression before (4:1-3; 5:8), but this is the first time he speaks of its impact on the wise. The relationship of the parallel line in verse 7b to verse 7a is not readily apparent. Receiving a bribe would not normally be paired with falling victim to oppression. It is possible that there is no strict symmetry between the two lines, rather each describes circumstances that may be the downfall of the wise person. An alternative is to read "oppression" as shorthand for "oppression's profit" (Alter 2010, 370), in which case the second line reiterates the idea of the first. Perhaps what is to be highlighted here, no matter which reading is chosen, is Qohelet's acknowledgment that under certain conditions or influences good character can be deformed. The significance of Qohelet's observation in its current context should not be overlooked. The cumulative effect of the proverbs beginning in verse 2 is to build up a pronounced contrast between two categories of people: those marked by sobriety and probity, and those characterized by debauchery and flattery. Now the sage suggests that, given certain conditions, such categories may collapse (cf. 7:1). The discernment and good judgment of the wise person is not invulnerable to circumstance or temptation (compare Prov 30:7-9).

7:8-10 Keeping Perspective

The situation in the background of these three proverbs is a change in fortune, as is made apparent in the concluding admonition of verse 10: "Do not say, 'Why were the former days better than these?'" The three proverbs commend the values of patience and matter-of-fact acceptance in responding to misfortune. In this way the unit anticipates the conclusion of the entire sequence, in which Qohelet will elaborate further on the best response to the downs *and* ups of life (7:14).

The declaration that the end of a thing is better than its beginning harks back to the lesson of 7:1 and reminds once again that "the best perspective one can hope to attain on a matter is its outcome" (Towner 1997, 326). Life is unpredictable. In this context, the meaning suggested for the second line of verse 8 is that it is better to wait patiently for the end of a thing than to presume to know the outcome (compare 10:14 where it is fools who presume to know the future). Qohelet's praise for perseverance is followed up by two warnings on how *not* to respond to the situation: first, one should not fly off the handle in anger (v. 9), and second, one should not lament or pine after days gone by ("Why?"). In other words, the wise person will not expend energy either nursing rancor or questioning the turn of fortune's wheel. The "do nots" of these verses will be matched by "dos" in the final verse of the unit.

7:11-12 Wisdom's Advantage over Money

The proverbs of verses 11 and 12 ponder the value of wisdom by a comparison with material wealth. Similar assessments are found throughout the book of Proverbs, as one reads in 8:11: "Wisdom is better than jewels, and all that you may desire cannot compare with her" (see further Prov 3:14; 8:19; 16:16). As becomes readily apparent, the proverbs from Ecclesiastes 7 do not express the matter quite so unequivocally. What does it mean to say that "wisdom is *as good as* an inheritance" (v. 11a, emphasis added)? The second proverb also undercuts wisdom by making material wealth the assumed value point—the bar against which wisdom is measured (v. 12a). In the final analysis Qohelet (or the tradition he transmits) does find in favor of wisdom with the concluding line of the sequence: "But the advantage of knowledge is that wisdom nourishes the life of its possessor" (AT). Wisdom has an edge over wealth: while both can be said to provide "cushion," wisdom can nurture and sustain a life in a way that wealth cannot. In a nutshell the two proverbs taken together make this positive statement: money is useful, but wisdom is more so.

In the chapters leading up to this passage Qohelet has not only disallowed that wealth will bring fulfillment, he has mounted a psychologically probing analysis of the acquisitive urge (4:7-8; 5:10-17). The inherent assumption of the merits of money in 7:11-12 is not in contradiction with his views on the issue. His comments merely reflect a pragmatic recognition of the benefits of having some means. In putting wisdom on a trajectory with money—perhaps the more striking feature of the sequence—he is also viewing it from this more commodious angle, for its utility and insurance benefits (see Brown 1996, 126–29).

A closer examination of these two verses suggests the possibility of a double-edge to their meaning. One may note that the proverb of verse 11 describes wisdom and, by extension, inheritance, as advantages to "those who see the sun"—in short, the living (compare 4:15). That specification, seemingly gratuitous, puts one in mind of the introduction to the book, where Qohelet bitterly lamented that neither material gains nor wisdom shield one from death (1:12 –2:23). Here in chapter 7 he presents the value of these more from a glass-half-full perspective, but the larger context of the book makes us aware of the equivocal nature of his valuation. In fact, the suggestion of a double-edge is further supported by the choice of vocabulary in verse 12, where Qohelet likens the "protection" of wisdom to that of money. The Hebrew word translated "protection" can indeed refer to the protective cover of shade (e.g., Ps 80:10). Alternately it can mean "shadow" with the connotation of transience (e.g., Job 14:2). Thus Qohelet, while acknowledging the protecting aegis of these two entities, at the same time alludes to their impermanence (the word is indeed the same used in 6:12 to convey the fleeting nature of humanity's days). Such details as these suggest that, like other skilled forgers and purveyors of proverbs, Qohelet prods his readers, testing us for our alertness.

7:13-14 Considering the Work of God

However one takes the estimation of wisdom in 7:11-12, the auspicious statement following hard on them draws an unmistakable boundary to wisdom's efficacy: "Consider the work of God; who can make straight what he has made crooked?" When it comes to the mysterious work of God, wisdom runs up against a decisive barrier. In the first chapter of the book Qohelet quoted a pithy saying about the impossibility of straightening "what is crooked" (see 1:15). Whereas in that passage responsibility was assigned only by inference, here in 7:13 the responsible party is named and the crooked thing explicitly identified. God is responsible, and the crooked thing is God's work.

An illustration of such baffling work is evident in the turns of fortune that one may experience in the course of life. Such alternations are far beyond the control of people, who cannot straighten out the work of God by wisdom or any other means. Since one cannot predict, much less control, such occasions, one should accept each as it comes, enjoying the good day fully and taking the bad day in stride. Qohelet's specific counsel for the day of misfortune is, as the NRSV translation reflects, to remember that it is indeed God who has sent this day, as well as the day of blessing. The Hebrew of this phrase might also be rendered: "God has set the one next to the other" (compare Gordis 1968, 176; Ogden 1987, 111; Fox 1999, 257). The difference here is in nuance (the emphasis in this case is on the juxtaposition of opposites), but perhaps it places the emphasis more precisely: Qohelet's advice for the day of trial reinforces the alternation of fortune and misfortune in all its confounding mystery. Qohelet's ensuing statement of the divine rationale for such activity, while admittedly ambiguous, seems to imply that the presence of such ebb and flow in human experience makes it impossible to tell what will happen next (reading "afterward" for "after them"; see commentary on 6:12). Stated more broadly, such vicissitudes of existence provoke an acute awareness of one's epistemological limits. As Robert Gordis paraphrases, "God sends good and evil into the world in bewildering array, so that man cannot gather from the flux of events the meaning of things" (1968, 295). Having warned us against asking after bygone days (7:10), and having reminded us of the utter futility of discerning the future (7:14b), Qohelet's advice has the effect of drawing us to reside in the present.

Qohelet's assertion that all occurrences come from God and that humans can do nothing in the face of such sovereign decrees is ultimately an encouragement to take the ups and downs of life as they come. Accordingly, some discussions of these key verses from the sage summarize their message as a call to adopt a degree of stoical distance amid such vacillations. Such a characterization is potentially misleading. To state the obvious, the directives Qohelet gives for navigating through the fluxion are customized, one to the day of good and one to the day of misfortune. It is on the day of adversity that one is called to "consider"—that is, a bit of philosophical distance is reserved for the difficult times. On the good day, however, the only mandate is to "be in good" (AT), the Hebrew here being an expression without exact parallel elsewhere in the Old Testament. Whereas times of suffering call for a modicum of critical distance or perspective, times of good, by their nature, beckon full immersion. This is the wisdom Qohelet offers in the face of human limits.

Elusive Wisdom

Literary Analysis

The preceding unit (7:1-14) culminates in a reflection on the incomprehensible activity of God. So 7:15-29 commences with a reflection on an instance of such enigmatic work, namely, lapses in the operation of retributive justice (vv. 15-18). This first subunit is followed by an interlude consisting of disparate wisdom sayings (vv. 19-22). In substance these offer both affirmation and reminder: affirmation of the value of wisdom for human endeavor, and reminder of the limitations of human righteousness. Though it is difficult to discern how this sequence connects with what precedes and what follows, it is possible that this sampling of sayings serves as prelude to Qohelet's summary assessment of his quest for wisdom in the conclusion of the unit.

The unifying topic of the concluding unit in verses 23-29 is the elusiveness of wisdom. Qohelet's admission of his failure to achieve the wisdom he sought after in verses 23-24 states the central theme and is in fact the climactic statement of 7:15-29. In view of the phrase "I turned" at the beginning of 7:25, some commentators designate the conclusion of a major segment at verse 24; however, this expression does not necessarily designate a new beginning (compare 2:20). The relationship between verse 23—"All this I have tested by wisdom"—and verse 25—"I turned my mind to know and to search out and to seek"—is a parallel one. Verse 25 provides further elaboration on the process of investigation, detailing its rigors. The unity of verses 23-29 is confirmed by the presence of the key word "find" (or "discover"), which occurs in verse 24 ("Who can find it out?") and is repeated no fewer than seven times in the ensuing verses.

Exegetical Analysis

7:15-18

The fear of the LORD prolongs life, but the years of the wicked will be short.

Proverbs 10:27

Proverbs 10:27 expresses a central tenet of the wisdom tradition: the wicked are ultimately bound for destruction, but the righteous are on a path to well-being and life. The sages are persistent in their efforts to instill this fundamental lesson (e.g., Prov 10:2; 11:4, 8, 21; 12:21; 16:22; 18:10). Indeed the book of Proverbs is introduced with this theme: those who attend to the voice of wisdom will come into a safe haven; those who ignore it will meet with destruction (1:8-33). Qohelet addresses a challenge to these foundational suppositions of wisdom thinking in 7:15, arguing that sometimes the righteous die young even as the wicked enjoy longevity. As is clear from his formulation of the observation, Qohelet is not stating a general principle here but rather observing troubling exceptions to what should be. Nonetheless, his prefatory reference to his *fleeting* life (literally, "life of vapor"—see 6:12 and 9:9, as well as Psalm 78:33 and Job 7:16, for analogous meanings for the phrase) might imply that such exceptions are not as scarce as one might hope. Such cases are at least common enough to be observed within a single human life span, brief as it is. Qohelet's testimony poignantly contravenes that of the psalmist in 37:25, who declares: "I have been young, and now I am old; yet I have not seen the righteous forsaken, or his descendants begging bread" (NASB).

The puzzling counsel offered in the three verses that follow has sparked considerable debate among interpreters. Qohelet appears to advise that one be neither too good nor too bad! A common reading of this sequence is that it in some manner reflects the Greek philosophical notion of moderation, in which virtue is located at the mean between an excess and a deficiency. The application of this notion to these verses is inappropriate, however, since the golden mean does not refer to the middle way between virtue and vice; rather, achieving virtue is precisely the goal of exercising moderation. In arriving at an understanding of verses 16-18 it is important to see that they are entrained in the lead idea of verse 15 and are to be interpreted in that light. The point of Qohelet's observation in verse 15 is that the deed/consequence connection cannot be assumed; there are no guarantees that a particular act generates a particular consequence. The ensuing warnings against too much wisdom or too much folly should, first and foremost, be understood as a rhetorical strategy for elaborating on the dilemma inherent in verse 15, namely, what is one to do?

Qohelet warns against being too righteous or too wise; the concepts are in parallel here and are to be considered synonymous. According to the NRSV and numerous other translations, one should avoid overdoing righteousness/wisdom, lest one "destroy" oneself. But the verb refers, more precisely, to the state of being dumbfounded or appalled, usually in response to a terrible or marvelous sight (see Isa 59:16; 63:5; Dan 8:27; Sir 43:24; cf. Ps 143:4). This connotation for the verb suggests that Qohelet's caution is in line with his previous reminders that the clarity of vision afforded by wisdom is accompanied by painful awareness of life's enigmas and inequities (1:18; 2:13-15). In a world where retribution malfunctions (7:15), Qohelet warns once again that acute discernment may issue in acute disillusionment.

The counterpart to this warning is that one should also avoid the opposite extreme of being very wicked or a fool (as in verse 16, the two concepts are in parallel). Here, too, it is apparent that Qohelet's words are not to be taken literally, but rather as a rhetorical means of exploring the ramifications of verse 15. Qohelet has testified that the operation of retributive justice has serious glitches. Here in verse 17 he would seem to preempt one possible response to such a breakdown in affairs: if those doing evil get off scot-free, why not act as one pleases? The answer implicit in Qohelet's warning is simple, and it in no way contradicts his statement concerning exceptions in verse 15: sometimes the wicked *do* get their just deserts.

Needless to say, Qohelet's admonitions have an ironic tinge. He does not actually warn against too much righteousness/wisdom (he does not believe such is humanly possible; e.g., 7:20, 23-24), or too much wickedness/folly (he would not sanction even a little of such). The admonitions not to be too good or too wicked are attention-getting devices to pique the reader's interest. In this way Qohelet explores the ramifications of the troubling acknowledgment of verse 15. The sum effect of these three verses taken together is to convey the problematic absence of any assured consequence for a given action. Will being righteous/wise guarantee security or a sense of well-being? It will not. But one who banks his or her course of action on the erratic operation of retributive justice just might discover it is functional! There are no assurances that a particular course of action leads unquestionably to a particular end. In short, humans live their lives and make their choices in a world where there are no guarantees, one way or another. The one thing that is certain about this situation is an absence of certainty.

The concluding counsel of verse 18 is somewhat cryptic. The initial phrase implies a tension between the "one" and the "other" that one should lay hold of, but what is the referent of these two pronouns? Usually they are seen to refer in some manner to the two preceding counsels, elaborating in some fashion on the admonition to avoid too much righteousness on the one hand, and extreme wickedness on the other (compare NIV "It is good to grasp the one and not let go of the other. Whoever fears God will avoid all extremes"). Yet those espousing this line are hard-pressed to articulate how such advice plays out in concrete terms. What does it mean to advise that one should not be too righteous while not being too wicked? As a response to the breakdown of retributive justice, the suggestion that one should hedge one's bets (by tempering righteousness with a bit of wickedness?) is bizarre, to say the least. If, as proposed here, Qohelet's "counsel" is primarily a rhetorical device for expressing the tenuous nature of the deed/consequence nexus, then an alternative interpretation of verse 18 is possible. The warnings of verses 16-17 taken together recognize both the reality of divine justice and its apparent lapses. Possibly Qohelet suggests that the one who fears God is cognizant of both, living in awareness of this enigma (in fact a more literal translation of the final phrase of v. 18 is "goes forth with both"). In this construal the "one" and the "other" are not, strictly speaking, the counsels themselves but rather, respectively, the negation and affirmation of divine justice implicit in them. Such a reading may take verse 18 to a higher level of abstraction than is warranted; yet it may be observed that the tension expressed here is found in other key passages in the book (see especially 8:11-14).

7:19-22

A logical progression in these sayings is not immediately apparent. The unit may represent a wisdom dialogue, that is, a sequence in which a conventional wisdom saying is followed by one which in some way challenges or modifies it (see introductory remarks to 6:10–7:14). Qohelet will once again explore the interplay between wisdom's efficacy and its limits in 9:13–10:2.

In the first saying Qohelet affirms the effectiveness of wisdom for the wise by means of a comparison. As the NRSV has it, the strength wisdom brings to the wise is deemed superior to the aid of ten rulers. The comparison is peculiar. As has been observed, rulers are not a likely source of aid for the wise. With minor emendation the text reads: "Wisdom gives strength to the wise more than the *wealth of the* rulers who are in the city." In this case the meaning of the passage is similar to other places in wisdom instruction where wisdom is more valued than wealth (Prov 3:13-15; 16:16; cf. Job 28:15-19). Perhaps it even ups the ante in that the wealth is not just any wealth, but the wealth of the ruling elite.

The optimistic comment on the empowering potential of wisdom for the wise person is followed by a sobering comment on human limitation (v. 20). Qohelet's recognition of human susceptibility to sin echoes other passages from biblical tradition that assert that no one is entirely righteous (e.g., 1 Kgs 8:46; Ps 143:2; Prov 20:9; Rom 3:10). To err is human, Qohelet seems to suggest.

With the admonition of verses 21-22 Qohelet turns to a specific instance of such inevitable moral frailty: disparaging talk of others. Somewhat surprisingly, his warning focuses not on the speaking, but on the hearing of it. The situation is that of hearing oneself insulted by subordinates. Qohelet recommends an attitude of tolerance, reminding the listeners of their own culpability in such behavior. His reminder is a pronounced summons to honest self-examination, directing the listener to what the heart knows. It can be noted moreover that the syntax of the Hebrew in this final sentence places emphasis on the frequency of such lapses (Crenshaw 1987, 143). Implicit in the admonition of these verses is the insight that vigilant introspection behooves the person who exercises authority over others.

7:23-29 Elusive Wisdom

At the beginning of the book Qohelet has introduced the entirety of his observations and teachings as an investigation: "by wisdom" the sage will assay to grasp all that occurs under heaven (see 1:13). Ecclesiastes 7:23-25 hearkens back to this framework in which all his reflections are presented, as he recounts his quest and summarizes its findings (compare also 8:16-17). A prominent feature of the unit is the recurrence of the word *find*, which occurs no less than eight times in these seven verses. But the emphasis is on that which is *not* discoverable rather than on that which is.

One of the central questions in this sequence has to do with the identity of the woman "more bitter than death" in verse 26.[2] Given that she is often seen to represent womankind in general (see, for instance, the JB and NEB translations), the passage has generated much discussion about Qohelet's attitude toward women (see, e.g., Koosed 2006, 77–87; Dell 2013, 74–94). In ascertaining the identity of this female figure it is helpful to survey the movement of the opening lines. In two verses Qohelet synopsizes both his aspiration and failure: he set out to be wise, but it was beyond his reach (vv. 23-24). The utter inaccessibility of the goal is conveyed with two different spatial figures, which emphatically express both its distance and its depth (Crenshaw 1987, 145). The wisdom Qohelet sought was nothing less than a comprehensive understanding of the "sum" of it all (7:25). The word "sum" (*ḥešbôn*) occurs only in this book in the Old Testament (7:25, 27; 9:10), but in later Hebrew it means "account, calculation, sum." In fact it is not unlike the English words *calculation* and *accounting* in that it can refer not only to the final solution of a computation but to the *process* of reckoning itself. Used here in conjunction with "wisdom" it adds the nuance of an understanding arrived at by means of a highly deliberate process of accounting and reasoning, a dimension that is brought to the fore in Qohelet's self-characterization of 7:27: "adding one thing to another to find the *sum*." The latter half of verse 25 may be read as an enumeration of things in the realm of folly, rather than two sets of double accusatives as in the NRSV, a reading that results in assertions of the obvious (compare NJPS and Fox 1999, 267). In this way Qohelet conveys the comprehensiveness of the undertaking; he determined to leave no stone unturned (see similarly 1:17). In complementary fashion the series of verbs denoting intellectual effort ("to know," "to search out," "to seek")

---

2. This passage has a particularly malignant legacy, being cited in the fifteenth-century Inquisitors' witch-hunting manual *Malleus Maleficarum*. See Fontaine 1988, 137–68.

underscore its rigors. The search to understand "that which is" is not only exhaustive, but exhausting. In all events, disillusionment is the dominant mood of these opening lines.

Does Qohelet then descend from this lofty prospect to engage in complaints about the opposite sex? Such a shift in scope seems unlikely. Moreover, the use of the definite article with "woman" ("the woman") suggests that this figure is familiar to the readers. The characterization of this figure, predatory in nature and associated with death, calls to mind the *topos* of the temptress figure in Proverbs 1–9 (Prov 2:16-19; 5:3-14; 6:24-35; 7:4-27). This woman is powerfully alluring. Indeed the imagery associated with her is erotic (Prov 5:3; 6:25; 7:16-17; cf. 9:13-18). The man who succumbs to her charms will meet with destruction. He is compared to an ox going to the slaughter or a bird rushing into a snare (Prov 7:22-23). This woman is the original *femme fatale*, enticing but death-dealing (Prov 2:18; 5:4-5; 6:26). In the opening nine chapters of Proverbs she is set up as the very antithesis to Woman Wisdom (see especially chapter 9).

The characterization of the figure of the temptress in traditional wisdom literature suggests the possibility that Qohelet's woman, "more bitter than death," of ensnaring heart and hands, is an allusion to this persona (e.g., Dell 2013, 93–94; Bartholomew 2011, 266; Brown 2000, 83). In fact, one sees indication that Qohelet has already made implicit reference to her positive counterpart, Woman Wisdom, in 7:23-24. The pertinent background for understanding these verses is Proverbs 1–9. In these chapters Woman Wisdom calls out her invitation to "all that live" (Prov 8:4). Moreover, she is situated variously in the city squares, on the busiest street corner, at crossroads, and at the city gates. In other words, wisdom is in public, open, and unrestricted arenas, where anyone can view her and attend to her instruction. Wisdom is accessible, readily available to any who would seek her, even the simple (Prov 8:5, 17; 9:4; cf., e.g., Sir 6:27; 51:23-27). It is possible that Qohelet's assertions in 7:24-25 are a contentious rejoinder to this characterization. Wisdom, the sage contends, is anything but accessible. It is not at hand, it is "far off, and deep, very deep" (7:24). Wisdom as a goal is elusive.

The possibility that Qohelet has already alluded to Woman Wisdom lends credence to the idea that the dangerous woman of verse 26 is a reference to her negative counterpart. Yet one must ask how such an about-face in focus would fit within the flow of the passage. Read thus, Qohelet, in the midst of recounting his unremitting quest for wisdom, suddenly warns against (or confesses to?) falling prey to Wisdom's foil. The sudden appearance of Woman Folly at this moment is abrupt and unintegrated. Nor does it cohere well with the larger context of the book. It is not the snares of folly that have been Qohelet's major preoccupation. Throughout his investigation it is *wisdom* (its merits, demerits, advantages, disadvantages) that has occupied his attention (e.g., 1:13, 1:17-18; 2:13-15; 8:16-17; 9:13-16; 9:17–10:1).

An alternative proposal is that verse 26 continues the sage's disillusioned reflection on his failed enterprise by offering up complaint on Woman Wisdom herself, characterizing her in the predatory terms normally reserved for her antithesis (compare Kruger 2004, 145–47). It is Woman Wisdom who turns out to be the proverbial snare and delusion. She is *worse* than death (cf. Prov 2:18; 5:5; 6:26). Verse 26b continues in the ironic vein by depicting the God-pleasing (i.e., fortunate) person as the one who escapes her, and the "sinner" (i.e., unfavored one) as falling prey to her allure (see 2:26 on Qohelet's use of these terms). The speaker quite obviously categorizes himself as the latter. It is he, after all, who has laboriously engaged in adding "one thing to another" to find the sum (*ḥešbôn*) of it all (v. 27), and to no avail.

Under this identification of the woman "more bitter than death," the ensnarement imagery has a slightly different import. Her threat lies not in her aggressive pursuit of humans (as is the case with the temptress figure of Proverbs 1–9), but rather in the charismatic draw she exerts on mortals to pursue, thus engaging them in a futile venture. In the apt characterization of William Brown, wisdom is for Qohelet a kind of *fata morgana*—"a destination that dissipates like mist once the first steps are taken toward it" (Brown 1996, 125). In sum, verses 23-26 plot a steep plunge from aspiration ("I will be wise") to actual outcome. Qohelet began his grand venture enthralled by the objective of wisdom, but instead found himself in thrall to something illusory, a chimera.

The concluding three verses of the chapter present a few interpretive difficulties and ambiguities: "(27) See, this have I found, says *Qohelet*, adding one thing to another to find the sum (*ḥešbôn*): (28) that my mind sought continually, but I did not find. One man among a thousand I found, but a woman among all these I have not found. (29) See, this alone I found: That God made human beings straightforward, but they have sought out grand solutions (*ḥiššěbōnôt*)" (AT).

While the particle at the beginning of verse 28 is usually translated as a relative pronoun ("which"), it may also function to introduce a perception or realization (as it does in verse 29: "*that* God made humans"). What Qohelet has understood is just this: that he did not understand (so Kruger [2004, 147], who cites the Socratic dictum, "I know that I know nothing"). Thus verse 28a reiterates and encapsulates the report of verses 23-25 (note how the adverb "continually" captures the unremitting nature of his quest as portrayed there).

But what did Qohelet find? His ensuing statement in verse 28b is obscure but seems to suggest the realization that while a good man (*'ādām*) is scarce, a good woman (*'iššāh*) is virtually nonexistent. It is hard to see how the comment coheres with the larger movement of the unit. As noted, it seems unlikely that the focus of this passage is a complaint about womankind. Some commentators have suggested that Qohelet here introduces a snippet of popular wisdom to which he does not necessarily subscribe. It is difficult to make a judgment on this, since there are no clear indicators that he disassociates himself from the assertion, but it is certainly possible that Qohelet draws on a ready-made adage of some sort that laments the scarcity of a good woman. It is interesting, however, that the saying does not in fact specify the particular quality that makes the hard-to-find man or woman desirable. Readers must supply the idea of *worthy* or *good* on the assumption that this is Qohelet's point (compare Prov 20:6 and 31:10, where the positive value is made explicit). As it stands, the saying only reports that a woman could not be found in a thousand. Perhaps it is this very indeterminacy that has commended the saying to Qohelet's use: as it stands in the current context of verses 23-29 its associative effect is to echo the elusiveness of Qohelet's intended objective, *the* Woman herself, Wisdom (compare Dell 2013, 94). Whatever the import of this cryptic reference, and the interpretation remains highly uncertain, it continues the thematic thread of a diligent, determined, all-encompassing search that yields minimal findings (continued in the ensuing conclusion: "See, this alone I found").

The precise import of Qohelet's final discovery is unclear. Does he mean that God originally made humans "upright" (so NIV), but they have become devious or corrupt? This is one possible reading but, as can be seen from a comparison of translations, other understandings are possible. The adjective *yāšār* (NRSV "straightforward") very often has moral connotations of *upright* or *just*, but it may also have the concrete meaning of *straight, level, smooth*. Both the NRSV and the NJPS tend toward the latter domain. The NJPS applies the term to the intellectual faculties of humans, at least by implication: "But see this I did find: God made men plain, but they have engaged in too much reasoning" (compare Fox 1999, 265: "God made people straight, but they seek out great solutions"). In these interpretations the emphasis is more on simplicity or directness rather than on moral rectitude per se.

The NRSV translation of "devised" in the final phrase contributes to a more negative interpretation of the human activity in question, but in fact the word may equally well be translated more neutrally as "seek," as it is in verses 25 and 28 (compare NIV). Furthermore, the word translated as "schemes" in the NRSV reflects a Hebrew word (*ḥiššəbonot*) occurring only one other time in the Old Testament, where it refers to some sort of weaponry for war (2 Chron 26:15). We cannot be sure of the meaning here. In any case this word is related in origin to *hešbôn* in verses 25 and 27 ("sum"). Both words derive from the verbal root *hašab*, which means "to think, plan, reckon." What can be said with certainty is that the author has twice used *hešbôn* to refer to his own calculations to comprehend the grand scheme of things. As Michael Fox has noted, the word-play constituted by *hešbôn* and *hiššĕbōnôt* suggests that the final sentence contains a "self-directed irony" (1999, 267). It is Qohelet who has found himself unable to refrain from calculations and analysis. It would seem humans are so inclined. In other words it is possible that the remark, rather than carrying a weight of moral judgment on human perverseness, is more a matter-of-fact comment on the human inclination to try to figure things out, despite considerable evidence this is not a route to fulfillment.

Theological and Ethical Analysis

You look on my calamity, and are afraid.

Job 6:21

On a Saturday evening in Brooklyn, New York, seven siblings, aged five to sixteen, died in a fire in their home. The fire was caused by faulty wiring in an electric hotplate. The hotplate was in use, keeping food warm from sundown Friday until Saturday night, to enable the Orthodox Jewish family to observe the prohibition against igniting a flame on the Sabbath. It is such a tragedy as this, and the anguished questions it raises, that Qohelet ponders in his candid preliminary observation: "There are good people who perish in their righteousness, and there are wicked people who live long in their evildoing" (AT). The occurrence of such events sunders the link between a person's ethical conduct and that person's fate (see also 8:14; 9:11).

In pursuing the import of such happenings as this, Qohelet poses a challenge to conventional wisdom teaching, which affirms a morally ordered creation in which good and reprehensible acts each reap their due consequences. Both the books of Ecclesiastes and Job insistently challenge this doctrine, each in its way posing the evidence of experience to challenge the viability and truth of its claims. The book of Job provides an illuminating complement to Ecclesiastes in that the problem is dramatically portrayed in the plight of its central character. Job the righteous man suffers calamitous loss of his fortune, his family, and his health. He then engages in an extended dialogue with his friends who have come to provide comfort. The position of the friends is that he is guilty of some sin that has brought about his calamity, a stance they maintain for the duration of the debate, even in the face of Job's impassioned protests of innocence. Chapter 6 of the book contains Job's response to Eliphaz's speech in chapters 4–5. Job pleads for understanding from his companions, characterizing their failure to see his side as a betrayal (6:14-30). Like desert streambeds that abound with water in cool seasons but that, to the dismay of parched travelers, run dry in summer heat, Job's friends have failed him just when he most desperately thirsts for their sympathy and understanding. In the pivotal moment of this sequence he confronts them directly: "You see my calamity, and are afraid." The suggestion that the friends' stance toward Job is motivated by fear is an arresting one. Though just what they fear is not explicit in the text, the author, in naming the response as such, suggests at the very least that there may be something self-preserving in their dogged insistence on his guilt. As commentators remark, the ascription of fear to the friends' response is reflective of a worldview in which suffering is, *ipso facto*, a sign of divine displeasure. The friends must therefore keep a certain distance from Job since to side with him is, in effect, to side against God, a risk they dare not take. More fundamentally, it may be observed that the very fact of Job's situation—a man to all appearances innocent, yet smitten by unthinkable disaster— threatens the depth-level belief structures that give order and coherence to their existence.

The law of cause and effect propounded by conventional wisdom—that righteous living brings well-being and wrongdoing brings punishment—does indeed witness to a truth of life: deeds *do* have consequences, as any elder steeped in life experience will warrant. But the template is inadequate as an explanation of human suffering. When applied as an all-encompassing lens to human experience, it is grossly distorting and deleterious in that it tends to cordon off the sufferer of misfortune from the solace that comes of true empathy.

There is, in fact, a self-perpetuating dynamic to the view that tragedy can be located in the fault of the afflicted one. The presumption of guilt on the part of a suffering victim creates a sense of taboo and induces those around that person to keep her or him at a psychic distance. In turn that very distance encourages the objectification of that person and reinforces the ability to maintain a theoretical framework over against a person's experience. I suggest that the conclusion of Job's speech in chapter 6 gestures toward this very dynamic (vv. 28-30).

> But now, be pleased to look at me;
>> For I will not lie to your face.
> Turn, I pray, let no *deceit* be done.
>> Turn now, my *vindication/integrity* is at stake.
> Is there any *deceit* on my tongue?
>> Cannot my taste discern calamity?
> (Based on NRSV)

A few terms in these verses remain tantalizingly bivalent; nonetheless certain key motifs are evident. Most salient in this concluding unit is Job's poignant adjuration to "turn." The verb is richly connotative in the Hebrew. First, it can refer to the physical act of turning or returning. In this case it is suggestive of a setting in which the friends have actually turned away or moved apart from Job in the course of his response to them. Such a scenario is supported by Job's initial request, which can be translated, "But now, be pleased to *face* me" (AT). The word "turn" also has the conceptual meaning of "reconsider" or "relent" (so NIV, NJPS); in this latter sense the word is used in the prophetic and Deuteronomic literature to call for repen-

116

tance—for a full-scale reversal of one's moral and ethical orientation. There is no need to choose between these resonances: Job is calling on the friends to radically alter the stance they have taken toward him. Significantly, he asks that they do so by looking directly into his face (Newsom, 1996, 390). Inherent in his request—"Face me, for I will not lie to your face" (AT)—is a knowledge that there is something in this face-to-face intimate address of the sufferer that, by its very nature, disallows deception. This encounter has its own kind of veracity, a truth of its own, that cannot be accessed by reflecting on general paradigms about sin and suffering. When Job asks that his friends look at him, he is asking that they look away from their theories and paradigms and see *him*. The underlying intimation is that the cycle set in motion by assuming guilt on the part of the sufferer can be broken when we dare to turn and look into that person's face.

The dynamics of sufferer/observer intimated in this sequence merit careful consideration. Contrary to the impression left by some discussions of retributive justice, the view that misfortune is connected to an individual's actions is not confined to the thinking of ancient cultures. It is alive and thriving, manifesting itself in various attitudes and philosophies, both religious and secular. In contemporary American culture such assumptions can be found all over the map, fueling such popular dictums as, "You draw all happenings to yourself," and "There are no accidents." The very persistence of this worldview is of course witness to the crucial ordering and protective function it fulfills. At its heart it reflects the profound human need to imagine ourselves reasonably safe in the world. Belief in a world where terrible suffering can be linked to the actions of the sufferer shields us from a nightmarish world in which things happen merely at random. To contemplate this is to contemplate the abject vulnerability of ourselves, and our loved ones.

The teaching that abusive, violent, selfish actions come home to roost and that, conversely, acts of nurture, generosity, and empathy engender well-being and healing in their wake, is a tried and true wisdom, itself amply witnessed to by the experience of generations. For many of us such a view is a testimony to faith in a God who is both sovereign and just, immanently involved in human history and human affairs. Yet, as is tacit in the voices of such biblical witnesses as Ecclesiastes and Job, there is a dark underside to this worldview. In the face of inexplicable suffering and loss it can mutate to become, in substance, a defense mechanism for the observer. I am reminded of one woman's account of her painful physical and emotional recovery from a brutal rape. One day while taking a morning walk in the countryside of southern France, Susan Brison was savagely attacked, strangled to unconsciousness, and left for dead. The assault occurred in broad daylight, and the perpetrator was a complete stranger; nonetheless in the ensuing legal proceedings a female court official, observing that she herself had never been a victim, suggested that Susan might benefit from the experience by learning to be less trusting and to take basic precautions such as not going out alone at night (Brison 1993, 20–21). The reason we cling to the view that tragedy is in some sense a consequence of a person's choices is that letting go of such a view requires us to acknowledge the inherently fragile nature of our own well-being.

It is for this reason that the books of Ecclesiastes and Job are as disquieting to readers today as they were to readers of ages gone by. With their radical challenge to the connection between the sufferer and the sufferer's actions, they eliminate the safe buffer between the victims of tragedy and onlookers. To have one's safe place in the world taken away is a deeply disquieting thing; it is in fact a profound loss, a loss of innocence. And yet it is only by relinquishing the "myth of our own immunity" (Brison 1993, 21) that we can find our way toward a place beside the sufferer and become true comforter to her.

Injustices Revisited

Literary Analysis

Chapter 8 divides into two major subunits, with verses 2-9 reflecting on human power and human limits, and verses 10-17 taking up the topic of justice and retribution. The final thought of verse 9, the exploitation of power to the harm of others, leads to a searching reflection on the inadequacy of divine retribution. The Hebrew conjunction at the beginning of verse 10 (NRSV "then" or "thereupon") supports a link between the two units. These two segments are bracketed by references to the sage and his vocation (vv. 1, 16-17), with the (apparent) affirmation of his unsurpassed understanding being answered by an assertion of its limits.

Exegetical Analysis

8:1a Who Is Like the Wise Man?

The initial rhetorical question affirms the elevated vocation of the wise man: *no* one is like the sage. Though the second question—in essence an assertion that *no* one knows the interpretation of a matter—does not sit easily with the first, it may be taken as elaboration on the sage's unparalleled status (no one else *but* the sage). The ensuing tribute of the second half of the verse to the sage's "soft" or well-disposed demeanor, affected by wisdom's sway, seems to continue in a positive vein. Nonetheless, the broader context of this opening gambit raises questions about Qohelet's deployment of such statements. He has just testified that, even with all his considerable effort, he could not attain the status of "wise" (7:23). Indeed, he describes the goal he sought as altogether elusive, leading him to exclaim that *no* person can obtain it (7:23-24). A more subtly compromising element is found in the continuation of 8:2-5, which offers instructions for prudent behavior in the royal court. Woven through these directives is an awareness of the sage's abject vulnerability before the ruler, with the accent tending toward the monarch's supreme power (vv. 3-4). True, the caveats offered in these verses do not necessarily undermine claims for the sage's incomparable insight—some would even see them as tribute to his capacity for shrewd assessment of risk and benefit. Still the sum effect of 8:2-5, following on the lofty accolades of 8:1, is that of anticlimax. The tension intimated here becomes more prominent as Qohelet's ruminations progress (vv. 6b-9).

8:1b-9 The Great Reach of Power; the Greater Reach of Death

King: *Now Hamlet, where's Polonius?*
Hamlet: *At supper.*
King: *At supper! Where?*
Hamlet: *Not where he eats, but where he is eaten: a certain convocation of politic worms are e'en at him. Your worm is your only emperor for diet: we fat all creatures else to fat us, and we fat ourselves for maggots: your fat king and your lean beggar is but variable service, two dishes, but to one table: that's the end.*
William Shakespeare, Hamlet Act IV, Scene 3

Verses 1b-5 reflect on proper conduct before a powerful monarch. Such counsel to those standing in the presence of the king is familiar discourse from wisdom texts of the ancient Near

East, including Proverbs (e.g., Prov 16:14; 24:21-22; 25:6). Not surprisingly, Qohelet puts his own distinctive twist on the topic, parlaying it into reflection on those things that render *all* humans subject, namely contingency and death (vv. 6-9).

The maxim commending wisdom's power to transfigure the wise person's demeanor for the better (v. 1b) serves as preface to Qohelet's pragmatic comments on discretion and judicious comportment before royal power: the wise person knows better than to display an inimical ("hard") countenance before such a powerful presence. Indeed, verses 2-5 offer a kind of survival manual on behavior in the presence of royal power. Though the import of verses 2-4 is unclear at points, the emphasis on the supreme authority of the king comes through distinctly (v. 4). His word and command are final. Qohelet's counsel is pragmatically motivated, for the king's power is absolute (vv. 3-4). In tenor the passage is not unlike chapter 5, where Qohelet gives instruction concerning conduct before God (vv. 1-7). In both passages he shows the same honed awareness of the power differential, and his counsel is based on an acknowledgment of who can do whom harm (see 5:2, 6b). The fact that social and political structures are lamented but not challenged is in continuity with the rest of the book. Qohelet is aggrieved by the existence of abuses and oppression but never advocates social revolution (4:1-3; 5:8-9; 8:9).

Verse 5 maintains an optimistic view of the sage's ability to negotiate the challenges of the royal court, and the arbitrary exercise of power. The assurance that he will know the "time and way" is bolstered by the continuation in verse 6: "For every matter has its time and way." The thought reflects the adage of a propitious moment for action in situations, one that the wise heart will be able to discern. It is an idea we have seen expressed in the poem on the times in 3:1-8 (compare 3:1: "For everything there is a season, and a time for every matter"). Yet Qohelet's ensuing comments do not bear out this optimism. Instead, in a movement akin to his coda to the poem on the times (see 3:9-15) Qohelet rejoins this idea by pointing to the human situation of ignorance: "Indeed every matter has its time and way. Yet the misfortune of mortals lies heavy upon them. For they do not know what is to be, for who can tell them how it will be?" (AT).

Or as Qohelet has put it in 3:11: people cannot find out what God has done from start to finish. However astute the sage may be in his judgments, he does not know the future and hence is subject to the human condition and its limitation (compare 8:17).

A sequence of four negations follows on this observation. While these are sometimes read as reference to four different circumstances of human impotence, they are best understood as a triple scoring of a single theme: human powerlessness before death. Verse 8a contains two occurrences of the Hebrew term *rûaḥ*, which may mean "wind" (NRSV, NIV; see also 1:6; 11:4) or "life-breath" (NJPS, REB; see also 3:19; 11:5). Hence it could function as a general image for human impotence (no one controls the wind; so NRSV), or it could refer more specifically to our helplessness before death (so REB). Qohelet's ensuing contention in the parallel line that no one governs the day of death (v. 8b) suggests the latter, more specified meaning of impotence before the death hour. Moreover, the conception of restraining the *rûaḥ* found in the first line of the verse coheres with the author's image elsewhere of the death process as a release and return of the life-breath to God (3:21; 12:7). Read in this vein, Qohelet asserts that humans can in no way forestall this release. The first two lines, then, underscore the inevitability of death, expressed as human powerlessness to postpone it. No person forestalls the time of death, by so much as a day, by so much as an hour (compare 9:12).

In the following line (v. 8c) Qohelet speaks of the battle from which there is no "discharge." The phrase is difficult and the meaning assigned to it must be tentative, but given the immediate context, it is more likely that his reference to war is figurative, an allusion to death, *the* confrontation from which no person can be excused (compare NJPS: "There is no mustering out from that war" and GNT: "That is the battle we cannot escape"). In these final two clauses of verse 8, historical evidence and spare textual clues converge to suggest an evocative image. The reference to release from battle may in fact refer to the contracting out of one's military obligation, an option granted beneficiaries of land grants during the Persian period (see Seow 1997, 28–30). Is it possible Qohelet alludes to such a practice, expressively underscoring the inescapability of death, the one "obligation" that cannot be contracted out or fulfilled by proxy? This point of reference lends support for emendation of the otherwise baffling reference to wickedness (v. 8d) as the other human ploy that will not ward off death. The reminder is a banal truism, which might commence such a sequence but as a crowning statement is anticlimax. Some interpreters emend the Hebrew word for "wickedness" to read "wealth"; thus: "and *wealth* will not deliver its master" (so REB: "No wealth will save its possessor"; compare Ps 49:6-9 [Heb. 49:7-10] for a similar view). By alluding to such a practice in these final two lines Qohelet reinforces the universality of death, which is no respecter of persons. Every individual—wealthy or poor, high or low, sovereign or subject (wise or foolish)—must bow to death.

Chapter 8 has begun on a high-flown note, with words touting the acumen and *savoir faire* of the wise man. In a somewhat unexpected turn, Qohelet brings the focus round to the sobering reach of the ruler's authority, the one whose word is power and who brooks no challenge whatsoever. Though the passage progresses in disjointed manner, and interpretation of it in its details is not agreed upon, one thing is clear: by the time Qohelet reaches the end of verse 8, his emphasis has turned from the scope of human capability to the limits of such, be one wise man or potentate. What has begun under the guise of guidance on court etiquette has moved a good distance beyond that topic.

At verse 9, Qohelet makes one more unexpected turn, doubling back to the topic of human power and its exercise. In mood the latter half of verse 9 echoes thoughts from the beginning of chapter 4. There, as here, Qohelet laments the exploitation of power to another human's harm (4:1-3). The difference is that in chapter 8 Qohelet has relativized this seemingly absolute authority of the powerful with his reflections on those things that no mortal controls (vv. 7-8). Yet in his parting remark, placed almost as an afterthought, he returns the focus to the very real problem of the abuse of power and its pernicious consequences (cf. vv. 2-4). While such power does go unchecked, be it in the form of tyranny or some other form of control, humans will violate fellow humans.

True, even the most powerful despot will one day bow to death. Yet (Qohelet seems to suggest) such a long view of the matter does not mitigate or alleviate the evils of oppression while it exists. That this is the tack in his thinking is intimated by the recurrence of a particular verbal root for "power," late and relatively rare vocabulary, that he first uses to speak of the absolute authority and power of the king's word (v. 4), then to speak of the "power"-lessness of all humans before death (v. 8, twice), and finally to speak of the exercise of power over another (v. 9), hence hearkening back to the initial context in verse 4.

8:10-17 Bearing Witness

Though some commentators identify a new literary unit in verses 10-17, the Hebrew conjunction employed in verse 10 implies some sort of continuity with what has preceded. Perhaps the medieval commentator Ibn Ezra was correct in assuming a link between the dominating powerful of verse 9 and the wicked who are accorded honors in verse 10. In that case Qohelet observes not only the propensity to exercise power at the expense of others (v. 9b) but also—adding insult to injury—the way society turns a blind eye to such abuses, even paying homage to the perpetrators. Whatever the precise connection between these two verses, Qohelet uses the spectacle of society's skewed values as bridge to one of his most poignantly candid deliberations on the inadequacy of divine justice.

The meaning of the Hebrew text for verse 10 is not at all certain, but the majority of recent commentators agree that Qohelet speaks of some inequity that is connected to the burial of the wicked. Though the NRSV makes the wicked the subject of the comings and goings from the holy place, this is unlikely to be the case since their interment has just been observed. Instead this going to and fro most likely refers to the processing that accompanies funerals. One may compare Job 21, which is also a complaint about attentions lavished on the wicked at their burial: "Everyone follows behind him. Innumerable are those who precede him" (21:33 NJPS; see also Eccl 12:5, where mourners process in the streets). In similar fashion, Qohelet laments the fact that the corrupt are accorded honors at their death, celebrated even in the very city where they have committed their offenses. In the ensuing verses he turns his examination to a more fundamental miscarriage of justice. More disturbing than the burial of the wicked with honors is the fact that corrupt people commit their crimes with impunity, experiencing no consequences for their actions. Contrary to the teaching of the sages, the wicked are *not* always cut off in their prime; indeed they would seem to flourish by their misdeeds (v. 12a; cf. 7:15). Hence, evildoing begets evildoing (v. 11). When Qohelet observes that such people enjoy long lives he is mounting a challenge to his wisdom forbears, who teach, "The fear of the LORD prolongs life, but the years of the wicked will be short" (Prov 10:27). In verses 12b-13 one glimpses an undercurrent of theodicy dialogue that surfaces at other points in Israelite tradition as well. One response to the prospering of the wicked was the reassurance that punishment was yet to be (e.g., Pss 37; 92:7; Sir 5:4; 9:12). Qohelet recognizes a troubling flaw in this scheme: the problem with delayed punishment is that it provides no deterrent in the moment. Job says something similar as he addresses one version of the traditional response, which is that punishment will fall on the *offspring* of the wicked:

> You say, "God stores up their iniquity for their children."
> Let it be paid back to *them*, so that they may know it.
> Let their *own* eyes see their destruction,
> and let *them* drink of the wrath of the Almighty.
> For what do they care for their household after them,
> when the number of their months is cut off?
> (Job 21:19-21, emphasis added)

In both Job and Ecclesiastes, the underlying problem is the same: a justice in which there is no immediate consequence for the evildoer lacks teeth. Here, as in other places where Qohelet addresses injustice and suffering, one sees his nagging concern with the "meantime" (3:16–4:3; 8:9). The notion of a reckoning to come may balance out the record in the larger scheme of things; meanwhile, human nature being what it is, it leads to more wickedness.

Interpreters have long puzzled over this sequence of statements in verses 11-14. In fact the reader may feel buffeted by the abruptly shifting perspectives of these verses. There are few rhetorical markers that might signal how Qohelet relates the different perspectives, and those present are ambiguous. For instance, when Qohelet moves from his affirmation that justice will prevail and the wicked will not thrive (vv. 12b-13), to his observation of moral inversions—the good suffering the fate of the bad, and vice versa (v. 14)—there is little to guide the reader in terms of understanding how he adjudicates these two assertions. The impression of two tensive views is marked enough that commentators have sometimes posited the presence of another voice in the positive affirmations of divine justice. Some identify these as an insertion by an orthodox editor. Others suggest that Qohelet quotes an opposing view for the purpose of refuting it. The problem with these approaches is that there are no textual markers or cues to suggest verses 12b-13 belong to another party, either as interpolation or quotation. Therefore one should be wary of disassociating Qohelet from them. Instead the tensions expressed in the text should be left intact. The passage reflects a cognitive dissonance—a disparity between what the sage experiences in the world, and what he holds to be true about God as just judge. Take a closer look at the sequence of statements in verses 11-14: in verses 11-12a, Qohelet deplores the thriving of the wicked and the absence of swift justice. He testifies to what he knows through observation. In verses 12b-13 he states something that he also knows. It is not what he sees at the moment, but it is something he holds to as a tenet of his tradition—the principle of just retribution. In verse 14 he speaks once again of something he knows. What he sees going on around him is in dissonance with this principle.

In reflecting on the question of Qohelet's stance in this passage it is useful to compare it with his deliberations in 3:16–4:3. Here, too, Qohelet contemplates rampant injustice under the sun, and here, too, this observation is followed by an assurance of a reckoning to come: "I said in my heart, God will judge the righteous and the wicked, for he has appointed a time for every matter, and for every work" (3:17). Note that Qohelet's preface to this affirmation ("I said in my heart") makes the reader aware of it as a part of a dialogue within himself. Part of the effect of this is to hedge off the closure that might come from an impersonal or *ex cathedra* pronouncement (contrast the tone and effect of the epilogist's words in 12:13-14). It may be suggested that "yet I know" in 8:12 functions in a comparable manner. Qohelet goes on record, so to speak, testifying both to what he has received in his tradition and to what he observes around him. What he assents to is the principle of just retribution, and what he sees are gross violations of that principle. Both are evidence for consideration. In both 3:16–4:3 and 8:10-17 Qohelet initiates the reader into a dilemma, a dilemma that remains such. In fact one may say that, whatever the state of the author's mind on the issue, his rhetorical strategy is to bring the reader into the midst of the strait and to deny us easy resolution.

Verse 15 presents a marked change of key, though one by now familiar: "So I praised enjoyment" (AT). Qohelet once again advocates taking pleasure in life. Although the context of previous exhortations has varied at some points, the constant in all of them is that Qohelet urges enjoyment in the midst of voicing constraints on the human situation; the possibility of enjoyment is lifted up in the midst of impasse (see 9:1-12). In chapter 8 the impasse is the radical disjunction between what is and what should be, an impasse that defies comprehension (strikingly, the exclamation of verse 14 is hemmed by a pronouncement of *vapor* on both sides; see Excursus at 1:2). The tone of the exhortation, it may be argued, continues the subtle heightening evident in prior expressions (see 5:18). Qohelet now *lauds* enjoyment. The robust emphasis is lost in most translations, which tamp it down to "commend" or the like. The verb is relatively rare in the Old Testament. Apart from one other occurrence in Ecclesiastes (4:2) it is found only in the worship language of the Psalms in the context of praise of God and God's works (Pss 63:3 [Heb. 4]; 117:1; 145:4; 147:12). One wonders if Qohelet has made use of a specialized vocabulary, intentionally borrowing on elevated hymnic language to mark his own emphasis on the goodness of the plain and tellurian gifts of food, drink, and enjoyment (on Qohelet's use of religious vocabulary, see Gordis 1968, 87–93; cf. 9:7). The thought must remain conjectural given the limited linguistic evidence. What is true to pattern is Qohelet's recourse to this theme of enjoyment in response to those things that humans cannot control or fathom.

Qohelet concludes his discussion with a reassertion of the implacable limits on human understanding (vv. 16-17, cf. v. 7). Humans cannot fathom the mysterious divine activity. Once more and finally, Qohelet makes reference to the concerted nature of his effort to gain understanding of what happens on earth (see 1:13-18; 7:23-25). The image of sleeplessness conveys determination even as it exudes fatigue; the endeavor to comprehend takes its toll and, in the end, proves thankless, as seen in the use of the theme word "toil" (v. 17), which refers, as it has in chapter 3, to the futility of any attempt to comprehend God's doings (see 3:9-15).

With the final phrase of verse 17 Qohelet asserts the boundary that is placed on every human. Just as all humans are subject to the boundary of death (8:8), so all humans are subject to the boundary on human understanding. Of all humanity one might hope that the sage could be that hero who would breach this boundary. But the sage enjoys no privileged status. Qohelet has begun this passage by saying, "No one is like the wise man." He ends it by saying that the wise man is like everyone else.

To Life!

O my soul, do not aspire to immortal life, but exhaust the limits of the possible.

Pindar, Pythian III

This passage is the culmination of Qohelet's assertions on the limits that circumscribe and define us as humans. He begins with reflections on death as the inevitable fate of every human (vv. 1-6). He ends with a rejoinder on the contingent nature of all human endeavor, with incalculable death the ultimate contingency (vv. 11-12). All the more arresting, then, that in between these two reflections is his most impassioned invitation to live. The force of this passage inheres in this dramatic interplay between shadow and light, death and life, sunlight and the grave. It is a tension that is woven throughout the book but achieves its most cogent expression here.

Literary Analysis

Many commentators designate a separate unit for verses 11-12. On the literary level, two framing features support verses 1-12 as a unity (Murphy 1992, 89). The first is the noun "fate" and its related verb "happen, befall," occurring in verses 2 and 11 respectively (*miqreh/yiqreh*). The second is the phrase "no human knows" in verses 1 and 12 (NRSV "One does not know. . . . No one can anticipate").

It can be argued, furthermore, that the phrase "Again I saw" at the beginning of verse 11, rather than demarcating a new segment, marks a shift of focus within the unit, as does the same expression in 4:1 (see 3:16–4:3). In both instances Qohelet employs the phrase to resume a topic from the beginning of the passage. In this chapter Qohelet has begun by dwelling on death as the fate of every human. This is a situation that eradicates all moral distinctions. As such it signifies a rupture in the causal connection between a deed and its consequence. Verses 11-12 pursue this same theme, widening the scope of assessment beyond moral merits. Talent, strength, expertise: none of these *ensures* a correlative outcome. There is no necessary symmetry between who we are and what befalls us. To be human is to be vulnerable to factors beyond our control. Qohelet concludes this final assessment by returning to the ultimate contingency: death.

Exegetical Analysis

9:1-6 The Same Fate Comes to All

Qohelet's protest against the universality of death reaches its climax in chapter 9. Translations of the end of verse 1 in relation to verse 2 vary, as there is some debate about the coherence of the Hebrew as it stands. One possible literal translation is: "(1b) Everything is before them. (2a) All is as to all." By slight emendation (supported from some ancient textual witnesses), the two verses can be read as a continuous thought: "(1a) Everything before them (2a) is *vapor*, since to all . . . " (compare NRSV). The choice of reading here does not greatly alter the main point of verses 1-3, which is summed up at the opening of verse 3: "This is an evil in all that happens under the sun, *that the same fate comes to everyone*" (emphasis added). The fact that all human endeavor, aspiration, and accomplishment must end in death is a tragedy for Qohelet. But the universality of death has a particular ramification for the Israelite sage. In biblical tradition, foolishness and wickedness are punished by premature death (e.g., Prov 2:22; 10:27; 11:19).

Qohelet is intent on examining this principle in light of the universal nature of death (compare 2:12-17; 3:16-22). Qohelet begins his reflection with a focus on the righteous and the wise in particular. To be "in the hand of God" (v. 1) in biblical tradition means to be subject to God's power, be that for good or for ill. In a positive context it refers to God's redeeming and providential care (e.g., Ps 31:5 [Heb. 6]; Ezra 8:22; Wis 3:1). Certainly it is the "righteous" and the "wise" who may be expected to repose in such safekeeping. And yet— Qohelet probes—just what *is* the meaning and substance of divine favor in the light of universal death? *The same fate comes to everyone.* Ultimately, the consequence of living righteously and living without scruples is the same: death. The ramification of this is that the divine attitude toward persons is obscured (v. 1b). "Love from hatred human beings cannot tell," translates Roland Murphy (1997, 88). Divine favor looks the same as divine antipathy, viewed in the light of universal death. Qohelet laments a world bereft of the recognizable signs of curse and blessing. He laments a world devoid of a fundamental coherence.

In the end the same fate comes to all. Qohelet is not content to stop at his assertion of one fate to "the righteous and the wicked" (v. 2). The ensuing litany of moral opposites, invoking both general and specified categories of ethical conduct (e.g., the good and the evil, and one who swears versus one who prudently refrains from such) has a cumulative effect, underscoring and reiterating the absurdity of the situation. Despite the fact that some of Qohelet's categories are of limited relevance to the modern reader, the sequence retains its impact: universal death means that the conscientious are as the unscrupulous, the judicious as the reckless, the kind as the mercenary, the compassionate as the cruel.

Verses 1-3a are, in sum, a protest against the irremediable injustice created by the fact of universal death. It is therefore somewhat unexpected when in the second half of verse 3 Qohelet speaks of the corruption of the human heart. Qohelet is not tacitly justifying human mortality by citing human iniquity; if he subscribed to such an explanation he would not be so deeply vexed by the fact of death. Rather, as in 8:11, where he observed a symbiosis between the apparent moral anarchy of the world and the proliferation of human wickedness, he now draws a connection between the indiscriminateness of the universal death sentence and the debauchery and madness to which humans sink. Qohelet's comments here put one in mind of philosopher Thomas Hobbes's memorable description of human existence as "nasty, brutish and short." Fittingly, Hobbes's statement is a description of the condition to which humans regress when they live "without a common power to keep them all in awe" (*Leviathan*, chapter 8). For Hobbes that power is the protective and restraining authority of a sovereign government. Qohelet does not have Hobbes's faith in political structures; however, he would agree that when rules are not enforced—when no moral law is in evidence—humans become yet more degenerate.

In this bleak outline of humanity's prospects, Qohelet posits one "trustworthy thing" (a better translation than "hope" [NRSV] for the Hebrew word in verse 4) for those still among the living. Instead of immediately identifying that, however, he offers a tersely suggestive proverb that deems a live dog better off than a dead lion. In ancient Near Eastern culture the dog is a despised animal (e.g., 1 Sam 17:43; 2 Sam 3:8), while the lion is a beast of grandeur, an emblem of royal might and majesty (Gen 49:8-10). The valuation implied is that life—life on *any* terms—is superior to death with honor. Qohelet seems to confirm the modest margin inherent in the proverb when he goes on to define the edge the living have on the dead—as the knowledge that they *will* be dead! This, on the face of it, is not much to write home about. And yet Qohelet is not being glib or offhand. His manner of making the point may be ironic, but this margin of advantage possessed by the living he advocates in all earnestness. Some might understandably counter that certain awareness of death as one's destiny serves only to cast a pall over all existence, thus seeing in Qohelet's comments only bitterness and sarcasm. This is one possible consequence of such knowing, of which our sage is aware. At the same time, germinating throughout the book has been the thought that this is not the necessary or inevitable outcome of such consciousness.

"The living know that they will die, but the dead know nothing" (v. 5). In the immediately ensuing comments it is the nonsentient state of the dead, indeed the utter nullity of death, that Qohelet dwells upon to cinch his orientation toward life. Qohelet is trying to impart the unimaginable. Is it possible? The final destination of our existence is . . . nonexistence. Our loves, animosities, sorrows, and strivings, all effaced in a moment. Qohelet preempts the suggestion that one can hope for survival in one's legacy or reputation (v. 5b), asserting, as he does elsewhere (1:11; 2:16), that the dead are eventually forgotten.

Death is not only the extinction of all those relationships that constitute us as unique, unrepeatable selves; it is the unequivocal end of all potentiality (no more reward [v. 5b]), a theme he will enlarge on in verse 10. Whatever our aspirations, plans, or hopes—great or modest—they are finished with death. There are no second opportunities beyond the grave (v. 6b).

9:7-10 Humanity's Portion

In the wake of this brooding portrait of the void of death, Qohelet returns to his theme of enjoyment. The motif is expressed more fully than in any of its previous occurrences. Moreover, the manner in which it is offered is unprecedented. On previous occasions Qohelet has spoken in the form of commendation, advice to be overheard by the implied audience. Now he hails his listener directly and in the imperative mode.

There is urgency here. In the immediate context of chapter 9 these rhetorical shifts occur on the very pulse of his summating thought on the finality of death. Upon saying, "never again will they have any share in all that happens under the sun," Qohelet turns to address his listener directly. Moreover, his first word is "Go!" Inherent in this movement is awareness that profound certitude about death's finality can be galvanizing.

The themes and language of this sixth call to enjoyment are, it may be argued, chosen to evoke a particular setting. Eat your bread with joy, enjoins Qohelet, "and drink your wine with a merry heart" (v. 7). Elsewhere in the Old Testament references to drinking wine with a merry heart occur in the context of feasting, indeed, exuberant feasting (Ruth 3:7; 1 Sam 25:36; 2 Sam 13:28; Esth 1:10). White garments are the festal attire of the ancient Near East (compare Esth 8:15). The practice of anointing the head with oil is likewise connected with feasting and joyful occasions in the Old Testament (e.g., Pss 23:5; 45:7 [Heb. 8]; Prov 27:9; Isa 61:3). In Ecclesiastes 9:8 the specifications accompanying these two practices—"Let your garments be white *at all times,* and oil on your head, *let it not be lacking*" (AT)—are in themselves an acknowledgment that such things are normally reserved for special occasions. In other words, Qohelet's response to the certainty of coming death is that we should make *each* day a feast day.

In the course of discussing this segment, commentators often quote an intriguing passage from the ancient Mesopotamian Epic of Gilgamesh (see introduction). The passage, coming from the Old Babylonian version of the story, portrays an encounter between Gilgamesh and a wise woman, the tavern-keeper, Siduri. Gilgamesh has watched the slow, debilitating death of his beloved friend and comrade in arms, Enkidu. Grief-stricken and horrified, he has set upon a frantic quest to find the secret of immortality. His plan is to search out the hidden dwelling of Utnapishtim the flood hero, the one human who has obtained the status of immortal. Encountering Siduri at the nadir of his sorrow and terror, he pleads with her for help. Siduri responds thus (author's translation):

Gilgamesh, where are you going?
The life you pursue you will not find.
> When the gods made humankind,
> Death they assigned to humankind,
> Life they kept in their own hands.

You, Gilgamesh, let your stomach be full.
> Day and night enjoy yourself,
> Of each day make a festival,
> Dance and play, day and night.
> Let your garments be sparkling fresh,
> Bathe your head, may you wash yourself in water.
> Look on the little one holding your hand,
> Let the wife in your embrace have pleasure time and
> again.

This is the task of [humankind].

Although many scholars do not see evidence of a direct borrowing from this text, there are features that suggest that the author of Ecclesiastes is familiar with this passage (see Jones 1990, 349–79). First the progression of themes (defined broadly) is the same: feasting, the donning of fresh or bright garments, bathing/anointing of the head, and joy in one's loved ones (9:7-9). Perhaps most significantly, both sequences conclude with a similar synopsis—that these things are the lot of humanity (Eccl 9:9: "because that is your portion in life"). A second striking feature is a shared motif: namely the initiation of celebratory activities and customs into day-to-day life. Admittedly the motif is more prominent in the Epic: "*Day and night* enjoy yourself. *Of each day* make a festival. Dance and play *day and night*." Nonetheless Qohelet's references in verse 8 (white garments *always*, oil *never lacking*) may be seen as an echo of this familiar motif in Siduri's speech.

In sum, Qohelet's words of counsel are rich with the resonances of Siduri's speech to Gilgamesh. Indeed, they may be a kind of homage to her sage counsel. While it is not uncommon for Siduri's counsel to be cited in commentary discussions of these verses from Ecclesiastes 9, it is rare that the immediate context of this counsel is brought to bear. This larger context is illuminating for the tenor of her message to Gilgamesh and helps, I believe, to reveal more subtle ways in which Ecclesiastes is redolent with the themes of the myth. Gilgamesh has described his plight in the following terms (author's translation):

> Enkidu, whom I love so dearly,
>> who went with me in all hardships,
>> has now gone to the fate of humankind.
>
> Days and nights I wept over him.
>> I would not give him up for burial,
>> As if he would rise up to me at my cry,
>> Seven days and seven nights,
>> Until a maggot fell down from his nose.
>> Since his passing, I have not found life;
>> I have roamed like a hunter in the midst of the wild.
>
> O tavern-keeper, now that I have seen your face,
>> Let me not see the death that I ever dread.

There are two dimensions to Gilgamesh's anguished state, his bereavement and his own death anxiety. That is to say, the experience of Enkidu's death has had a compound effect on him. It is not just that he has suffered the loss of a dear one; it is also that through this he has come to have a taste of what death really is. It is final and irrevocable (he cannot bring his loved one back by dint of will) and quite truly the dissolution of the person (as seen in the graphic depiction of decomposition). As for Siduri, it is her task to offer the antidote to Gilgamesh's predicament. Notably she does not speak directly to his condition of bereavement but rather to his death terror and his determined mission to thwart mortality. Her reply is plain, strong medicine: to be human is to die. Immortality is reserved for the gods. "Deal with it," says Siduri. Issuing directly from this is her charge to Gilgamesh to fill his stomach, don fresh clothing, and bathe, making each day a celebration. Within the context of the storyline her exhortation is layered: at one level it bids Gilgamesh put away mourning rites for Enkidu. Yet even more profoundly, it illuminates the significance of accepting death as an implacable boundary. Each day should then be lived to its fullest ("Of each day make a festival, Dance and play, day and night"). What emerges here, if subtly, is that Gilgamesh's refusal to come to terms with inevitable death has also kept him from life (notice his account of his wanderings after Enkidu's death is portrayed as a liminal state between life and death: "Since his passing, I have not found life; I have roamed like a hunter in the midst of the wild"). This is in fact poignantly drawn out in Siduri's concluding injunctions, which direct his attention to the loved ones who do remain to him, the little child at his side and his wife. There is a suggestion or implication, one not without irony, that Gilgamesh's obsession with eluding ineluctable death has in some sense exiled him from life and its possibilities in the present.

Qohelet has learned the lessons Siduri offers, and he seeks to impress them upon his listeners. In the continuation of his exhortation he invokes *vapor* to speak of the boundaries of human existence and their claim on us. It is, in fact, the fleeting nature of one's life (literally "life of vapor"; NRSV "vain life") that fuels the injunction to eat, drink, celebrate, and enjoy love's companionship. The idea is repeated for emphasis, a component not reflected in the NRSV: "Enjoy life with the wife whom you love, *all the days of your fleeting life* that are given under the sun—*all your fleeting days*—for that is your portion in life and in your toil at which you toil under the sun."

Qohelet's impassioned behest climaxes in a summons to *do*—to do what we would with our strength. Already in earlier counsels Qohelet has advocated enjoyment *in* one's work (see 3:22; 5:18-19 [Heb. 17-18]). Now he goes further, explicitly encouraging his listeners to invest with vigor in the task at hand. The reason for doing such is simply stated: our inescapable destiny is the vacuum of death. It is such a recognition that inspires the passionate challenge of the Greek poet Pindar: "O my soul, do not aspire to immortal life, but *exhaust the limits of the possible*" (emphasis added). Immortality has not been granted to humans. Other things have. When we accept this limit we are released; those energies that were syphoned off in the pursuit of what is not possible can be harnessed for what is.

At the beginning of his hearty summons to enjoy life's bounty Qohelet has offered a theological endorsement, citing divine approbation in the matter of human enjoyment: "for God has long ago approved what you do" (v. 7). The Hebrew verb *rāṣāh*, which the NRSV renders as "approved," means not only to accept or to favor, as often noted, but in fact, yet more actively, can connote *delight*. For instance it is used of God's joy in his chosen servant in Isaiah (Isa 42:1), of his pleasure in his people (Pss 44:3 [Heb. 4]; 149:4), and of a father's loving delight in his son (Prov 3:12). In addition, the Hebrew verb has a more specified function in cultic contexts in that it denotes God's approval of right and appropriate sacrifices. This latter usage suggests the intriguing possibility that Qohelet intentionally borrows on this theological background to configure human enjoyment as, quite truly, an appropriate and felicitous offering to one's God (see further the discussion by Robert Gordis on Qohelet's use of religious terminology, 1968, 87–93; see 8:15 for another proposed instance in which Qohelet draws creatively on theological vocabulary to convey his own distinctive values).

The phrase affirming God's prior approval of human enjoyment bears further examination as it reflects an element appearing in other statements of the enjoyment theme. In three of the five commendations occurring to this point Qohelet attaches a qualifier. It is expressed in varying ways but, in function, it is a reminder that ultimately God is the one who grants the conditions that make enjoyment possible (2:24-25; 3:13; 5:19–6:2). The sequence in 5:19–6:2 is especially pointed in this regard. After extolling the pleasures of eating, drinking, and work, Qohelet reiterates God's role as giver: "Likewise all to whom God gives wealth and possessions and whom he enables to enjoy them, and to accept their lot and find enjoyment in their toil—

this is the gift of God" (5:19 [Heb. 18]). The recognition that God grants the conditions that make enjoyment of the good thing possible entails the recognition that God sometimes denies these conditions as well. Qohelet examines just this in the scenario to follow, a man who has it all but is not allowed to enjoy what he has. Instead, someone else gets the benefits of what is his (see discussion at 6:1-6). Under the system of retributive justice one can ascribe such misfortune to wrongdoing, but Qohelet, having repeatedly mounted a challenge to this system in its conventional presentation, can no longer resort to this as a blanket explanation. He not only matter-of-factly ascribes the situation directly to divine action, he pointedly deplores it as a sickening tragedy (6:2).

In the end we are left with a kind of paradox or, better, a complexity in the divine character. Qohelet affirms to his listener that God is the source of that which is pleasurable and good in this life. But Qohelet does not let his listener forget that it is God who may also withhold the good and the pleasurable. Such a reminder does not arise from a morbid temperament or a gratuitous attraction to the negative side of the picture. For the candid sage it is a matter of record. What emerges from this view of things is a recognition of joy as *gift*. We cannot manufacture it, earn it, or save up for it. Our task as humans is to recognize the possibility when it comes to us, and enter into it with abandonment (see 7:14).

9:11-12 The Same Fate Comes to All

Though many commentators designate verses 11-12 as a separate unit, these verses resume the theme considered at the beginning of the chapter (9:1-3). Qohelet has begun this passage by protesting that the righteous and the wise meet the same fate as everyone else. Death levels out all distinctions. In verse 11 Qohelet continues to lament the rift between what we do and are, and what befalls us. It is important to discern the configuration of Qohelet's grievance here. His complaint is not that the mighty warrior *never* wins the battle or that the skillful *never* achieve success. What he points out is that there are cases in which this does not occur. Qohelet laments the fact that there is no necessary correlation between the character and abilities of a person and the fate that overtakes that person. The reason is that we, as humans, are ever subject to circumstances beyond our control (v. 11b). The runner, the warrior, the wise man: all are vulnerable to circumstance. A wise man might end up a pauper or a mighty warrior be struck down in the first moment of battle. Qohelet asserts that no amount of prowess—physical or intellectual—guarantees successful outcome. With his reference to a person's ignorance of the "time of disaster," Qohelet turns to contemplate *the* misfortune, namely precipitous death (v. 12). The comparison to the ensnarement of animals is poignant and profoundly expresses Qohelet's protest. Can it be so? When it comes to the hour of death, the ultimate calamity, humans are no different from insentient creatures (see 3:18-22).

It is intriguing that Qohelet's stark recognition of the tenuous connection between endeavor and result, between character and fate, is directly preceded by his vigorous exhortation to dedicate ourselves ardently to whatever we would do (9:10). What is the meaning of this in light of his assertion that human ability and endeavor do not necessarily win the day? One might more reasonably expect the sage to counsel a healthy measure of detachment, a more calculated expenditure of effort (see Davis 2000, 212). Unexpectedly Qohelet moves in the opposite direction, urging full investment in the task at hand. The move is paradoxical. Qohelet's thinking here is more fully explicated in a pivotal passage coming near the end of the book: "In the morning sow your seed, and in the evening do not let your hands be idle; *for you do not know which will prosper, this or that, or whether both alike will be good*" (11:6, emphasis added). In other words, Qohelet's surprising response to his painstaking interrogation of the unpredictable nature of our efforts is that we should give ourselves wholly to them. Who knows? One of them might take root and flourish (see 11:1-6).

Theological and Ethical Analysis

The signal theme of the book of Ecclesiastes is human limits, with the consummate limit being death. Juxtaposed with Qohelet's many observations on human finitude are his counsels to take hearty enjoyment in life's good things. Qohelet's meditation on human limits and death has never been so protracted and brooding as it is in chapter 9. At the same time his invitation to live has never been so emphatic.

In order to contemplate this dynamic further, I return to the Epic of Gilgamesh as discussed in the introduction. As suggested there, these two works share the same preoccupation. Like the book of Ecclesiastes, the Gilgamesh Epic charts a journey (in this case a literal journey) that is a struggle to come to terms with human mortality. The ancient epic is an illuminating heuristic lens for the book of Ecclesiastes. Having already drawn attention to some intriguing elements in the speech of Siduri, wise keeper of the tavern by the sea, I would like to consider a second speech from the Epic, situated at the conclusion of Gilgamesh's quest, upon his confrontation with the flood hero (this speech survives only in the later Standard Version of the epic; see introduction). Gilgamesh, with the guidance of the tavern-keeper, has been able to cross the sea and gain access to the remote dwelling place of his ancestor, Utnapishtim, the only human ever to have obtained immortal status. Utnapishtim replies to Gilgamesh's stricken appeal for help with a long poem that ends with a message similar to that of Siduri: humans cannot escape death; no exceptions apply.

> After they had pronounced the blessing on me,
>> The Anunnaku, the great gods, were assembled,
>> And Mammitum, creatress of destiny, decreed destinies with them.
>> They established death and life.
>> Death they fixed to have no ending.
> (Lambert 1980, 54–55)

141

To be noted is the opening of the speech, which responds specifically to the incessant questing of Gilgamesh in his attempt to avoid the inevitable. Here Utnapishtim draws out a particular irony in the situation of the hero: "You have toiled without cease, what have you got? Through toil you are wearing [yourself] out, you are filling your body with grief, *you are bringing forward the end of your days*" (Lambert 1980, 55; emphasis added). The irony is that the denial of death attenuates life.

A contemporary testimony to this insight into the human condition is found in the diaries of a young Jewish woman from the Netherlands. The journals of Etty Hillesum record her experiences in Amsterdam during the time of the Nazi occupation. They trace the spiritual and intellectual maturation of a gifted young woman, her intense quest for self-knowledge and for understanding of her fellow humans. However, in their oblique reflection of a young person's dawning awareness of imminent death, the journals also embody the themes of the more self-consciously crafted works of Ecclesiastes and the Epic of Gilgamesh.

While the early entries of the journal from summer of 1941 reflect little of the turbulence belonging to Etty's external world, the increasing hardships and abuses of the occupation gradually begin to impinge on her private world. Her entries during this period of increased hardship poignantly reflect the vacillating moods of optimism, frustration, denial, and anger. The dawning recognition of what this chapter in history portends for her personally is inchoate in an entry from autumn 1941: "Mortal fear in every fibre. Complete collapse. Lack of self-confidence. Aversion. Panic" (Hillesum 1996, 57). Yet the paralysis and abject terror so palpable in this entry, far from being the last word, mark the beginning of a change. Her writings in the ensuing months show a gradual shift in perception as she struggles to come to terms with this knowledge of her own demise. The culmination of this process is registered in an extraordinary confession of the following summer (July 3, 1942): "Something has crystallized. I have looked our destruction . . .

straight in the eye and accepted it into my life, and my love of life has not been diminished." Etty's direct confrontation with the ultimate limit is, in fact, her liberation from fear: "The reality of death has become a definite part of life; my life has, so to speak, been extended by death, by my looking death in the eye and accepting it, by accepting destruction as a part of life, and no longer wasting my energies on fear of death or the refusal to acknowledge its inevitability" (Hillesum 1996, 155).

The capstone to this series of realizations is sparely but eloquently delineated: "It sounds paradoxical: by excluding death from our life we cannot live a full life, and by admitting death into our life we enlarge and enrich it" (Hillesum 1996, 155).

The denial of death diminishes life. And strangely, a realization of death, the implacable boundary on life, extends life. The journal covers three more months of Etty's life. In this candid, unself-conscious record of daily experience in a time of suffering, vicissitudes of mood do persist. Nonetheless a perceptible shift in orientation is reflected in the entries of the final weeks. As Etty writes during this period, "Somewhere there is something which will never desert me again" (Hillesum 1996, 153). This underlying serenity is joined to an ardent *élan vital*. One discerns a more intense focus on the pleasures of the senses, a joyous reveling in starkly simple experiences of taste, sight, touch—the roundness of an orange, the morning cup of coffee, jasmine on a mud-brown wall, bathing with lilac soap. One might venture that the philosophical musings prominent in the earlier part of the diary give way increasingly to an experience of the moment at hand.

The diary ends, but her letters from Westerbork camp allow glimpses of what remains alive in her as death nears. In them Etty describes the world around her in passionate detail, not omitting the worst, but also able to take joy in the sky above the camp's barren landscape where "a different sunset is staged every night" (Hillesum 1996, 335). Within months of her death she writes, "I often walk with a spring in my step along the barbed wire and then time and again it soars straight from my heart—I can't help it, that's just the way it is, like some elementary force—the feeling that life is glorious and magnificent" (Hillesum 1996, 294).

The Epic of Gilgamesh and the journal of Esther Hillesum, divided by some three millennia, evince similar responses to the fact of mortality. Death is our inescapable human destiny. The denial of its reality vitiates life, and coming to terms with it makes living possible. Siduri's eloquent response to Gilgamesh the questing hero warrants another look. In her summation she refers to the activities she has described as the "task" of humanity. These words hearken back to her initial assertion: when the gods made humans they kept one destiny for themselves and "assigned" humans another. Siduri's ensuing call to Gilgamesh—to feast, to celebrate, to love with affection and passion—becomes in effect an amplification on mortal status. It is a description of what *is* properly the human domain. This is the task of humankind. Gilgamesh has wished to transcend his mortal nature. Siduri assures him he cannot. But she points out those other things that also belong to that status. In seeking to avoid death, the defining mark of his humanity, Gilgamesh has missed out on those *goods* that are the mark of humanness.

Though Qohelet does not voice his response to death in so positive a fashion, these three works are on a continuum of thought. The difference is largely a matter of the glass viewed half-empty or half-full. Would Qohelet say that by admitting death into our life we "enlarge and enrich it"? Not in so many words. Yet what reaches articulation in the writings of Etty Hillesum germinates in the contemplations of this author. Indeed it is difficult to read Ecclesiastes without confronting one's mortality. This biblical book urges its readers to a reckoning. It is such a reckoning that is potentially our liberation. As Leo Tolstoy has put it, "We can be lord of nothing so long as we fear death. When we no longer fear it, all things are ours" (cited in Thielicke 1983, xi).

The Value and Limits of Wisdom

Literary Analysis

This passage contains a series of proverbs and prose snippets that cover a variety of areas, including wisdom and folly, behavior in the presence of authority and power, and competent governance. There is no overarching design to the sequence and no apparent development of thought. However the saying of 10:14 is a functional rubric for this passage that, if not apt for every part of it, captures its overall tenor: "No one knows what is to happen, and who can tell anyone what the future holds?" In fact, the backdrop of so many of these sayings and vignettes is that of an unpredictable world in which existence is precarious and all human endeavor subject to turns of fortune. It is amidst all this uncertainty that Qohelet commends the value of wisdom. While wisdom is no panacea, it may prove efficacious in some life situations. Moreover Qohelet is adamant that it *is* superior to folly even though it takes so little foolishness to undermine it.

The segments, broadly summarized, are as follows. In 9:13–10:3 the theme is wisdom and folly. Ecclesiastes 10:4-7 offers counsel concerning behavior before rulers and comment on a situation of irresponsible rule. Ecclesiastes 10:8-11 focuses on the precarious nature of daily life, and 10:12-15 concerns wise and foolish speech. The final section is a reflection on proper and improper governance, ending with a warning to refrain from criticizing those in power (10:16-20).

Exegetical Analysis

9:13–10:3 The Value and Limits of Wisdom

Proverbs 21 recounts how one wise man went up against an entire city of warriors and prevailed (see especially v. 22). Qohelet's own tale about a poor wise man rescuing his city against great odds is in good company with this and a few other proverbs that assert that wisdom is mightier than the sword (e.g., Prov 16:32; 24:5). That wisdom is superior to sheer might Qohelet does not doubt (as he reaffirms in 9:18a). His departure from the sages is seen in his qualifying of such affirmations. In both his prose vignette (9:13-16) and the ensuing proverbs (9:17–10:1) he affirms not only wisdom's superiority but its limitations.

In the conclusion of Qohelet's prose scenario the poor wise man and his accomplishments are forgotten. Thus wisdom does not receive its proper due (there are no lessons of history learned here; one is reminded of the amnesia that plagues humanity in the opening poem). Qohelet's summation of the story juxtaposes both its positive and negative facets: "Wisdom is better than might; yet the poor man's wisdom is despised, and his words are not heeded." The ensuing proverbs do not reference the story explicitly, but they continue to play upon its tensions. The proverb of verse 17 maintains a positive assessment of wisdom by upholding the words of the wise over those of a ruler "among fools" (perhaps a comment on the constituency he attracts) and further underscores their currency by affirming that even softly spoken words of the wise are heard above the those shouted by a ruler. The fact that the counterpart of the wise person is a ruler, as opposed to the traditional sage/fool opposition, may have made the proverb especially suitable for this literary context, since it picks up on social status references in the prose tale. The proverb of verse 18 initially continues in this positive vein, reiterating the theme of wisdom's superiority to military might. But the second line provides a qualifier, proposing that it takes only one inept person to destroy "much good."

The Hebrew text of 10:1 is unclear, particularly in the first line. The overall point is generally agreed upon: just as it takes only one foolish person to destroy much good (9:18b), it takes only a tad of folly to nullify the efficacy of wisdom (10:1b). In fact, the first line of 10:1 may be emended to read: "A fly dies and makes the perfumer's vessel of oil stink." Read thus, it follows the pattern of the preceding line with the idea that it takes but a little of a bad thing to spoil something valuable (even a whole "vessel" of it). The vivid imagery of 10:1 paves the way for the final proverb in the series: "So a little folly outweighs wisdom and honor."

In 10:2-3 Qohelet ends his reflections on wisdom and folly with a compact contrast between the wise man and the fool. "Right" and "left" here denote the two diametrically opposed orientations of their "hearts," the heart being the seat of intelligence and the will in Israelite wisdom literature (often best translated as "mind"; Clifford 1999, 21). The contrast is expressed in a balanced couplet, but it is the conduct of the fool that becomes subject for comment in the following verse (compare 10:12-15), where the image of two paths that has been implicit in 10:2 becomes explicit and literal in the description of the fool walking on the road. Though the proverb allows for more than one understanding, it is likely that verse 3 means that even in the most common tasks the fool cannot help but advertise his folly (see Prov 12:23; 13:16; cf. 10:15).

10:4-7 Wise Counselors, Foolish Rulers

In verse 4 Qohelet turns to the topic of wise behavior in the presence of authority (compare 8:2-4). In the event of a superior's displeasure with him, the wise man should stand his ground with composure, "for calmness sets aside great offenses" (AT). In a similar vein the proverbs also suggest that soothing speech assuages wrath: "A soft response turns back anger, but a harsh word stirs up wrath" (Prov 15:1). Indeed a ruler can be won over by a "soft tongue" (Prov 25:15). Certain verbal echoes in 10:4 recall the contrast between the loud cry of the ruler and the quiet words of the wise in 9:17, hence reiterating the wise person's ability to persuade.

In verses 5-7 Qohelet deplores a disturbed social order. Fool and rich, slave and noble have exchanged status. For all his wariness of power and its potential abuses (e.g., 4:1; 5:8; 8:9), Qohelet's lament in these verses betrays his social conservatism (note that his chosen antonym for "folly" is the wealthy, and not the wise as one might expect [v. 6]). In this, too, he is in company with the traditional sages, who also read such abrupt reversals to be the sign of a world gone badly awry (e.g., Prov 19:10; 30:21-23; Job 12:17-19; Van Leeuwen 1986, 599–611). Qohelet ascribes responsibility for this societal upheaval to the ineptitude of a ruler (verse 5b is better read as an emphatic assertion—"indeed, an error issuing from a ruler!" AT). Thus these verses further illustrate that it only takes one bungler to wreak much havoc, and a little folly will undo much wisdom (9:18–10:1).

10:8-11 The Pitfalls of Everyday Life

The next grouping of proverbs is framed by references to the bite of a snake in verses 8 and 11. Various manual occupations with their attendant risks are introduced. The NRSV translation assumes the act and consequence connection: "Whoever digs a pit will fall into it." This follows the traditional image of the evildoer meeting destruction by the very snares he has laid for others (e.g., Pss 7:16; 9:16-17; 35:7-8; Prov 26:27; 28:10; Sir 27:25-27; compare Prov 1:18). Yet Qohelet does not seem to be using the example with its traditional freight of meaning, because there is no suggestion of misconduct in the activities of breaching a mortar wall, quarrying stone, and splitting logs. Thus the injuries described are misfortunes of the hapless, not retributions for wrongdoers. These are accidents that *may* happen: "Whoever digs a pit may fall into it." Such, says Qohelet, are the hazards inherent in daily occupations. He allows that certain precautionary measures can be taken; the implement can be sharpened beforehand to avoid having to exert excessive (potentially dangerous) pressure. Such foresight is the advantage of the wise. Qohelet's final aphorism could be read as a reinforcement of the need for *timely* application of one's skill: to avoid a snakebite the spell must be cast before it is too late. On the other hand, the example of the serpent's strike may evoke precisely those situations that cannot be prepared for, as in the opening scenario (v. 8) where the unlucky laborer is struck unawares by a snake nesting in a mud wall (compare Amos 5:19). Thus the final admonition may be a reminder that there are circumstances in which wisdom affords no remedy. Preparedness or foresightedness (sharpening the implement) can be effective for cases in which one can anticipate the need, but it is of limited value in the event of the unanticipated disaster. In this way Qohelet reminds the reader once again that the exercise of wisdom is subject to "time and chance" (9:11-12).

10:12-15 Words Can Surely Hurt You

In verse 11 Qohelet has employed a striking and anomalous expression for snake charmer, literally, "the master of the tongue." Pivoting on this last word, Qohelet launches a reflection on speech and its consequences, once again setting the wise person and the fool in diametric opposition (cf. 10:2). The sayings of the Proverbs are replete with such references to the mouth, lips, and tongue, all of which function as synecdoches for speech. One's speech betrays one's essential character (Prov 10:18; 12:18; 15:2, 7, etc.). With verse 12 Qohelet states the contrast memorably: "The words of the wise man's mouth bring him favor, but the lips of a fool are his destruction" (AT).

As in the wisdom tradition of the Bible and the rest of the ancient Near East, wordiness characterizes the fool (vv.13-14a). After describing the babbling fool, Qohelet revisits the theme of human ignorance of the future. The connection between this and the fool's chatter is not self-evident. Perhaps the suggestion is that the fool adds to the inanity of his endless talk with attempts to declare things to come (compare Brown 2000, 100). In any case, Qohelet has doggedly maintained the futility of such an endeavor for all mortals (compare 3:11; 6:12b; 7:14b). The ensuing proverb of verse 15 maintains the focus on the fool but shifts from his empty talk to his self-defeating toil. It may be an afterthought—a little proverbial tag that elaborates on yet another aspect of the fool's ineptitude. Or it is possible that "toil" refers to the futile enterprise of prognostication implied in verse 14 (compare 3:9 for this use of "toil"), indulged in by one who cannot even find the way to town, much less accomplish that which is beyond the sage (8:16-17).

10:16-20 Reflections on Misgovernment and the Wisdom of Reticence

These concluding verses take up the topics of governance and how to behave in the presence of authority and power, themes that Qohelet has touched upon earlier in the unit (10:4, 5-7).

Qohelet begins with two contrasting scenarios of government, a land with an upstart king (see 10:5-7) and a land with a king of noble birth. His respective assessments of the two situations ("Alas for you, O land" and "Happy are you, O land") reflect the assumption of an integral relationship between the welfare of a land and the quality and character of its king. When a king rules ably and justly he gives stability to his land and subjects; however, an unfit king brings the demise of all (compare Prov 29:4: "By justice a king gives stability to the land, but one who makes heavy exactions ruins it," and Sir 10:3: "An undisciplined king ruins his people, but a city becomes fit to live in through the understanding of its rulers").

These two scenarios are followed by a proverb (v. 18) in which the corrosive nature of misrule is portrayed as a house that deteriorates due to the laziness of its inhabitants. The saying, with its parallel warnings against laziness and its consequences, typifies a traditional proverb in both style and content. The image of a house is particularly apt for Qohelet's purposes, since the Hebrew term can also refer to a royal dynasty. Within the current context, the vices of "sloth" and "indolence" hearken back to the court decadence of the first scenario (v. 16), where the princes start their feasting when the day begins (as opposed to the princes of the highborn king, who feast at the proper time). The ensuing ode to food, drink, and money (v. 19) is best understood against this scene of laziness and carousing that eventually destroys the (royal) house. One might even interpret it as an illustrative vignette of the dissolute court members, who feast and drink even as the roof caves in.

Qohelet's reflection on governance at its best and at its worst brings him round to a final caveat regarding judicious behavior in the presence of power. As in previous passages on the topic, he encourages circumspection (8:2-4; 10:4). Here Qohelet advises extreme caution when it comes to criticism of the king (or anyone with political power or influence), lest one be overheard. He underscores his counsel with hyperbole: do not even harbor a disparaging *thought*, and do not speak a critical word even in the privacy of your own bedroom! The modern analog is "The walls have ears."

Qohelet's final image is of a winged creature bearing off words spoken in apparent safety and privacy. A saying from the Aramaic *Proverbs of Ahiqar*, a wisdom text circulating among a community of Jews in Egypt during the Persian period, also carries the association of words and birds (*TAD* III, 1.1.80–82). In fact the tone of this admonition is strikingly similar, in that the sage's rationale for careful speech is that there are eyes and ears everywhere! In this Aramaic text the injudicious speaking of a word is compared to the release of a bird, presumably with the idea that one can no more control a word once spoken than one can a bird set to flight. Other ancient Near Eastern texts have similar warnings about criticism of authorities, and Qohelet's versions may derive from this tradition (compare Prov 24:21-22). Yet it is also possible that they give evidence of a particular historical setting in which informants loyal to those in power were especially ubiquitous. As Seow points out, the writings of the Greek historians Xenophon and Herodotus tell of the existence of such informants during the Persian period, referred to as "the eyes and ears of the king" (1997, 341). Verse 20, with its emphatic cautions, might reflect such a climate.

A Modus Vivendi

Literary Analysis

The opening verses of chapter 11, which occur just before the concluding invocation to joy, are a pivotal passage in the book. The passage speaks of the uncertainty of future events and our inability to control or plan for them. Significantly, the refrain "you do not know" occurs four times in these six verses, standing at the beginning and end of the unit (vv. 2, 6) and occurring twice in verse 5. The theme of limitations on human knowledge and control is a familiar one (3:11; 8:17; 9:11, etc.). Even so, there is something new here that is signaled in the imperative verbs that begin and end the passage (vv. 1-2, 6): "Send out," "Give," "Sow." These imperatives are an insistent summons to act in the face of ignorance of how future events will play out (each command is joined to an acknowledgment of human ignorance). The sayings ensconced in these framing admonitions reinforce this message (vv. 3-5). Thus in this passage Qohelet both anticipates and counters one possible response to human impotence—that of paralysis or cynical apathy. In an unpredictable turn Qohelet avows that the answer to human impotence is not to withdraw from life but rather to invest deeply in it.

Exegetical Analysis

11:1-2

Send out your bread upon the waters;
for after many days you may get it back.
Give a portion to seven, or even eight,
for you do not know what disaster may happen on
the earth. (AT)

In verse 1b I propose the translation *"may get it back"* for "will get it back" (NRSV). This choice (that is, to adopt the modal meaning of the verbal form) is based on context. Elsewhere Qohelet denies that there is any certain connection between a deed and its consequence (7:15; 8:14; 9:11). In verse 2 the translation "Give a portion" (NRSV "Divide your means") represents a more literal translation of the Hebrew.

Verses 1-2 are in the wisdom form of an admonition: an instruction is followed by a clause that motivates the listener to follow it (e.g., 5:2; 7:9-10, 21, 9:7-10; 10:20; Prov 22:22-25; 23:10-11). The same form occurs at the end of the unit in 11:6. The content of the two admonitions in verses 1 and 2 is parallel. "Send out" (v. 1a) is parallel to "Give" (v. 2a; NRSV "Divide"), and "your bread" (v. 1a) is parallel to "a portion" (v. 2a). The latter half of each admonition motivates the recommended behavior by referring to a future eventuality. But the two proverbs are not entirely congruent in this last aspect. While verse 1 does acknowledge the uncertainty of the future, this is not the main point. In verse 2, the uncertain future *is* the motivation. This shift prepares the reader for the focal point of the passage, which will emerge as a tandem emphasis on the uncertain future ("you do not know") and the question of human response to that constraint.

The question is what, specifically, is the sort of action Qohelet wishes to advocate with these two sayings? This has been a matter of some debate. One interpretation is that Qohelet encourages the practice of liberal giving. This understanding represents the oldest interpretation of this section (seen in the Targum, rabbinic sources, Jerome, and other early commentaries on the text). A proverb from the Egyptian wisdom tradition is relevant to this interpretation in that it shares the same striking image of casting something in the water. In this teaching the thing thrown in the water is a good deed: "Do a good deed and throw it in the water; when it dries you will find it" (*AEL* III, 174).

In more recent treatments, however, the prevailing view understands the admonitions to be counsel about judicious and foresighted economic planning (e.g., Whybray 1989, 159; Towner 1997, 349; Bartholomew 2009, 337). The imagery is understood in a commercial context. Thus "bread upon the waters" refers to cargo (grain or merchandise) on ships. The advice is seen as an encouragement to invest abroad in order to get more lucrative return. The second verse follows this advice with a warning to diversify one's ventures in case of mishap. The NEB translation illustrates this view: "Send your grain across the seas, and in time you will get a return. Divide your merchandise among seven ventures, eight maybe, since you do not know what disasters may occur on earth."

Whether the advice is read literally as a word to merchants or as a figure of speech for life's various endeavors (interpreters differ on this point), it is generally taken as a balanced recommendation to risk some while still protecting one's interests.

A problem with this interpretation is seen in the motivation provided for sending out one's "bread." Verse 1b identifies the return on the investment as receiving it back again. But a return that promises nothing beyond one's capital outlay is no incentive for investment. As for verse 2, the view that it refers to diversifying one's portfolio would be a plausible interpretation if a context of commercial language were present, but such a context is not established by verse 1. As noted, the literal translation of verse 2 is: "*Give* a portion to seven, even eight." The idea that "seven" (or "eight") refers to business ventures is based on assumptions about verse 1 that the text does not support.

As mentioned, another interpretation of these verses is that they encourage giving liberally of one's means. In this case both admonitions make a similar point: give generously of your resources to others; in time such deeds may be rewarded in unexpected fashion (Seow 1997, 343; Fox 1999, 312; Enns 2011, 105). While Qohelet's counsel here might have a broader connotation than simply charitable giving, the general idea of this interpretation has more support in the text than the "calculated risk" interpretation. Another look at verses 1-2 is instructive. The first verse has the image of releasing one's bread on the surface of the water. Though we cannot be sure of the background of this image, it seems to be an observation that tides or floods might, against all odds, wash something back to shore or recede and leave it on dry land (note the Egyptian parallel just cited). The emphasis in 11:1 is on the unexpected nature of such an event: Qohelet says that after many days you may get it back, indicating the uncertainty of the prospect. In other words, to release something *on the water* is an image for giving something away without expecting its return. The image has been interpreted in just this way by the medieval Jewish commentator Rashi, who sums up this verse as follows: "Do good, act kindly to the person whom your heart tells you, 'You'll never see him again'—like a person who throws his sustenance upon the surface of the water" (cited in Davis 2000, 219).

In the parallel phrase of verse 2a the listener is admonished to give a portion to "seven, or even eight." The numerical parallelism here is a stylistic device in Hebrew poetry that is used for emphasis. Various (sequential) numbers may be paired in this convention (for example one/two, two/three, etc.). Although this device can emphasize the paucity of a thing (e.g., Isa 17:6), it may also be used to signify "much" or "many" (e.g., Amos 1:3–2:6). There is evidence that the latter is the case in 11:2. In Micah 5:5, the one other place where the pairing of seven/eight occurs, the emphasis is on plenitude. Moreover, seven is a symbolic number in the Old Testament, often carrying with it the concept of "much" (Cain is to be avenged sevenfold [Gen 4:15]) or of an ideal or full complement of something (in Hannah's thanksgiving song the barren woman bears seven children [1 Sam 2:5] and Job has seven sons [Job 1:2]). Thus there is some evidence that the encouragement here is not just to give, but to give abundantly. This understanding of v. 2a suggests that the combined emphasis of the two parallel lines—"Release your bread on the water!" and "Give to seven, even eight!"—is one of letting go of one's resources with an unreserved, unstinting generosity.

We may ask then about the meaning of the motivation that Qohelet appends to this second proverb, namely one's ignorance of what misfortunes may come. There is ambiguity here. Qohelet does not explicate the connection between generous giving and one's ignorance of future tragedies. We might speculate that, from a practical perspective, it is the person giving help who might receive help in his or her own time of need. The Egyptian instruction of Ptahhotep suggests just this in a context much like 11:2. The listener is encouraged to give generously of his earnings to his acquaintances in light of his ignorance of future events for "if misfortunes occur, it is [one's] acquaintances who say 'Welcome!'" (trans. Fox 1999, 313). This wisdom teacher spells out what is not stated in Qohelet's admonition of verse 2. It is possible, then, that Qohelet's words here presume such a tradition of teaching (Brown 2000, 101; Fox 1999, 312–13). On the other hand, it could be that the omission of any such pragmatic incentive leaves the passage open to a yet more radical interpretation. Ellen Davis elaborates on the observation of Rashi as follows:

> Not only should you give without certainty of repayment; you should give with the fair certainty of *not* being repaid. Disperse as widely as your means will stretch, "for you do not know what disaster may happen on earth" (v. 2). Our instinct is to hoard in anticipation of scarcity. Koheleth's reasoning is: give now; one day you may not have any more to give. No calamity, not even death itself, can strip us of what we have chosen to give away. (2000, 220)

11:3-6

In verse 3 Qohelet continues a thought from verse 2b, citing instances of those disasters the future might hold—drought and wind. The point of his observations in this verse is human powerlessness before these things. The clouds will bring rain at some point. The tree will fall someplace. But humans cannot control *when* the rain will come or *where* the tree will fall. Things will happen when and how they happen. As becomes explicit in verse 4, his point is that those who wait for certain knowledge or perfect conditions before taking action will never act. The direction and force of the wind (*rûaḥ*), the timing of precipitation—knowing these things would allow us to "sow" and to "reap" at the ideal time. Yet we cannot know such things. We do not have the crucial information that would guide us to act at the opportune moment. Qohelet allows that we can make certain general predictions regarding circumstance and consequence. When the clouds are full, it will rain. Yet we cannot be certain when that will be (compare 3:1-15). Qohelet has dwelt repeatedly on the limits of human knowledge and control. It is here in this passage that he overtly addresses one possible response to this realization, a state of paralysis or perpetual irresolution. His choice of agricultural imagery to represent the various endeavors of life is astute in that it brings out the absurdity of a response of inaction. The farmer cannot predict with any certitude the weather, the one thing that affects him most crucially. Yet what would happen if this uncertainty deterred him from sowing seed or bringing in harvest?

For the Hebrew audience there would have been an element of surprise in the opening phrase of verse 5. Once again Qohelet evokes the unpredictable and mysterious ways of the *rûaḥ*, the word that has just been used in the previous verse to refer to the wind. Thus Qohelet momentarily gives the impression that he continues the agricultural metaphor. However, the continuation of the phrase, "to the bones in the mother's womb," signals a shift in focus. Pivoting on the word to its alternate meaning, Qohelet speaks now of the animating life breath itself, granted by God alone. To signify decisively the limits of human control, the poet uses the ultimate mystery, the origination of a human life. Thus in these two verses (4-5) the sage builds his case for choosing action in the face of ignorance. On the formal level they are linked by the pun on the word *rûaḥ* (wind/life-breath). Yet the commonality, expressed in the imagery of germination and gestation, is nothing less than the continuation of life. In this way the sage conveys the dilemma at its most fundamental level. If there were no willingness to act despite uncertainty there would be no regeneration, no procreation. In short, no life.

In verse 6 Qohelet returns to the instructional form of the opening verses. He now states his conclusion: sow your seed in the morning and at evening. The reason given? One cannot be certain of the consequence of any particular action. In other words, the motivation for persistent action is precisely our absence of control. Qohelet proposes the somewhat paradoxical conclusion that persistent action is the antidote to human powerlessness. Stepping back to view the passage as a whole, one can see that the final injunction is on a continuum with the opening admonitions to send out with abandon and to give abundantly. The remedy for an uncertain future is not, as one might have supposed, a chary or stinting allocation of our energies and reserves. Instead one should let go, give, sow with boldness, persistence, and wholeness of heart (compare 9:10).

The language of this final injunction merits further examination, as it would seem to indicate a shift in the book. Qohelet's theme that we are completely ignorant of what the outcome of our actions will be is a familiar one. However the specific manner in which he elaborates on it is not: we do not know which will *prosper* or whether *both* might! To one familiar with the sage's usual mode of exposition, this stands out. The Qohelet we are accustomed to might more likely have said that we do not know which will *fail* and both might. The slight shift in rhetorical mood here is suggestive. One sees further evidence of a shift in tone in the imagery of the preceding verse (v. 5). Here Qohelet has employed the familiar phrase, "the work of God" (compare 3:11, 7:13; 8:17). Throughout the book of Ecclesiastes God's mysterious action has so often had as its subtext the fact of human death. Here, in an arresting turn, the divine work is encountered in the mystery of life's inception. The point being made, that we can in no way comprehend the divine work, is the same as it has been in previous discussions. The imagery is new, however. The mystery signifying our limits is not that of death, but of birth. It is a minor point, but taken together with Qohelet's positive elaboration on the potential of a seed sown, it may represent a subtle development in the sage's long journey. The book, repetitive as it may seem on the face of it, is not static. The shift here is not dramatic, but one might say that the sage has moved from a focus on the inevitable to a view of the possible. True, he will ultimately conclude with a solemn meditation on death, but not before this expression of a *modus vivendi*, issuing in a simple affirmation of the sweetness of light (11:7).

Theological and Ethical Analysis

Throughout his book, Qohelet reflects an acute consciousness of the arbitrary nature of human existence. In the end, says Qohelet, we are not the masters of our destiny. Things beyond our power may have a decisive role in whether or not our dearest hopes and most passionate aspirations will reach fruition. Qohelet is neither the first nor last thinker to dwell on this predicament and its consequences for human existence. Such a worldview has engendered a variety of responses. One such response is seen in the retreat into nihilism, namely, the view that there is no inherent or transcendent meaning to existence, and therefore no moral imperative. Albert Camus probes this worldview in *Caligula*, a play written during the ascendancy of the Nazi party in Germany. In this imaginative view of history Camus focuses on a single event, the untimely death of Caligula's beloved sister, as the catalyst for all the emperor's subsequent demented and arbitrary exercise of power. The play is a penetrating exposition of the roots of nihilism. If it is indeed true that we live our lives at the mercy of powers beyond ourselves, if all that matters most to us in the world can be taken away in an instant, and if death has the final word, then where *is* the ground for moral behavior? Human life is cheap, and power over others—transient as it is—becomes the only means of expressing one's self as *subject*. Indeed, Qohelet has an acute awareness of such cynical exercise of power (e.g., 4:1-3; 5:8; 8:9; cf. 9:3).

Another response to the radically contingent nature of human effort and existence is paralysis, an abdication of all action. This is the stance of the third servant in Jesus's parable of the talents in Matthew 25:14-30. Instead of trading with his talent as his fellow servants do, he stows it away in the ground for safekeeping. In the concluding confrontation between the servant and his lord, the servant explains his motivation: "Master, I knew that you were a harsh man, reaping where you did not sow, and gathering where you did not scatter seed; *so I was afraid*" (25:24, emphasis added). The risk was too great. Where the stakes are so high and uncertainty abounds, it is better to hold on to what one has than to risk loss of even that ("Here you have what is yours," he says to his master, v. 25). In a scathing response to the servant the master addresses him as "wicked" and "lazy" (v. 26). It has been observed, however, that the Greek underlying "lazy" derives from a verb that may also mean "to hesitate or shrink, as from fear or timidity" (Patte 1987, 352).

To hesitate, to shrink: such words bring to mind T. S. Eliot's "Love Song of J. Alfred Prufrock," with its indelibly etched figure of fear and perpetual retreat from choice:

> And indeed there will be time
> To wonder, "Do I dare?" and, "Do I dare?"
> Time to turn back and descend the stair.
> (Eliot 1915, lines 37–39)

The phrase "there will be time" (or "there is time") is a refrain in the early stanzas of the poem. However, this provision of time is to allow for "a hundred indecisions":

Do I dare
Disturb the universe?
In a minute there is time
For decisions and revisions which a minute will reverse.
(Eliot 1915, lines 45–48)

Prufrock, "politic, cautious, and meticulous" (line 116), cannot in the end muster the strength to "force the moment to its crisis" (line 80), lest he hear the dreaded words of demurral: "If one, settling a pillow by her head, / Should say: 'That is not what I meant at all. / That is not it, at all'" (lines 96–98). Various images of the poem, for instance the miasma of yellow fog and the evening sky laid out like an etherized patient, as well as the references to Hamlet and to "the overwhelming question," portray an existence suspended between death and life.

It is important to acknowledge that both of these texts are, by virtue of their respective literary genres, laden with multiple levels of meaning. In the reading offered here it is proposed that each in its own fashion mines the same vein of human experience—the posture of paralysis and abdication induced by fear of a world beyond our control. Qohelet's directives in chapter 11 are an eloquent and passionate address of just such deep-seated fears, the sins of omission: those ventures not dared because we are overcome by anxiety of failure and loss. To this Qohelet responds: without action, without risk, life could not go on. To be sure, there are no guarantees; on this point Qohelet has not wavered. But who knows? The right time may be now.

Accepting Death, Embracing Life

This section marks the last words of Qohelet. The *vapor* refrain at the end of 12:8 forms a frame with the opening introduction of Qohelet's words in 1:2, mirroring it both in its reference to Qohelet in the third person and in its use of the superlative form (*vapor of vapors*) paired with the comprehensive pronouncement (*all is vapor*).

Qohelet's final words to his listeners are a vigorous summons to enjoy life to the fullest before it is too late, a message brought into relief by a solemn meditation on our ultimate destination.

Literary Analysis

The macrostructure of this section reflects the wisdom form of an instruction: an exhortation followed by a motivation. In 11:7–12:1 Qohelet exhorts the listener to enjoy life *now*. In the ensuing poem of 12:2-7 he offers the motivation for this: death awaits you. The focus of each of these segments is expressed by the imagery of light and darkness. In 11:7 the sweetness of "light" and "sun" is affirmed as a prelude to the summons to enjoy life while one can. In 12:2 "light" and "sun" (in reverse order) are now darkened, along with the moon and stars.

The images and obscure references of the poem of 12:2-7 have generated considerable debate. A dominant line of interpretation, prevailing since early stages of interpretation, is that it is in some way an allegory of the physical decline of aging. In this reading the various images of the poem, particularly in verses 3-7, are correlated with body parts deteriorating with age. For instance, the trembling "guards of the house" are legs or arms, and the dwindling grinding women are teeth (12:3). Though there is plausibility to this idea in a few cases, it is difficult to derive such a reading from other elements in the poem. A more overarching objection to this view of the poem is contextual. Qohelet has not shown much concern for the problem of aging in his other reflections. It seems unlikely that the book should culminate in an extended lament on the woes of advancing age.

A few scholars have identified death as the predominant theme of this final passage, a concern that has indeed been a central preoccupation of the sage. This approach directs attention to the latter part of verse 5 as a guide to the location and context of the preceding descriptions: "For the human is going to his eternal home; and the mourners process in the streets" (AT). On the basis of this passage it is suggested that the context of the poem's images is that of a funeral procession (Fox 1999, 319–32 and references cited there). The grammatical structure of verses 3-5 supports this reading and is a key factor in this argument. The initial line of verse 3, "In the day when," establishes a time frame that extends through the end of verse 5. Thus the ensuing events—the cowering of the men, the cessation of work, the shutdown of the marketplace—occur on this single day. This day is the day of death and mourning (12:5c): a person is being taken to her grave.

Yet this is not just any funeral procession. Sun and moon turn black and clouds lower. Grown men double over in fear, and daily routines are disrupted. Recent scholarship has identified the background of such images in prophetic depictions of the day of God's judgment (Seow 1997; Fox 1999). The darkening of the heavenly lights is a theme found throughout such eschatological scenes: "The sun and the moon are darkened, and the stars withdraw their shining" (Joel 2:10; see also Isa 13:10; Ezek 32:7-8; Amos 5:18-20; Zeph 1:15). The human community responds with fear and dismay, as in Joel 2:6 where people's faces "gather blackness" (Fox 1999, 340) or Isaiah 13:7-8 where hearts melt in fear and people writhe as if in labor. In this cataclysmic state all signs of normalcy, including the rhythms of daily existence, are absent: "And I will banish from them the sound of mirth and the sound of gladness, the voice of the bridegroom and the voice of the bride, the sound of the millstones and the light of the lamp. This whole land shall become a ruin and a waste" (Jer 25:10-11). The prophets use this language of cosmic calamity to depict the terrible day of Yahweh that brings about the end of a nation or the world as it is known. Qohelet draws on this fund of imagery to depict another kind of destruction, the extinction of the individual (Fox 1999, 343).

In further entertaining this particular approach to 12:2-7 a few observations on the nature of poetic communication are pertinent. At the risk of stating the obvious, reading a poem is a temporal process. As opposed to encountering a work of the visual arts, our experience of a poem is linear. Each successive line supplies more information, adding to, revising, or focusing what has come before. Poets exploit this dynamic to its limit. Thus we as readers do not always know where we are being taken. This suggests that we should not necessarily assume that the obscurity of the images and references in this passage is entirely due to our own cultural distance. Perhaps some of the imagery is strategically obscure. We as readers absorb the poem's shades and moods, its aura, before we can identify specifics of circumstance and location—the plot, so to speak. We encounter images of darkness, consternation, debilitation, and fear before we understand their source or context. These take hold before we know where we are being taken. By the time we see the person being carried to the tomb it is too late for defense mechanisms. We have already felt something of death, even if we have not been able to name it. Poetry has the potential to take us beyond intellectual acknowledgement to a visceral experience of a reality. Qohelet's poem is a conjuration, an attempt to make real and present the event of death.

The poetic strategy employed here is that of defamiliarization. The artist takes something seemingly ordinary or routine and transforms it in such a way that we are caught unaware and compelled to see it anew. In the case of Qohelet's poem, we apprehend an event that shrouds the cosmos in darkness, terrifies those who witness it, and brings all things to a standstill. This event, it becomes evident, is not the end of the world, but someone's death. The poet invokes images of universal destruction to communicate the extinction of a human life, a most mundane event and yet one that, viewed from a subjective perspective, is indeed the expiration of a world (see further the analysis of Michael Fox, to which this discussion is indebted, 1999, 333–49).

Who is being carried to the grave? The poem is, in its immediate context, addressed to a young man. But the audience tends to merge with the addressee as the poem progresses. What ensues then may be viewed as Qohelet's invitation to his listener to imagine the inconceivable—his or her own death (Fox 1999, 338). In his opening monologue of chapters 1–2, spoken in the voice of the great king Solomon, we have overheard Qohelet's confrontation with his own mortality. Now in this final section, he speaks to us of our own.

Exegetical Analysis

11:7–12:1 Remember Your Destination That You May Live Now

"Sweet is the light," declares Qohelet. His unequivocal affirmation of the experience of being alive is prelude to a two-part segment, demarcated by the audience addressed. In 11:8 the focus is on humanity in general (Heb. *'ādām*); in 11:9–12:1 Qohelet turns his attention to the young man. Each part carries the counsel to "rejoice" (11:8-9), then concludes with the counsel to "remember" one's ultimate destination (11:8b; 12:1a). But it is the young man who sustains Qohelet's attention and to whom he speaks with the most urgency.

11:8 "Sweet Is the Light"—Even When . . .

Qohelet's first counsel acknowledges the plain fact that with advancing age enjoyment of life's pleasures wanes: "Even if a man lives many years, let him rejoice in them all; let him remember that the days of darkness will be many. Whatever comes is *vapor*" (11:8, AT).

The rationale for enjoying *all* of one's years is expressed by way of wry understatement: no matter how many years one lives, the years spent in the dark grave will exceed them! In the summation of Elsa Tamez: "Live Intensely in the Present . . . the Days of Darkness Are Infinite" (2000, 132). Qohelet's initial declaration hales the sweetness of the light, even in the context of aging with its accompanying decline in certain pleasures. It is still simply good to be alive and feel the sun on one's face. The message here has been somewhat obscured by the NRSV translation "*Yet* let them remember," as if the remembrance of death should somehow temper enjoyment of one's waning years (the Hebrew conjunction on "remember" should be left untranslated, as it is in 12:1). This is not the point. Rather one remembers death—its permanence and finality—*in order* to take full enjoyment in one's years, even those of old age.

11:9–12:1 "Sweet Is the Light"—Especially When . . .

In 11:9 Qohelet turns his focus to the young man, the presumed recipient of his admonitions. Qohelet's heightened emphasis is seen in the fact that he addresses him directly and speaks in the imperative: take joy, he says, and let your heart cheer you while you are young. The ensuing injunctions elaborate on this initial exhortation. Qohelet's words to the young man are perhaps best appreciated in the context of typical admonitions directed to the youthful audience of Proverbs, such exhortations as to rise early, work energetically, and avoid all forms of idleness (e.g., Prov 10:4; 12:24; 20:13). Qohelet, however, has nothing whatsoever to say with respect to the work ethic of the sages. Rather he bids the youth to (translating more literally) go in the "ways" of his heart and in the "sights" of his eyes—that is, to pursue his desires. It is perhaps no surprise that uneasiness about Qohelet's counsel is apparent in various phases of interpretation. The rabbis even questioned the soundness of the book's teaching on the basis of this passage (see introduction), responding with Numbers 15:39 as rebuttal (*Midrash Rabbah Kohlelet* on Eccl 1:3): "Recall all the commandments of the Lord and observe them, so that you do not follow your heart and your eyes in your lustful urge" (NJPS). Qohelet's troubling of the interpretive waters is demonstrated in additions made in some Greek translations of the verse: the youth is instructed to follow the ways of his heart *blamelessly* and *not* the desire of his eyes! Ben Sira, a more conventional sage of a subsequent generation, also overturns the advice of Qohelet: "Do not go after your heart and your eyes, to go in the delights of evil" (Sir 5:2 [Heb., Ms A]; Beentjes, 1997). Such interpretive repercussions as these give us an insight into the very distinctive nature of Qohelet's counsel.

Qohelet follows his bold advice to pursue one's desires with a reminder of divine judgment (v. 9d). Some scholars have suggested that this portion is the addition of an orthodox editor. Yet here one should take pause and consider the teachings of Qohelet carefully, for the notion of accountability for one's deeds is not at all foreign to his thought, as seen in such passages as 3:17, 5:4-7, and 7:17. Still one may ask, what *is* the relationship of this reminder of divine judgment to the ebullient charge to follow one's desires? To some degree the tonality hinges on the translation of the particle attached to "know" (v. 9d). This is translated as a disjunctive in the NRSV: "*But* know that for all these things . . ." (emphasis added). Here the relationship is a tension: the charge to follow one's desire is quickly qualified by a reminder not to get *too* carried away. But the particle is equally well translated as conjunctive:

"*And* know that for all these things. . . ." When it is read in this way, this directive to be aware of accountability before one's creator is not in tension with the mandate to enjoy life to the fullest; it may be taken instead as an intrinsic part of it. The notion of boundaries or limits as inherent in the human status is, as we've seen, very much a part of Qohelet's anthropology (see especially 9:1-12). To live in such mindfulness is consonant with the conditions of being human. Though Qohelet has often been in protest of certain aspects of such limits, in admonition mode he "gets real" and solicits recognition of them (compare 5:1-7).

Qohelet concludes his advice to the youth by affirming a holistic approach to enjoyment: one should keep both mind and body free of unnecessary discomfort (v. 10). The Hebrew word "pain" (v. 10) is repeated in the first verse of chapter 12 (NRSV "trouble") but this time with reference to impending old age ("before the days of trouble come . . . when you will say, 'I have no pleasure in them'"). The point then is that one day the young man will have no choice about removing pain/trouble from his body. He should thus act now while such things are within his power. The urgency is underscored with lyric simplicity: "For youth and the dawn of life are fleeting [*vapor*]" (NRSV "vanity"). The address to the young man continues into 12:1, closing with the injunction "remember," as has the first unit (11:8).

Some readers have been puzzled by the reference to the creator as motivation here. However, in the larger context of the poem, to remember one's source is to remember one's end. This is made apparent by the climax of the poem in 12:7, where dust returns to dust and the life-breath "returns to God who gave it." The reference to God as creator anticipates this conclusion. Thus "remember" functions here as it does in 11:8, to remind one of death so that one will live fully now. This understanding is in fact made apparent by the continuation of the verse, which specifically adjures one to this consideration *before* old age. The point is that it is best to realize one's finite existence in the time of youth, while one is still possessed of the capacities to enjoy life to the fullest.

12:2-8 For This Is the End of Everyone (7:2)

The evocation of old age provides a segue into death as the topic of the concluding poem. In verse 1 the Hebrew phrase underlying "before" ("before the days of trouble come") is a unique construction in the Hebrew ('ad 'ăšer lō'); this same phrase commences 12:2 as a means of signaling a transition to the final movement of 11:7–12:8. The demarcation at 12:2 is also seen in the repetition of the two light entities from 11:7, "light" and "sun" (here announced in reverse order): the light that signified the realm of the living is now extinguished; contemplation of the dark begins. Finally, it may be noted that in 12:1 Qohelet acknowledges his addressee overtly for the last time ("the days of which you will say"). Beginning at 12:2 he ceases to speak to a "you." Still this slight shift away from his listener is more apparent than real. The poem that follows is meant to be overheard. The striking images that follow are an attempt to make real and present what has been intimated by "days of darkness" (11:8) and "your creator" (12:1). In this way the second major section (12:2-8) functions as the motivation for all that has been said in the first (11:7–12:1; see "Literary Analysis").

The series of vignettes set forth in verses 3-5 are located on the day of darkness heralded in verse 2. Verse 3 describes the repercussions of some event in the human community. The event itself is not disclosed. We know only that it instills dismay and grief and disrupts daily routine. The image of an estate appears to be the backdrop, at least initially. The guards or stewards of the house quake in terror, and their superiors (NRSV "strong men"; see Ruth 2:1 for a meaning associated with social status) likewise cower in fear. The next two lines feature the women of the household. The reason the grinding women have dwindled is not apparent, but the salient point here is that milling has ceased. The chore of milling was necessary to the basic sustenance of a household (see the legal provision in Deut 24:6). The halt of this activity is therefore ominous. At the same time, women peering through the windows are said (in the Hebrew) to have "become dark" (NRSV "see dimly"). The phrase is odd but suggestive. In Lamentations this same verb is used for eyes darkened by grief (Lam 5:17). But the verb is most commonly used for the darkening of light, such as the celestial lights snuffed out in verse 2. In this passage the "darkening" of the peering women may function polysemously—conveying human grief even as it evokes darkened windows in a once-inhabited household. The two groups of women may reflect two social classes, thus functioning as counterparts to the two classes of men. Grinding was a task often left to servants and slaves (Exod 11:5; Job 31:10). By contrast, those who peer through the lattice would be women of leisure (compare Judg 5:28; 2 Sam 6:16-23; 2 Kgs 9:30). In other words, the poetic strategy of these four vignettes is to convey the effect of an event leaving no sector of society untouched: men and women, servants and highborn (Fox 1999, 324).

Verse 4 continues the theme of a kind of portentous silence. The human realm is still the subject of attention, but the poet widens the purview beyond the happenings of a single estate. The word "street" here may refer to the main thoroughfare of the city, the location of commerce and social intercourse. These doors are now shut, and the grinding has stopped. The sound of scraping grindstones would have been a familiar background noise, a sign of society in its right state, and of business as usual. Jeremiah 25:10 offers good illustration of the significance with its reference to the silencing of the sound of joyous occasions and of the sound of the millstones. The absence of such is meant to dramatize a situation in which there are no vestiges of civilized culture, including the comforting rhythms of ordinary routine.

Still, various aspects of verse 4 remain obscure. Who is the one who rises "at the sound of a bird"? Who are the "daughters of song," and what is the significance of their being "brought low"? It is in fact grammatically possible to read "the sound of the bird" as the subject of the verb "rises up" in verse 4c (Seow 1997, 358). Thus we may translate: "The sound of the bird goes aloft." In terms of literary movement this phrase appears to be placed in a contrast with the preceding clause: the "voice" (*qôl*) of grinding has dropped low, even as the "voice" (*qôl*) of the bird ascends. A society/nature contrast is suggested; in the void left by the steady hum of milling, one hears the sound of hooting birds. In prophetic passages portraying ravaged cities, wild animals and birds of prey move in where people once lived (Isa 13:21-22; 18:6; 34:13-15; Jer 12:9; 50:39; Ezek 39:4). Qohelet's choice of vocabulary for the decline of the mill sound is intriguing. This Hebrew verb (*šāpal*), which means "to be, or become low," is nowhere else used to refer to the recession of sound. In fact the verb is most often employed in a figurative sense to describe the humbling or abasement of proud humans (e.g., 2 Sam 22:28; Isa 2:9, 17; 5:15; Job 40:11; Prov 29:23). Perhaps Qohelet has intended just such resonances in his extended image of humanity's encounter with *the* great leveler.

The subsequent references to the "daughters of song" and to "those who fear heights" (AT; the verb "fear" is plural though this is not reflected in the NRSV) is one of the most disputed passages in the sequence. There are no exact biblical parallels for "daughters of song" and some have suggested it continues the reference to birds. The verb translated "brought low" appears in contexts of mourning in the Psalms (Pss 35:14; 38:6; 44:25), where it refers to being bent over in sorrow. In three other occurrences it is paired with the verb *šāpal* (the same verb used for the cessation of the milling) in a context of once-proud humans being humbled (Isa 2:9; 5:15; 29:4). These contexts suggest the possibility that the daughters of song are female singers who are bowed low in the posture of mourning (see 2 Chron 35:25, where singers and songstresses utter laments).

The appearance of female mourners in verse 4d suggests a pattern in which the lines of this verse alternate between the human and natural realm—from the marketplace and milling to the sound of hooting birds and back again to female mourners prostrating themselves. While the reference to fear of heights in verse 5 is odd and makes little sense in context, the verb "they fear" (NRSV "one is afraid") may alternatively be read as "they look" without any change to the Hebrew consonantal text (this is also the interpretation of the Greek translators). In this case the undesignated subject might be the birds (v. 4c) who look down from a height upon the dreadful sights in the road, presumably the distress and lamentation of the human community.

The meaning of the subsequent lines in verse 5 is also disputed. The position adopted here follows Fox (1999, 328) in taking all three references to be to plants—the almond blossom, the locust tree (NRSV "grasshopper"), and the caperberry (NRSV "desire"). These "blossom," "become laden," and "bud" (for "bud" see Fox 1999, 328). In this they are set forth as a counterpoint to the human who is going to his eternal home. As these things bud forth again after a period of dormancy, the human (NRSV "all") is carried to her permanent resting place.

A final repetition of "before" (*'ad 'ăšer lō'*), the distinctive Hebrew phrase that marked a shift to the poetic section in 12:2, now marks a transition to its final stanza (v. 6). Now we view a series of objects: a cord, a bowl, a pitcher, a jug (NRSV "wheel"), each one destroyed. The identification and function of these is debated. The bowl of gold may refer to a lamp, and the silver cord to the stand that supports it (see Seow 1999, 227–28). The snuffing out of light thus represents the end of life (compare Job 18:5-6; 21:17; Prov 20:20; 24:20). The second pair of images draws on the symbolism of water as life source. Clay vessels for retrieving it—a pitcher and a jug—shatter to pieces, crumbling back to soil. The image merges seamlessly into the image of human death: "And the dust returns to the earth as it was, and the breath returns to God who gave it" (v. 7). The various figures in this climactic moment of the poem are richly allusive, reflecting a poignant awareness of both the elegant splendor of a human and our abject vulnerability—"a masterpiece as delicately wrought as any work of art, yet as breakable as a piece of earthenware" (Kidner 1976, 103). Such is the human status (compare Pss 8:3-9; 144:3-4).

Qohelet's description of the death process comports with its portrayal in other Old Testament passages: the animating life breath granted by God returns to its source, and humans return to the dust whence they came (Job 34:14-15; Ps 104:29-30; cf. Gen 2:7). Contained within such language is the recognition of an absolute distinction between divine and human, creator and creature. Humanity is defined by its boundaries, a beginning and an end in the earth: "You are dust, and to dust you shall return," says the Yahwist in the creation story (Gen 3:19; see also Gen 18:27; Job 10:9; and Ps 22:29 [Heb. 30]).

"Vapor of vapors," says Qohelet, "all is vapor.". The theme statement that introduced Qohelet's words now concludes them, forming a frame around them. At the same time, the statement is a fitting climax to this final contemplation of the transitory nature of human existence. Thus the *vapor* pronouncement of 12:8 has a double valence. Specifically it concludes the poem of 11:7–12:8, while generally it concludes all the words of Qohelet, setting the stage for the ending tribute to his work and thought (12:9-14).

In his opening poem of chapter 1, Qohelet viewed the question of meaning as if from a promontory (1:4-11), against the backdrop of the cycles of nature, the march of generations, and the scheme of history, all sweepingly evoked to depict a world that, despite incessant activity, remains in stasis. In his closing poem Qohelet steps close and views the question of meaning at the level of the individual human life cycle. The human, like the sun and the wind of the opening poem, can only return to her place of origin.

Theological and Ethical Analysis

Let us then resolutely turn our backs on the once-born and their sky-blue optimistic gospel; let us not simply cry out, in spite of all appearances, "Hurrah for the Universe!—God's in his Heaven, all's right with the world." Let us see rather whether pity, pain, and fear, and the senti-

*ment of human helplessness may not open a profounder view and put
into our hands a more complicated key to the meaning of the situation.*
William James, *Varieties of Religious Experience*

In Ecclesiastes 11:7–12:8 we once again encounter the sharp abutment of life and death. Qohelet's pronouncement on the goodness of being alive is followed by a solemn contemplation of death. It is on this note that the final reflection concludes. Dust returns to dust. Still, in searching out the tonality of this final section it is useful to revisit its formal literary features. Qohelet's poem on death is, in its current literary context, directed to the reader, and it has a function. It *motivates* the urgent exhortation to the listener to savor the sweet light of the sun *now*. A second consideration has to do with the (aesthetic) form that the motivation takes. Qohelet has chosen to use poetry. This choice is not without significance. Poetry is the medium of conjuration. Qohelet wants to take us beyond mere intellectual acknowledgment of our demise. He wants us to taste something of it.

What is highlighted by these observations on formal aspects of 11:7–12:8 is Qohelet's persuasion that for one to really enter into life one must truly believe in death. It is, in the end, only a realization of death that allows us to seize upon life. I have earlier spoken of the writer and philosopher Albert Camus, another probing thinker who insistently asked after the meaning of existence in the light of human limits. Near the end of his most noted essay on human finitude, he makes this climactic statement with respect to the plight of his human toiler, Sisyphus: "But crushing truths perish from being acknowledged" (Camus 1955, 90). What does Camus intend by this? Can he really mean that certain facts of our mortal existence evaporate? He cannot, for he recognizes, in characteristically paradoxical fashion, that these are *truths*. He means, I think, that these truths may no longer exert their power over us. His pronouncement reflects an awareness that we are most dominated by knowledge that we suppress. For Camus redemption from the limits of this existence is to be found only in our willingness to confront these directly—without illusion or fabricated solace. From this stark place we may begin to seek out the possibilities of a meaningful existence—to, in his words, "live and create, in the very midst of the desert" (1955, v).

Qohelet's place of beginning is not so stark as that of Camus. For Camus God is absent from the world, leaving humans to make their way in an indifferent universe. Qohelet still holds to belief in a creator who, even if inscrutable in deeds and responsible for limits, is the source of all good gifts we know. Still, one may discern the affinity between these two thinkers. For both it is necessary to confront all that is difficult and incomprehensible about human existence before coming to some sort of *modus vivendi*.

In his classic work, *The Varieties of Religious Experience*, William James identifies and explores two categories of religious temperament: the "healthy minded" and the "sick soul" (James 1929, 77–162). His probing delineation of these provides a useful lens on the mind-set of our sage and invites a contemplation of the potential witness of Ecclesiastes in confessing communities.[3] The healthy-minded person is one who is by temperament an optimist, one who looks on life and sees it as fundamentally good: "We find such persons in every age, passionately flinging themselves upon their sense of the goodness of life, in spite of the hardships of their own condition, and in spite of the sinister theologies into which they may be born. From the outset their religion is one of union with the divine" (James 1929, 78).

As for the evil aspects of this world and of human existence, the healthy-minded address these by minimizing them in one way or another "by systematically declining to lay them to heart or make much of them, by ignoring them in his reflective calculations, or even, on occasion, by denying outright that they exist" (James 1929, 125). The sick soul, on the other hand, is one who sees "that the evil aspects of this life are of its very essence" and "that the world's meaning most comes home to us

---

3. I am indebted to Michael Fox (1999, 135–36) for drawing my attention to affinities between William James's work and the book of Ecclesiastes.

when we lay them most to heart" (James 1929, 128). The sick soul suffers an acute consciousness of evil and cannot easily put it aside. Notably this temperament is not necessarily the result of a difficult life or of the absence of any happy experience. In fact, the sick soul may well have ample experience of the good things of this life, of contentment, success, happiness, and love, as James's various excerpts attest. The difference lies in his or her keen awareness that all such goods are vulnerable to circumstance, and that ultimately death takes all. James quotes the following from an acquaintance: "'The trouble with me is that I believe too much in common happiness and goodness, and nothing can console me for their transiency. I am appalled and disconcerted at its being possible'" (James 1929, 137). In other words, the disposition of the sick soul may arise precisely from a profound belief in the good that is part of life, for this makes all the more tragic and absurd the fact that it can be so arbitrarily withdrawn.

It would not be difficult to surmise how James would classify Qohelet, but in fact we need not speculate. As a means of conveying the lineaments of the sick soul he offers a compendium of passages from Ecclesiastes, following these with a provocative distillation of the sensibility reflected there: "In short, life and its negation are beaten up inextricably together. But if the life be good, the negation of it must be bad. Yet the two are equally essential facts of existence; and all natural happiness thus seems infected with a contradiction. The breath of the sepulcher surrounds it" (James 1929, 137).

I earlier quoted Thomas Hardy, who has written: "If way to the Better there be, it exacts a full look at the Worst." For the "sick soul," well-being is to be found only by traveling *through* acknowledgment of all that is dreadful, sorrowful, and absurd in this world. This is the path of the sage Qohelet.

In light of all these resonances, what does it mean that this book resides in our canon of scripture, claiming a voice in that witness to the divine/human relationship? Perhaps the most powerful thing is simply that it is included at all. Anyone who has suffered grief or depression understands the painful component of isolation. The language of our lectionaries, our liturgies, and our sermons does not always address the profound darkness that some of us experience. Some confess God even in their darkness, but find God remote, even hidden. Ellen Davis begins her commentary on the book of Ecclesiastes by telling of a Vietnam War chaplain who attests that "it was the only part of the Bible that his soldiers were willing to hear." She adds: "It is comforting that even the experience of total alienation from life (2:17) is given voice within the biblical tradition. Alienation and despair are recognized as one moment, at least, in the journey toward faith" (Davis 2000, 159). To read the book of Ecclesiastes is to admit the possibility that in no anguished question, in no searing encounter with senseless evil, in no sense of alienation, are we truly and utterly alone.

Epilogue: A Tribute to Qohelet the Wise

T he epilogue refers to Qohelet in the third person. A structural indicator of a divide at this point is the *vapor* pronouncement of 12:8, which echoes the beginning of the book in 1:2 (see 12:8). The final six verses of chapter 12 stand outside this envelope structure.

Literary Analysis

The fact that the conclusion of the book of Ecclesiastes is in a voice other than Qohelet's raises the intriguing question of perspective: what is the stance of this final speaker toward the contribution of Qohelet? A determination of this is not as easy as one might hope, due to certain grammatical and lexical ambiguities in these verses. The presence of both accolades and apparently critical statements has led some commentators to identify two writers in the final segment, one favorable to Qohelet's work (vv. 9-11) and one wary of it (vv. 12-14). Still others, recognizing these same tensions, posit a single source but allow for an ambivalent or at least more complex relationship on the part of the final commentator. Robert Gordis, for instance, characterizes the epilogist as "both fascinated and troubled by its contents" (1968, 200).

In view of certain textual features as well as matters of content, this treatment identifies two hands in the final section: an epilogue spanning verses 9-12 and an addendum or postscript from yet another source in verses 13-14 (see Seow 1997, 382–96; Fox 1999, 349–63). The epilogist thoughtfully reflects on Qohelet's contributions as sage. The author of the postscript attempts a concise summation of the message of the book. The sequence may be outlined as follows:

12:9-12 Epilogue—*Qohelet among the Wise*

> Qohelet endorsed as sage (12:9-10)
> The potent teachings of the wise (12:11)
> The hazards of intellectual exertion (12:12)

12:13-14 Postscript—*A Summation: All Any Person Needs to Know*

12:9-12 Epilogue—Qohelet among the Wise

The tribute to Qohelet's professional activity in verses 9-10 situates Qohelet squarely within the wisdom tradition. Qohelet is proclaimed as not only a sage, but as one who "taught the people knowledge" (v. 9). His pedagogical vehicle is identified as the proverb. We see Qohelet at work, thoughtfully studying proverbs and arranging (perhaps editing) them for presentation. The three Hebrew verbs used to convey his scholastic labors exhibit sound play (assonance)—*'izzēn/ḥiqqēr/tiqqēn*—a favored device of wisdom teachers (e.g., Prov 3:35; 6:21; 9:5; 13:24; Eccl 10:11, 18). The second verb (NRSV "study") means to search out or examine thoroughly (see Job 29:16 and Prov 18:17, where it refers to the thorough examination of legal cases). Thus the commentator draws attention to the conscientious, deliberate process behind Qohelet's contribution. The climactic verb in the series (NRSV "arrange") is unique to Ecclesiastes in the Hebrew Bible. It occurs two other times in the book, in both instances with the meaning "to straighten" (1:15 and 7:13). The rarity of this word suggests the possibility that the epilogist has consciously chosen it to resonate in some way with these two instances. In both 1:15 and 7:13 the verb is used in opposition to the word "crooked," and the context is human inability to make sense of God's mysterious works. "Who can make straight what he has made crooked?" asks Qohelet in chapter 7. Here, in the end, Qohelet *has* made something straight, the epilogist implies. It is a more modest venture to be sure, and that is the point. It is a task that a mortal might reasonably aspire to, and take satisfaction in.

Verse 10 expands upon Qohelet's contributions. "Pleasing words" (v. 10a) refers to the aesthetic quality of his writing, not an attempt to cater to his listeners. The second part of the tribute posits the truth of Qohelet's words (v. 10b). The Hebrew word used here ('emĕt) includes the idea of soundness and reliability (see Ps 132:11). In the words of Roland Murphy, it is meant "in the profound sense of capturing reality" (1992, 125). When Woman Wisdom extols her teachings offered to all humanity, she does so in similar accents (Prov 8:6-7a): "Listen, for I speak noble things; Straightforward discourse comes from my lips. My mouth utters what is *trustworthy* ['emĕt]" (trans. Clifford, 1999, 91).

The testimony to the credibility and soundness of Qohelet's words in verse 10b is sometimes understood to be in a qualifying relationship with the praise of his rhetorical skill in verse 10a ("pleasing words"), as if the epilogist hastened to add that Qohelet valued truth more than finely wrought phrases (compare, e.g., NEB; Farmer 1991, 195; Towner 1997, 359). Such an interpretation assumes a dichotomy between form and content that is alien to wisdom thought. That elegant presentation marks the reliable sayings of the wise is a given, as seen in the genres previewed in the prologue to Proverbs (proverbs, figures, riddles—1:6). Indeed the sages' attention to the artistry of their expression is evident throughout the sayings of Proverbs (Alter, 2011, 205–30). Hence, the tributes to Qohelet's craftsmanship and to the validity of his words are complementary and serve to reinforce Qohelet's status as sage par excellence. Still, the epilogist is not quite finished. He also provides an adverb for the manner in which Qohelet conducted his work. According to the NRSV, Qohelet wrote his words of truth "plainly," but the Hebrew word (*yōšer*) in context suggests that the point is not accessibility, rather, again, truthfulness and reliability (compare Ps 25:21,where this Hebrew word is in parallel with "integrity" [*tōm*]). The same verbal root is at play in Proverbs 8:6 in the phrase "straightforward discourse" (Clifford 1999, 91), where it functions as complement to Woman Wisdom's trustworthy (*'emĕt*) speech. The sum effect of verse 10b is to draw a line under Qohelet's credibility (NJPS translates: "And [he] recorded genuinely truthful sayings.")

In verse 11 the epilogist broadens the purview of his tribute to encompass the sayings of the wise. It is not by chance that the emphasis on truthfulness is followed by the recognition that wisdom can cause discomfort! The words of the wise are compared to implements used to prod along and guide livestock. Evidence from rabbinic literature indicates that such goads were implanted with sharp pricks on the tips (Seow 1997, 386–87; compare Fox 1999, 354). In that case the "goads" and the "nails" in verse 11 comprise a single image, with the nails being the pricks set in the tips of the goads (compare also 1 Sam 13:21). The source of such painful prodding is identified as "one" shepherd, referring, it would seem, to any sage who plies such potent speech ("one" in Hebrew may be used to mark a noun as indefinite [e.g., Judg 9:53; Ezek 8:8]), though some have seen in it a reference to God as the ultimate source of wisdom teaching. However one reads it, one cannot fail to recognize in this extended image an apt description of the effect of Qohelet's words in particular! The message is pertinent for the young listener who would grow in wisdom. The process is not always pleasant; it can even hurt (compare 1:18). The medieval interpreter Ibn Ezra amplifies by saying that goads both afflict and open the mind.

This tribute to the pedagogical efficacy of the words of the wise is followed by a warning or admonition of some sort. This much is generally agreed upon. But certain grammatical ambiguities have given rise to differing understandings of the nature of this caution. In what has become a somewhat standard interpretation, the reader is warned about something *over and above* the saying of the wise (so NRSV "Of anything beyond these . . . beware"). According to this reading, the statement is a warning about some collection of teachings beyond the traditional teachings of the sages. It has been suggested that the epilogist reflects an incipient "canon consciousness," warning against an open attitude toward its boundaries (e.g., Barton 1908, 198; Crenshaw 1987, 191). Any more specific identification of the literature in question has remained in the realm of conjecture; it has been speculated that the writer refers to apocryphal writings, or perhaps even to non-Jewish literature. More recently it has been proposed that the warning has a formulaic function and its primary purpose, more positive than negative, is to affirm the sufficiency of the writings of Qohelet (see Seow 1997, 388). Such formulaic endings appear in other wisdom writings, such as the Egyptian *Instruction for Kagemni*, which concludes with the admonition: "All that is written in this book, heed it as I said it. Do not go beyond what has been set down" (*AEL* 1, 60). As Seow observes, the point is that there is no need to supplement Qohelet's work; all that has been intended has been set down. Similar statements in biblical texts may have served the same function (compare Deut 4:2; 12:32 [Heb. 13:1]; Rev 22:18-19).

One's interpretation of the meaning and purpose of the warning influences one's understanding of the nature of the expansion on it (v. 12, cont.):

> The making of many books is without end,
> and to study much is a weariness of the flesh. (AT)

For those who see in verse 12a some sort of warning against a body of writings beyond the words of the book, this ensuing remark is a kind of footnote that acknowledges the profusion of such writings, and the pointlessness of applying oneself to them. While this is plausible, the rhetorical details of this couplet suggest another possibility. The elements placed in parallel are *activities*—making/studying—suggesting that it is the undertakings themselves that are the focal point (not the content produced/studied). Moreover, these activities are modified with the same Hebrew word (translated as "many" and "much"). In Hebrew parallelism the repeated or stable element between two lines may function as an interpretive clue. Thus we might deduce that it not just the activities, but the excessive nature of such that is at issue. In short, these features suggest that the caution is not about content but about behavior. This introduces a different possibility with respect to the relationship of the warning to the sage(s) held up to view. Reading along these lines, the epilogist, having held up the merits of Qohelet's teaching, also warns of the downside to writing and study. Such application, carried to excess, has a momentum of its own. The epilogist describes a kind of intellectual "dance of the red shoes" that leads not to enlightenment but exhaustion. It is not hard to espy the resonances with Qohelet's own themes. Qohelet, too, ponders the strain of certain sorts of endeavors (and executes a cost/benefit analysis of such). In fact, our epilogist here shows himself to be in sync with the arc of the book as a whole. Qohelet's narration of his quest for understanding has issued in words addressed directly to a young man, the first and only specification of his audience (11:9): his wisdom is that one should savor one's youth, banishing worry from the mind and pain from the body. Now the epilogist seconds this message with his own comment to the youth ("my son"; NRSV "my child") about strenuous endeavor, in particular strenuous *intellectual* endeavor. Such exertions are not the avenue to fulfillment (e.g., 1:16-18; 7:23-24; 8:16-17). The relationship between the epilogist and his subject here is paradoxical: Qohelet, who spent himself in such questing, is at once the cautionary tale *and* the model (he has learned the same lessons proffered by the epilogist).

12:13-14 Postscript–A Summation: All Any Person Needs to Know

Certain features suggest these verses are an addition from a later editor (compare Seow 1997, 382–96; Fox 1999, 358–60). Verse 13a begins succinctly: "The end of the matter; all has been heard." A similar expression in the book of Daniel marks the end of Daniel's first vision (translating more literally): "Here is the end of the matter" (Dan 7:28). In two other instances in the Old Testament there is evidence of a concluding formula marking the end of a major textual unit or perhaps the original end of a scroll. In the Psalms we find one at the end of the second of the five scrolls (72:20: "The prayers of David son of Jesse are ended"), and near the end of Jeremiah a concluding formula marks the end of Jeremiah's prophecies and signals the transition to an historical appendix (Jer 51:64: "Thus far are the words of Jeremiah"; see further Fox 1999, 358–60).

A second feature highlighting a transition or seam at 12:13a comes from the Masoretes, the scholars who added vowel points and other annotations to the biblical consonantal text in the early Middle Ages. The Masoretes have made the first letter of "end" (*sôp*) in "end of the matter" an enlarged letter. It is possible the large letter is intended to mark a new section, or to otherwise draw attention to this verse (for instances of the practice see Tov 2012, 53).

The condensed expression and brisk pace of verse 13a prepare us for a conclusion. To say "All has been heard" is to say, "Enough!" Now all that the listener needs to know and remember is distilled in a concluding summation. The editor here is well acquainted with the vocabulary of Qohelet, and he draws upon it to set forth his own emphases, aptly described by one scholar as a thematizing of the book (Sheppard 1977, 182–89). The thematization contains both something old and something new. The mandate to fear God is a basic theme in wisdom literature (Prov 1:7; 9:10; Job 1:1; 28:8). Qohelet, too, has spoken of the fear of God in his teaching (3:14; 5:7; 7:18; 8:12-13; see discussion at 3:14). But the mandate to obey God's commandments is not present in his writings. In linking the two, this final writer is intentionally interpreting Qohelet's teaching in terms of God's covenant demands. In this way the book is drawn more into conformity with the mainstream of biblical thought.

The clause that follows this admonition to fear and obey is sparely put (translating more literally than the NRSV): "For this is every person" (NRSV "For that is the whole duty of everyone"). Although we cannot ascertain the precise meaning of this elliptical phrase (it may be an idiom otherwise unattested in biblical Hebrew), the immediate context gives some sense of where the emphasis lies. The preceding statements and admonitions have pertained to the sages and their pupils. "Every person" may be a means of differentiating the focus from what has preceded: the stipulations of godly fear and obedience to the Law apply to everyone.

There follows now a ringing affirmation of judgment to come (v. 14). This parting assertion, brief as it is, is dialogical in its interaction with the ideas of Qohelet. The speaker, like Qohelet, can give no timetable for such a reckoning, placing his emphasis on thoroughness of judgment instead: it is every deed, good and evil, even secret ones. Qohelet, too, has spoken of a time in the future when justice will prevail (3:17; 8:12-13), but the ambiguity of the timeline has been more vexing to him. That "meantime" in which the wicked flourish and the innocent suffer has so appalled him that it threatens to strip any solace from the idea of ultimate justice (see 3:16–4:3; 8:1-17).

Another telling feature in terms of a distinction between this final declaration and Qohelet's statements is the mode of expression. Because Qohelet's thoughts are expressed in the subjective mode (as are all his reflections), we are aware of Qohelet as an individual expressing a perspective (see introduction). This impression is underscored by the fact that such acknowledgments are voiced as a debate within himself, a conflict between what he observes and what tradition has taught him (see 3:16-17; 8:11-14). In contrast, the statement of the final writer is presented objectively: the speaker does not make us conscious of himself, and therefore of a viewpoint, which thus leaves the impression of something finally authoritative, handed down from on high.

Verse 14 borrows specifically from the vocabulary and phraseology of Qohelet's own admonition to the youth coming at the end of 11:9: "Know that for all these things God will bring you into judgment." The context of this word to the young man is an exhortation to live life fully while one has the capacities to do so. Hence this final injunction of 11:9 is a reminder of creaturely finitude and accountability before God—the boundaries of humanness—which, as suggested there, functions in a complementary way to Qohelet's encouragement to follow one's heart desires: "Follow the inclination of your heart and the desire of your eyes" (11:9b). As noted, the language Qohelet employs in this latter phrase would have caught the attention of his audience. In fact, it is the way of the heart and eyes that is used in Numbers 15 to epitomize the path of disobedience to God and the covenant requirements: "Recall all the commandments of the Lord and observe them, so that you do not follow *your heart* and *your eyes* in your lustful urge" (Num 15:39 NJPS). The singular nature of Qohelet's advice perturbed interpreters from very early on, as seen in the Greek translators' attempt to amend it, in Ben Sira's reversal of it (Sir 5:2 [Hebrew text]), and in rabbinic discussions. It seems likely that the ripple effect of Qohelet's subversive counsel is also evident in 12:13-14. Now the writer who has the final say recontextualizes this reminder of accountability. When all is said and done, it is fear of God and obedience to God's laws that matters. Without contradicting Qohelet, the writer has decisively shifted the emphasis by putting the reminder of judgment in this new context. There should be no ambiguity about the criteria by which one will be judged before God. Godly fear, as expressed in covenant obedience, is the standard by which one will be held accountable.

This divine judgment is comprehensive in scope and piercing in depth; not only will every act be appropriately judged, but even hidden deeds will be requited. Once more there surfaces both a point of contact and a certain tension with the thought of the book. Qohelet would seem fully aware of the murky depths of the human heart (e.g., 7:22; 8:11; 9:3); more, however, than the furtive deeds of his fellow humans, it is the opacity of divine action that has concerned and perplexed him (Brown 2000, 119). The divine work is mysterious and incomprehensible to humans (1:15; 3:11; 7:13; 8:17; 9:1, etc.).

The conclusion of chapter 12 is thus fundamentally at odds with the temper of the book in its assured confidence of divine judgment on every deed, speaking in terms that would hedge off the ambiguity that Qohelet has introduced with his vigorous questionings of the system. As Sibley Towner observes, the ending of Ecclesiastes lacks "the nuance and probing energy of the rest of the book" (1997, 359). For Qohelet the relationship between human action and divine judgment is hidden from human apprehension. Divine judgment is ultimately a mystery, a part of that larger enigma, the work of God.

Still, in another regard, the postscript is not entirely alien to the complexion of the book. The thread of continuity is seen in the positive directive of verse 13. Qohelet's response to his failed quests for comprehension of the grand scheme has been to propose a way of happiness and meaning that is feasible within the unyielding boundaries placed on mortals. It is to inhabit fully the moments of our lives, ready to receive and savor gifts of sustenance and companionship. In similar manner the final writer also prescribes "what is good for humans to do under heaven" in their status as creatures. Following up on the recognition of the limits of rational inquiry in verse 12, he moves to articulate the basics: "Fear God, and keep his commandments." The content of the response is different, yet there is something like in spirit here. The limits of the human condition having been granted, we are given a definitive directive about what is to be done within such boundaries. In this regard it is significant that while the canonical book ends on the note of judgment in verse 14, in Jewish liturgical readings of the book verse 13 is repeated, becoming thus the final word. Therefore, within the setting of community expression and worship, the book concludes not with a warning of sure and thorough retributive justice, but with a constructive charge concerning that which is within the power of every person to enact.

Theological and Ethical Analysis

At the end of the book of Ecclesiastes we find both continuities and discontinuities, harmony and tension, with the thought of the sage Qohelet. The takeaway messages found in the ending of the book are not facile or naïve, as if to betray only a passing acquaintance with its contents. It is to be noted instead that each voice heard here shows familiarity with the contents of the book and the dilemmas posed there. Thus the conclusion of the book, through its various interactions with the thought of the sage, both subtle and overt, creates a textured antiphonal dialogue with the book.

All's Well That Ends Well?

Qohelet has said many provocative things in the course of his reflections on life under the sun. All the more interesting, then, that it is the lingering question of divine retribution that the very final writer has chosen to set straight (vv. 13-14). While it is difficult to establish the historical setting for this final contributor, it is less difficult to recognize humanity's deep-seated desire to articulate an ordered world in which everyone receives their just deserts in the end (see "Theological and Ethical Analysis" at 7:15-29). As observed above, while Qohelet, too, has spoken of a time in the future when God's justice will prevail (3:17; 8:12-13), the ambiguity of the time line has been more vexing to him. That interim in which the wicked flourish and the innocent suffer is invariably the place to which he returns. Qohelet remains unsettled by the sight of the vulnerable in the hands of the oppressor (see 3:16–4:3; 5:8; 8:1-17). He voices both the belief that God will judge and the reality of the sight before his eyes: the travesty of the good perishing in their goodness, and the evil flourishing in their wickedness. The tension between the teachings of tradition and the exceptions he observes remains unresolved. It is perhaps no wonder that the author of the final two verses has wished to put the matter to rest.

Some readers of Ecclesiastes have tended to highlight continuity over discontinuity between these final words on divine judgment and those of Qohelet's (see, e.g., Fox 1999, 363, cf. 144–45). I am wary of such a move, and even more wary of allowing this voice the last word on the matter (compare, e.g., Kidner 1976, 13–19; Longman 1998, esp. 15–22, 29–40; Shields 1999, 117–39). Qohelet has shown himself unwilling to affirm divine justice without also bearing witness to the suffering of the innocent. He refuses to mitigate this tension between the teachings of tradition and the world in which we live. It is imperative that we not lose this key witness in the book. To gloss over it is to betray one of its central themes. The crimes against humanity of the last decades—the Armenian massacre, the holocaust of the Jewish and other populations of Europe, the genocides of Cambodia and of Rwanda, the atrocities against children and women in Darfur and the Democratic Republic of Congo—in the wake of these and countless other travesties, I suggest that Qohelet's way of speaking of the collision between what is and what should be must be kept ever before us. This tension or "dis-ease" is poignantly encapsulated in Elie Wiesel's unadorned account of events taking place immediately upon his liberation from the concentration camp at Buchenwald, Germany, in 1945: "Some of us organized a minyan and said Kaddish. That Kaddish, at once a glorification of God's name and a protest against his creation, still echoes in my ears. It was a thanksgiving for having spared us, but it was also an outcry: Why did You not spare so many others?" (Wiesel 1995, 96).

Some were spared. Many were lost. Thanksgiving and lament must each have their expression.

To Life!

Is that all there is?
If that's all there is, my friends,
then let's keep dancing.
Let's break out the booze and have a ball
if that's all there is.

Jerry Leiber and Mike Stoller, "Is That All There Is?"

I drink not from mere joy in wine nor to scoff at faith—no, only to
forget myself for a moment, that only do I want of intoxication, that
alone.

Omar Khayyam

The Human Portion

Heinrich Böll writes that the artist "carries death within him like a good priest his breviary" (cited in Lifton 1996, 9). One might say this is the calling of the artist or poet, that is, to help us negotiate the truths of life that are too difficult, too terrifying to manage alone. Because we do not "stop for death" the poet stops for us, so to speak, with arresting figurations of our mortality. Qohelet reminds us of human limits at every turn, with the ultimate limit being that of death. Indeed the book ends with a solemn reflection on death as the end "of everyone" (7:2). Yet, as we have seen, interwoven with these somber themes are a series of invitations to take enjoyment in basic and elemental pleasures—in food, in drink, in work, in companionship (2:24-26; 3:12-13, 22; 5:18-20; 8:15; 9:7-10; 11:9-10). Moreover, these summons to enjoy life often occur at the very points where Qohelet sounds the theme of death most clearly (see especially 1:12–2:26; 3:16-22; 9:1-12; 11:7–12:8).

As observed in the introduction, these two strains of thought produce a tension, and the question of tonality comes to hinge primarily on how one perceives their relationship to one another, and where one places the emphasis. For many interpreters the pessimistic themes strike the dominant chord in the book. As Roland Murphy observes, "The grim perspective of death conditions the strong recommendation to 'take joy' in all one's years—before old age and death set in (12:1-7)" (1992, lx). Peter Enns, in his nuanced treatment of the epilogue to the book, writes in a similar vein: "Qohelet the sage has journeyed to the very edges of despair and found only absurdity and death, with a small 'portion' thrown in along the way" (2011, 113). In addressing the exhortations, Shannon Burkes concludes that, within the larger context of the book, "these notes of joy are a meager tune in a work that plays in a somber key" (1999, 74). Within such views as these, the theme of enjoyment is offered in the mood of simple resignation, as consolation prize, a small one at that, for all the ways in which human longings are disappointed.

Some readers will recall the song "Is That All There Is?" that was made famous by Peggy Lee. In its own fashion this song captures something of the tonality of the view expressed by these commentators. The stanzas occurring in between the doleful refrain, "Is that all there is?" relate what we might think of as pinnacle moments or experiences—for instance, going to the circus as a child, or falling deeply in love—only to return to the refrain of disillusionment: "Is that all there is?" Life is ultimately disappointing, with death being "that final disappointment." If that is so, one might as well lose oneself in wine and song and other pleasurable activities, as the poet Omar Khayyam intones in the epigraph quoted above. Read through this lens, Qohelet offers pleasurable pursuits as a diversion or as a kind of anodyne for the harsh realities of existence. As Michael Fox writes, "One benefit of pleasure that Qohelet mentions is distraction. Pleasure anesthetizes the pain of consciousness" (1999, 127–28).

Pleasure taken in this way, as distraction from sorrow, as an aid to forgetting, is an old friend of the human race, a well-worn path to that state of blunted awareness in which death and all other human limitations fade for a while from view. The author of Ecclesiastes sees all our creative protective mechanisms for what they are. He notes that both the hero and the hedonist, the one who strives to outflank death by great achievement and the one who drowns awareness through pleasure, meet the same end. Deep inside we know we can never entirely distract ourselves from or truly suppress the knowledge of our death, for "despite the staunchest most venerable defenses . . . it is always there lurking in some hidden ravine of the mind" (Yalom 2008, 5). Hence, we can only escape death consciousness by stifling something that we know to be essentially true. Both the hero and the hedonist might end by asking, *Is that all there is?*

And yet from our earliest stories there are hints of a more profound relationship to the tasks that are set to humans to do, and the joys that are given to humans to feel. We die, each of us. Addressing this truth, and accepting it—as Siduri bids the questing Gilgamesh to do—frees up our energies to turn to life and embrace the gifts that do belong to us as humans.

Earlier in the book I discussed the journals of Etty Hillesum, a young Jewish woman who lived in the time of the Nazi occupation of the Netherlands. While her journals initially reflect a paralyzing terror as she comes to understand that she will not survive this chapter in history, they eventually record her acceptance of this: "Something has crystallized. I have looked our destruction . . . straight in the eye and accepted it into my life, and my love of life has not been diminished" (Hillesum 1996, 155). As the world darkens around her, the analytical intensity of the earlier part of the diary increasingly gives way to an experience of the moment at hand, a joyous reveling in the sensory details of commonplace joys; the scent of jasmine, a cake covered in strawberries, the "riot of bird song on the flat graveled roof." The encroaching shadow of death, rather than crowding out all else, brings into relief the delicate shimmer of the small daily gifts of life.

In a poem published a year after her death from leukemia, Jane Kenyon reflects on such mundane gifts:

"Otherwise"

I got out of bed
on two strong legs.
It might have been
otherwise. I ate
cereal, sweet
milk, ripe, flawless
peach. It might
have been otherwise.
I took the dog uphill
to the birch wood.
All morning I did
the work I love.

At noon I lay down
with my mate. It might
have been otherwise.
We ate dinner together
at a table with silver
candlesticks. It might
have been otherwise.
I slept in a bed
in a room with paintings
on the walls, and
planned another day
just like this day.
But one day, I know,
It will be otherwise.

(Kenyon 1996, 214)

Qohelet is ever cognizant of the "otherwise" that shadows our lives. The value of this heightened awareness of our terminality lies in its potential to *revive* us, and thus to refocus our attention on ordinary pleasures—the bounty of the near and familiar, the simplest gifts of life. Our "assignment" is only to be ready to recognize and fully savor such moments when they come to us. Be it a shared meal with silver candlesticks or a well-brewed cup of tea, the author of this book invites us to live each such moment to its deepest core. This is the wisdom of Qohelet.

WORKS CITED AND CONSULTED

Alter, Robert. 2010. *The Wisdom Books: Job, Proverbs, and Ecclesiastes*. New York: W. W. Norton & Co.

——. 2011. *The Art of Biblical Poetry*. 2nd ed. New York: Basic Books.

Anderson, Gary A. 1991. *A Time to Mourn, a Time to Dance: The Expression of Grief and Joy in Israelite Religion*. University Park, PA: Pennsylvania State University.

Barbour, Jennie. 2012. *The Story of Israel in the Book of Qohelet: Ecclesiastes as Cultural Memory*. Oxford: Oxford University.

Bartholomew, Craig. 2009. *Ecclesiastes*. Grand Rapids: Baker Academic Press.

Barton, George. 1908. *A Critical and Exegetical Commentary on the Book of Ecclesiastes*. International Critical Commentary. Edinburgh: T&T Clark.

Becker, Ernest. 1973. *The Denial of Death*. New York: Simon and Schuster.

Beentjes, Pancratius C. 1997. *The Book of Ben Sira in Hebrew: A Text Edition of All Extant Hebrew Manuscripts and a Synopsis of All Parallel Hebrew Ben Sira Texts*. Leiden: E. J. Brill.

Borg, Marcus. 2001. *Reading the Bible Again for the First Time*. San Francisco: Harper.

Brison, Susan. 1993. "Survival Course." *New York Times Magazine*, March 21:20–21.

Bronner, Stephen. 1996. *Albert Camus: The Thinker, the Artist, the Man*. Danbury: Franklin Watts.

Brown, William P. 1996. *Character in Crisis: A Fresh Approach to the Wisdom Literature of the Old Testament*. Grand Rapids: Eerdmans.

———. 2001. "'Whatever Your Hand Finds to Do': Qoheleth's Work Ethic." *Interpretation* 55:271–84.

Burkes, Shannon. 1999. *Death in Qoheleth and Egyptian Biographies of the Late Period*. Atlanta: Society of Biblical Literature.

———. 2003. *God, Self and Death: The Shape of Religious Transformation in the Second Temple Period*. Leiden: E. J. Brill.

Camus, Albert. 1955. *The Myth of Sisyphus and Other Essays*. Translated by Justin O'Brian. New York: Random House.

Christianson, Eric. 2007. *Ecclesiastes through the Centuries*. Oxford: Blackwell.

Clifford, Richard. 1999. *Proverbs*. Old Testament Library. Louisville: Westminster John Knox.

Cone, James H. 2009. *The Spirituals and the Blues: An Interpretation*. New York: Orbis.

Crenshaw, James. 2013. *Qoheleth: The Ironic Wink*. Columbia: University of South Carolina Press.

Dell, Katharine J. 2013. *Interpreting Ecclesiastes: Readers Old and New*. Critical Studies in the Hebrew Bible. Winona Lake, IN: Eisenbrauns.

Dyer, Wayne. 2003. *Manifest Your Destiny: Nine Spiritual Principles for Getting Everything You Want*. London: HarperCollins.

Eliot, T. S. 1915. "The Love Song of J. Alfred Prufrock." Pages 130–25 in *Poetry: A Magazine of Verse* VI.

Farmer, Kathleen Anne. 1991. *Who Knows What Is Good? A Commentary on the Books of Proverbs and Ecclesiastes*. Grand Rapids: Eerdmans.

Felstiner, John. 1995. *Paul Celan: Poet, Survivor, Jew*. New Haven: Yale University Press.

Fontaine, Carol. 1988. "'Many Devices' (Qoheleth 7:23–8:1): Qoheleth, Misogyny and the *Malleus Maleficarum*." Pages 137–68 in *A Feminist Companion to Wisdom and Psalms*. Edited by A. Brenner and C. Fontaine. Sheffield: Sheffield Academic.

Frankl, Viktor E. 1984. *Man's Search for Meaning*. 3rd ed. New York: Simon and Schuster.

George, Andrew. 1999. *The Epic of Gilgamesh: A New Translation*. London: Penguin.

Gordis, Robert. 1968. *Koheleth: The Man and His World; A Study of Ecclesiastes*. New York: Schocken.

Hardy, Thomas. 1920. *Collected Poems of Thomas Hardy*. London: Wordsworth Editions Limited.

Harrison, R. C. 1991. "Qohelet in Social-Historical Perspective." PhD dissertation, Duke University.

Hillesum, Esther. 1996. *An Interrupted Life: The Diaries of Etty Hillesum 1941–43 and Letters from Westerbork*. Translated by A. J. Pomerans. New York: Owl Books.

Ingram, Doug. 2006. *Ambiguity in Ecclesiastes*. New York: T&T Clark.

Jacobsen, T. 1990. "The Gilgamesh Epic: Tragic and Romantic Vision." Pages 231–49 in *Lingering over Words: Studies in Ancient Near Eastern Literature in Honor of William Moran*. Edited by Tzvi Abusch et al. Atlanta: Scholars Press.

James, William. 1929. *The Varieties of Religious Experience*. New York: Random House.

Jones, B. W. 1990. "From Gilgamesh to Qohelet." Pages 349–79 in *The Bible in the Light of Cuneiform Literature: Scripture in Context II*. Edited by W. H. Hallo et al. Lewiston, NY: Edwin Mellen.

Kenyon, Jane. 1996. *Otherwise: New and Selected Poems*. St. Paul: Graywolf Press.

Koh, Yee-Von. 2006. *Royal Autobiography in the Book of Qoheleth*. New York: De Gruyter.

Koosed, Jennifer. 2006. *(Per)mutations of Qohelet: Reading the Body in the Book*. New York: T&T Clark.

Kovacs. Maureen. 1989. *The Epic of Gilgamesh*. Stanford: Stanford University.

Kugel, J. 1981. *The Idea of Biblical Poetry: Parallelism and Its History*. New Haven: Yale University Press.

———. 1989. "Qohelet and Money." *Catholic Biblical Quarterly* 51:32–49.

Lambert, W. G. 1980. "The Theology of Death." Pages 53–65 in *Death in Mesopotamia: Papers Read at the XXVI Rencontre Assyriologique Internationale*. Edited by B. Alster. Copenhagen: Akademisk Forlag.

Lee, Eunny P. 2005. *The Vitality of Enjoyment in Qohelet's Theological Rhetoric*. Beihefte zur Zeitschrift für die Alttestamentliche Wissenschaft 353. Berlin: De Gruyter.

Lichteim, Miriam. 1973–1980. *Ancient Egyptian Literature.* 3 vols. Berkeley: University of California Press.

Lifton, Robert Jay. 1996. *The Broken Connection: On Death and the Continuity of Life.* Washington, DC: American Psychiatric Press.

Limburg, James. 2006. *Encountering Ecclesiastes: A Book for Our Time.* Grand Rapids: Eerdmans.

Longman, Tremper III. 1998. *The Book of Ecclesiastes.* New International Commentary on the Old Testament. Grand Rapids: Eerdmans.

Marglin, Stephen. 2008. *The Dismal Science: How Thinking Like an Economist Undermines Community.* Cambridge: Harvard University Press.

McKenzie, Alyce M. 2002. *Preaching Biblical Wisdom in a Self-Help Society.* Nashville: Abingdon Press.

Miller, Douglas B. 1998. "Qohelet's Symbolic Use of *hbl.*" *Journal of Biblical Literature* 117:437–54.

——. 2002. *Symbol and Rhetoric in Ecclesiastes: The Place of Hebel in Qohelet's Work.* Boston: E. J. Brill.

Moran, W. L. 1987. "Gilgamesh." Pages 557–60 in *The Encyclopedia of Religion.* Edited by M. Eliade et al. New York: MacMillan.

Newsom, Carol. 1995. "Job and Ecclesiastes." Pages 177–94 in *Old Testament Interpretation: Past, Present, and Future; Essays in Honor of Gene M. Tucker.* Edited by James L. Mays, David Petersen, and Kent Harold Richards. Nashville: Abingdon Press.

——. 1996. "The Book of Job." Pages 319–637 in *The New Interpreter's Study Bible.* Volume 4. Nashville: Abingdon Press.

——. 2012. "Positive Psychology and Ancient Israelite Wisdom." Pages 117–35 in *The Bible and the Pursuit of Happiness: What the Old and New Testaments Teach Us about the Good Life*. Edited by Brent A. Strawn. New York: Oxford University Press.

Noegel, Scott B. 2007. "'Word Play' in Qoheleth." *Journal of Hebrew Scriptures* 7:1–28.

Nussbaum, Martha C. 1986. *The Fragility of Goodness: Luck and Ethics in Greek Tragedy and Philosophy*. Cambridge: Cambridge University Press.

Ogden, Graham. 1987. *Qoheleth*. Readings: A New Biblical Commentary. Sheffield: JSOT Press.

Perdue, Leo G. 1994. *Wisdom and Creation: The Theology of Wisdom Literature*. Nashville: Abingdon Press.

Provan, Iain. 1999. *Ecclesiastes/Song of Songs*. The NIV Application Commentary. Grand Rapids: Zondervan.

Robinson, H. W. 1946. *Inspiration and Revelation in the Old Testament*. Oxford: Clarendon.

Rudman, Dominic. 1999. "A Note on the Dating of Ecclesiastes." *Catholic Biblical Quarterly* 61:47–52.

——. 2001. *Determinism in the Book of Ecclesiastes*. Sheffield: Sheffield Academic.

Schoors, Antoon, ed. 1998. *Qohelet in the Context of Wisdom*. Leuven: Leuven University Press.

——. 2013. *Ecclesiastes*. Historical Commentary on the Old Testament. Leuven: Peeters.

Seow, Choon Leong. 1995. "Qohelet's Autobiography." Pages 275–87 in *Fortunate the Eyes That See: Essays in Honor of David Noel Freedman*. Edited by A. B. Beck. Grand Rapids: Eerdmans.

——. 1996. "Linguistic Evidence and the Dating of Qohelet." *Journal of Biblical Literature* 115:643–66.

——. 1996. "The Socioeconomic Context of 'The Preacher's Hermeneutic.'" *Princeton Seminary Bulletin* 17:168–95.

——. 1999. "Qohelet's Eschatological Poem." *Journal of Biblical Literature* 118:209–34.

——. 2000. "Beyond Mortal Grasp: The Usage of *Hebel* in Ecclesiastes." *Australian Biblical Review* 48:1–16.

——. 2008. "The Social World of Ecclesiastes." Pages 189–217 in *Scribes, Sages, and Seers: The Sage in the Eastern Mediterranean World*. Edited by Leo G. Perdue. Gottingen: Vandenhoeck and Ruprecht.

Shaffer, A. 1967. "The Mesopotamian Background of Eccl. 4:9-12." *Eretz Israel* 8:247–50.

——. 1969. "New Light on the 'Three-Ply Cord.'" *Eretz Israel* 9:159–60.

Shaw, George Bernard. 1942. *Nine Plays by Bernard Shaw*. New York: Dodd, Mead & Company.

Shead, Andrew G. 1997. "Reading Ecclesiastes 'Epilogically.'" *Tyndale Bulletin* 48, no. 1:67–91.

Sheppard, Gerald. 1977. "The Epilogue to Qohelet as Theological Commentary." *Catholic Biblical Quarterly* 39:182–89.

Shields, M. A. 1999. "Ecclesiastes and the End of Wisdom." *Tyndale Bulletin* 50:117–39.

Sinaiko, Herman L. 1998. *Reclaiming the Canon: Essays on Philosophy, Poetry, and History*. New Haven: Yale University Press.

Spiegelman, Willard. 2009. *Seven Pleasures: Essays on Ordinary Happiness*. New York: Farrar, Straus, and Giroux.

Tamez, Elsa. 2000. *When Horizons Close: Rereading Ecclesiastes*. New York: Orbis.

Thielicke, Helmut. 1983. *Living with Death*. Grand Rapids: Eerdmans.

Tigay, Jeffry. 1982. *The Evolution of the Gilgamesh Epic*. Philadelphia: University of Pennsylvania Press.

Tillich, Paul. 1952. *The Courage to Be*. New Haven: Yale University Press.

Tolstoy, Leo. 1967. "The Death of Ivan Ilych." In *Great Short Works of Leo Tolstoy*. Translated by Louise and Aylmer Maude. New York: Harper and Row.

———. 2003. "How Much Land Does a Man Need?" In *Walk in the Light & Twenty-Three Tales*. Translated by Louise and Aylmer Maude. New York: Orbis.

Tov, Emanuel. 2012. *Textual Criticism of the Hebrew Bible*. 2nd ed. Minneapolis: Fortress Press.

Towner, Sibley. 1997. "The Book of Ecclesiastes." Pages 265–360 in *The New Interpreter's Bible*. Volume 5. Nashville: Abingdon Press.

Van Leeuwen, R. C. 1986. "Proverbs 30:21-23 and the Biblical World Upside Down." *Journal of Biblical Literature* 105:599–611.

Watson, Wilfred G. E. 1984. *Classical Hebrew Poetry: A Guide to Its Techniques*. Sheffield: JSOT Press.

Whybray, R. N. 1982. "Qoheleth, Preacher of Joy." *Journal for the Study of the Old Testament* 7, no. 23:87–98.

———. 1991. "'A Time to Be Born and a Time to Die,' Some Observations on Ecclesiastes 3:2-8." Pages 469–83 in *Near Eastern Studies*. Edited by M. Mori et al. Wiesbaden: Harrassowitz.

Wiesel, Elie. 1995. *All Rivers Run to the Sea: Memoirs*. New York: Schocken.

Yalom, Irvin. 1989. *Love's Executioner & Other Tales of Psychotherapy*. New York: HarperCollins.

———. 2008. *Staring at the Sun: Overcoming the Terror of Death*. San Francisco: Jossey-Bass.

Select Bibliography

Alter, Robert. 2010. *The Wisdom Books: Job, Proverbs, and Ecclesiastes*. New York: Norton & Company.

Bartholomew, Craig. 2009. *Ecclesiastes*. Grand Rapids: Baker Academic.

Brown, William. 2000. *Ecclesiastes*. Interpretation: A Bible Commentary for Teaching and Preaching. Louisville: Westminster John Knox.

Crenshaw, James L. 1987. *Ecclesiastes: A Commentary*. Philadelphia: Westminster Press.

———. 2013. *Qoheleth: The Ironic Wink*. Columbia: University of South Carolina Press.

Davis, Ellen F. 2000. *Proverbs, Ecclesiastes, and the Song of Songs*. Westminster Bible Companion. Louisville: Westminster John Knox.

Enns, Peter. 2011. *Ecclesiastes*. The Two Horizons Old Testament Commentary. Grand Rapids: Eerdmans.

Fox, Michael V. 1999. *A Time to Tear Down and a Time to Build Up: A Rereading of Ecclesiastes*. Grand Rapids: Eerdmans.

———. 2004. *Ecclesiastes*. The JPS Bible Commentary. Philadelphia: Jewish Publication Society.

Gordis, Robert. 1968. *Koheleth: The Man and His World; A Study of Ecclesiastes*. New York: Schocken.

Kidner, Derek. 1976. *The Message of Ecclesiastes: A Time to Mourn, and a Time to Dance*. Westmont, IL: InterVarsity Press.

Krüger, Thomas. 2004. *Qoheleth: A Commentary*. Hermeneia. Translated by O. C. Dean Jr. Edited by Klaus Baltzer. Minneapolis: Fortress Press.

Miller, Douglas B. 2010. *Ecclesiastes*. Believers Church Bible Commentary. Scottdale, PA: Herald Press.

Murphy, Roland E. 1992. *Ecclesiastes*. Word Biblical Commentary. Volume 23a. Dallas: Word Books.

Schoors, Antoon. 2013. *Ecclesiastes*. Historical Commentaries on the Old Testament. Leuven: Peeters.

Seow, Choon Leong. 1997. *Ecclesiastes: A New Translation with Introduction and Commentary*. Anchor Bible. Volume 18c. New York: Doubleday.

Tamez, Elsa. 2000. *When the Horizons Close: Rereading Ecclesiastes*. Translated by Margaret Wilde. New York: Orbis.

Towner, Sibley. 1994. "The Book of Ecclesiastes." Pages 265–360 in *The New Interpreter's Study Bible*. Volume 5. Nashville: Abingdon Press.

Whybray, R. N. 1989. *Ecclesiastes*. New Century Bible Commentary. Grand Rapids: Eerdmans.

CPSIA information can be obtained
at www.ICGtesting.com
Printed in the USA
LVOW08s2233100417

530329LV00001B/1/P